William Spotswood, Henry Rice, Patrick Rice

The Golden Cabinet

First Part

William Spotswood, Henry Rice, Patrick Rice

The Golden Cabinet
First Part

ISBN/EAN: 9783337258030

Printed in Europe, USA, Canada, Australia, Japan

Cover: Foto ©Thomas Meinert / pixelio.de

More available books at **www.hansebooks.com**

THE
GOLDEN CABINET:

BEING THE
LABORATORY,

OR
HANDMAID to the ARTS.

CONTAINING

Such *Branches* of *Useful Knowledge,*

As nearly concerns all Kinds of People,

From the S Q U I R E to the P E A S A N T:

AND WILL AFFORD BOTH

PROFIT and DELIGHT.

PART THE FIRST.

PHILADELPHIA:
PRINTED AND SOLD BY WILLIAM SPOTSWOOD,
AND H. AND P. RICE, MARKET-STREET.

1793.

TABLE of CONTENTS.

PART I.

Of gilding, filvering, bronzing, japanning, laquering, and the ftaining different kinds of fubftances, with all the variety of colours.

A 3

CONTENTS. iii

TABLE of CONTENTS.

PART II.

CONTENTS.

TABLE of CONTENTS.

PART III.

)f the nature and compofition of Glafs, and the art of counterfeiting Gems of every kind.

CONTENTS.

Compoſitions of GLASS, or PASTE, of a red colour.

Compoſitions of GLASS, and PASTE, of a blue colour.

Compofitions of hard GLASS and PASTES, of a yellow
colour.

Compofitions of hard GLASS, and PASTE, of a green
colour.

Compofitions of GLASS and PASTES, of a purple colour.

CONTENTS.

Of CEMENTS.

THE
SCHOOL of ARTS.

Of gilding, filvering, bronzing, japanning, laquering, and the ftaining different kinds of fubftances, with all the variety of colours.

PART I.

Of gilding in general.

THE gilding different fubftances is performed by a variety of means accommodated to the nature of each. But the principle is the fame in all ; (except with refpect to one kind practifed on metals, where quickfilver and heat is ufed, which I omit here as not properly a part of the fubject of this work ;) being only the putting fome proper cement on the body to be gilt ; and then laying the gold either in the form of leaves, or powder, on the cement ; which binds it to the body. The principal kinds of gilding are thofe called *oil gilding ;—burnifh gilding ;—*and *japanners gilding*, or *gilding with gold fize.* Thefe may be promifcuoufly ufed on grounds either of wood, metal, or any other firm or rigid body : but paper and leather require a treatment in fome cafes peculiar to themfelves. The firft attention, in moft kinds of gilding, is the choice of leaf gold : which fhould be pure, and of the colour accommodated to the purpofe, or tafte of the work. Purity is requifite in all cafes : for if the gold be allayed with filver, it will be of too pale and greenifh a hue for any application ; and if it contain much copper, it will in time turn to a yet much ftronger green. The purity may be afcertained with accuracy enough for this purpofe, by the touchftone, and *aquafortis*; and the fitnefs of the colour, to any particular purpofe, may be diftinguifhed by the eye. The full yellow is certainly the moft beautiful and trueft colour of gold : but the deep reddifh caft has been of late moft efteemed from the caprice of fafhion. Whichever may be chofen, the colour ought neverthelefs to be good of the kind ; for there is a great variation in the force and effect of different parcels of the fame teint ; fome appearing more foul and muddy ; others bright and clear. The beft method however of judging of the colour of leaf gold with nicety, is by keeping a fpecimen of fuch as is perfect ; with which any frefh parcel may be occafionally compared. There is, befides the true leaf gold, another kind in ufe, called Dutch gold : which is copper gilt, and beaten into leaves like the genuine. It is much cheaper ; and has, when good, greatly the effect of the true, at the time of its being laid on the ground ; but with any accefs of moifture, it lofes its colour, and turns green in fpots ; and, indeed, in all cafes, its beauty is foon inpaired, unlefs well fecured by laquer or varnifh. It is neverthelefs ferviceable for coarfer gilding, where large maffes are wanted ; efpecially where it is to be feen by artificial light, as in the cafe of theatres : and if well varnifhed, will there in a great meafure anfwer the end of the genuine kinds. The other preparations of gold, belonging to particular kinds of gilding, I fhall treat of them, as likewife the cements or other fubftances employed, in their refpective places ; and proceed now to fhow, what the inftruments are, which are common to the three principal methods.

Of the inftruments that are common to oil, burnifh, and japanners, gilding.] The firft neceffary inftrument is, a cufhion for receiving the leaves of gold from the paper, in order to its being cut into proper fize and figures, for covering the places to be gilt. This cufhion fhould be made of leather, and faftened to a fquare board, which fhould have a handle. It may be of any fize, from fourteen inches fquare to ten ; and fhould

)e ſtuffed betwixt the leather and board with fine tow
ir wool; but in ſuch a manner, that the ſurface may be
perfectly flat and even. A proper knife is the next,
ind an equally requiſite inſtrument; as it is neceſſary in
ill caſes to cut or divide the gold into parts correſpond-
nt to thoſe, which are to be covered. This knife
nay be the ſame in all reſpects as thoſe uſed in painting,
alled *pallet knives;* the blade of which may be four or
ix inches long, and ſomewhat more than half an inch
n breadth, with a handle proportionable. A ſquirrel
ail is likewiſe generally provided, for taking up the
whole leaves, and for compreſſing the gold to the ſur-
ace where it is laid, and giving it the poſition requir-
d. It is uſed alſo by ſome for taking up the parts of
eaves; but this is better done by means of a ball of
:otton wool; which will both anſwer this end, and that
if compreſſing the gold in a more eaſy and effectual
manner. This ſquirrel's tail is cut ſhort, and ſometimes
ſpread in the fan-faſhion by means of a piece of wood
ormed like a pencil ſtick, but broad at one end, and
ſplit to receive the tail; but it will equally ſerve the
ſurpoſe in its own form, when the hair is cut to a pro-
ſer length. This inſtrument is by ſome called a *pallet;*
ſut improperly; as the board for holding the colours
n painting, and which is frequently in uſe along with
his, being called by the ſame name, would neceſſarily
ſroduce a confuſion in ſpeaking of either. A bruſh
if very ſoft hog's hair, or of the fitch kind, made
arge, is likewiſe commonly uſed for paſſing over the
vork when it is become dry, in order to take off the
ooſe gold. Some fine cotton wool is alſo neceſſary for
aking up the ſmaller parts of the leaves, and laying
hem on the work: as alſo for compreſſing and adjuſt-
ng them when laid on. The cotton ſhould be formed
nto a ball, by tying it up in a piece of fine linen rag;
or if it be uſed without the rag, the fibres adhere to
:he gold ſize, and embarraſs the work. A ſmall ſtone
ınd mullar, with a proportionable palate knife, are re-
juired for grinding and tempering the mixtures made of
:he fat oil, or gold ſize, with each other, and the co-

lours that may be added to them. Proper brushes' are
also wanted for laying on, and spreading the fat oil, or
size, on the work : and some of these should be fitch-
es of different sizes; in order to convey and settle the
gold, where the relief of carved work forms deep hollows. These are all the instruments that are common
to all the three principal kinds of gilding ; such as are
peculiar to each, I shall take notice of where they more
properly occur.

*The manner of oil gilding, and the preparation of fat
oil.*] The gilding with oil is the most easy and cheap,
as well as most durable kind ; and therefore, is most-
ly applied to common purposes. It is performed by cementing the gold to the ground, by means of fat oil.
The preparation of which is, therefore previously neceffary to be known ; and may be much better managed in the following manner, than by any method hitherto taught, or commonly practiced.———" Take
any quantity of linfeed oil, and put it into an earthen,
or any other veffel of a broad form, fo that the oil
may lie in it with a very large furface ; but the proportion should be fo limited, that the oil may be about an
inch thick in the veffel. The earthen pans ufed for
milk, in the forming cream for butter, are very well
accommodated to this purpose. Along with the oil as
much water fhould be alfo put into the veffel, as will
rife fix inches or more above the bottom. Place the veffel then, with the oil fwimming on the water, in any
open place where the fun and rain may have accefs to
it ; but where it may be as free from receiving duft and
filth as poffible. Let it ftand in this condition, ftirring the contents on every opportunity, for five or fix
weeks, or till it appear of the confiftence of treacle.
Take the oil then from off the water into a phial, or
bottle of a long form, or what is better, into a feparating funnel, fuch as is ufed by the chemifts, and there
draw off the remainder of the water. Place it afterwards, being in the long bottle or phial, in fuch heat
as will render it perfectly fluid ; and the foulneffes it
may contain will foon fubfide to the bottom ; when the

elear part muſt be poured off ; and the remainder ſtrained through a flannel, while yet water, and the whole
will then be fit for uſe."——It is to be obſerved, that
this method is only practicable in ſummer ; as the ſun
has not ſufficient power in winter to produce a due
change in the oil. This method differs from that commonly practiſed, in the addition of the water ; which
ſuffers the foulneſs to ſeparate from the oil, and ſink to
the bottom ; where it remains without being again mixed with the oil every time it is ſtirred, as is unavoida-
ble where no water is uſed. The water likewiſe greatly
contributes to bleach the oil, and improve it in other
reſpects. The beſt previous preparation of the piece to
be gilded, if it have not already any coat of oil paint,
is to prime it with drying oil mixed with a little yellow
oker ; to which, alſo, a very ſmall proportion of vermillion may be added. But where greater nicety and
perfection is required in the work, the wood ſhould be
firſt rubbed with fiſh ſkin ; and then with Dutch ruſhes. This priming being dry, the next part of the operation is the ſizing the work ; which may be done, either with the fat oil alone, (but diluted with drying oil,
if too thick to be worked without) or with fat oil,
and the japanner's gold ſize, (of which the preparation, is below taught) either in equal quantities, cr in
any leſs proportion, with reſpect to the gold ſize.
The difference betwixt the uſe and omiſſion of the gold
ſize, in this way of gilding, lies in two particulars.
The one is, that the ſizing dries faſter according to
the proportion of the quantity of the gold ſize to the
fat oil, and is conſequently ſo much the ſooner fit to be
gilded. The other is, that the gilding is alſo render-
:d, in the ſame proportion, leſs ſhining and gloſſy ;
which is eſteemed a perfection in this kind of gilding :
hough, taking away the prejudice of faſhion, I ſhould
hink the moſt ſhining the moſt beautiful ; and of the
ſtrongeſt effect. The fat oil, or the compound of that
and the gold ſize, muſt be ground with ſome yellow
oker ; and then by means of a bruſh, laid thinly over
he work to be gilt. But, in doing this, care muſt be

B 3

taken to pafs the brufh into all the hollows and cavities,
if the fubject be carved, or have any other way, pro-,
jecting parts.   For where the fize fails to be laid on,
the gold will never take till the work be again repaired,
by going over the defective places with frefh fize : which
fhould be avoided as much as poffible.   Where great
perfection is required, the gold fhould not be laid on
the firft fizing ; but that being fuffered to dry, the
work fhould be again fized a fecond time : and fome
who are very nice even proceed to a third.   The work
being thus fized, muft be kept till it appear in a proper
condition to receive the gold : which muft be diftinguifhed by touching with the finger.   If it appear then
a little adhefive or clammy, but not fo as to be brought
off by the finger, it is in a fit condition to be gilt.   But
if it be fo clammy as to daub or come off on being
touched, it is not fufficiently dry, and muft be kept longer : or if there be no clamminefs or fticky quality remaining, it is too dry, and muft be fized over again
before it can be gilt.   When the work is thus ready to
receive the gold, the leaves of gold, where the furface
is fufficiently large and plain to contain them, may be
laid on entire, either by means of the fquirrel's tail ;
or immediately from the paper in which they were originally put : a method, that, by thofe who have the
proper dexterity of doing it, is found to be much the
fimpleft and quickeft, as well as beft, for the perfection
of the work.   Being laid on the proper parts of the
work, the leaves muft then be fettled to the ground, by
compreffing thofe, which appear to want it, gently
with the fquirrel's tail or cotton ball ; and if any part
of the gold has flown off, or been difplaced, fo as to
leave a naked or uncovered fpot, a piece of another
leaf, of fize and figure correfpondent to fuch fpot, muft
be laid upon it.   Where the parts are too fmall to admit of the laying on whole leaves, or where vacancies
are left after laying on whole leaves which are lefs than
require others to cover them, the leaves which are to be
ufed muft be firft turned from the paper upon the cufhion (defcribed above amongft the inftruments).   They
muft then be cut, by fcoring over them, with the knife

(above defcribed likewife) into fuch divifions or flips as may be moft commodioufly laid on the parts of the work to be covered. After which being feparated, and taken up as they are wanted by means of the cotton wool, to which being breathed upon they will adhere, they muft be laid in the places they are defigned to cover ; and gently preffed by the cotton, till they touch every where, and lie even on the ground. Where the work is very hollow, and fmall pieces are wanted to cover parts that lie deep and out of the reach of the fquirrel's tail or the cotton, they may be taken up by the point of a fitch pencil (being firft breathed upon) and by that means conveyed to and fettled in their proper place. Thofe who are accuftomed to it, ufe the pencil commodioufly for a great part of the work where large parts of the leaves cannot be ufed. The whole of the work being thus covered, fhould be fuffered to remain till it be dry ; and it may then be brufhed over by a camel's hair pencil or foft hog's hair brufh, to take off from it all loofe parts of the gold. If, after the brufhing, any defective parts, or vacancies appear in the gilding, fuch parts muft be again fized ; and treated in the fame manner as the whole was before : but the japanner's gold fize alone is much better for this purpofe than either the fat oil alone, or any mixture.

Of burnifh gilding ; with the preparation of the proper fizes, &c.] The gilding with burnifhed gold is feldom practifed, but upon wood ; and at prefent moftly in the cafe of carved work, or where carved work is mixed with plain. The chief difference in the manner betwixt this and old gilding lies in the preparing the work to receive the gold ; and in the fubftituting a fize made of parchment, or the cutting of glover's leather in the place of the fat oil, as a cement. The preparation of this fize fhould, therefore, be previoufly known ; and may be as follows.—" Take a pound of the cuttings of parchment, or of the leather ufed by glovers ; and, having added to them fix quarts of water, boil them till the quantity of fluid be reduced to two quarts : or till, on the taking out a little, it will appear like a jelly on growing cold. Strain it through flannel while hot ; and it will then be fit for ufe.''——This fize is employed in burnifh gilding, not only in forning the gold fize, or cement for binding the gold to the ground ; but alfo in priming, or previoufly preparing the work. But before I proceed to fhow the manner of ufing it fo, it is neceffary to give the compofitions for the proper cement or gilding fize employed in this kind of gilding. There are a multiplicity of recipes for this compofition, which are approved of by different perfons : but as in general they vary not effentialy from each other, I will only give two, which I believe to be each the beft in their kinds. ——" Take any quantity of bole armoniac, and add fome water to it, that it may foak till it grow foft. Levigate it then on the ftone, but not with more water than will prevent its being of a ftiff confiftence ; and add to it a little purified fuet or tallow fcraped ; and grind them together. When this is wanted for ufe, dilute it to the confiftence of cream, by parchment or glover's fize, mix'd with double its quantity of water, and made warm. Some melt the fuet or tallow, and mix it previoufly with five or fix times its weight of chalk before it is put to the bole, to facilitate their commixture ; to which in this wet ftate they are otherwife fomewhat repugnant. It is alfo fometimes practifed to put foap fuds to the bole ; which will contribute to its uniting with the tallow. ——This is the fimpleft compofition, and equaly good with the following, or any other ; but for the indulgence of the variety of opinions, which reigns in al thefe kinds of matters, I will infert another " Take of bole in fine powder one pound, and of black lad two ounces. Mix them well by grinding ; and then add of olive oil two ounces, and of bees-wax one ounce melted together ; and repeat the grinding till the wiole be thoroughly incorporated. When this mixture is to be ufed, dilute it with the parchment or glover's fize, as was directed in the former recipe. But till the time of ufing them, both this and the foregoing fhould le kept

immerſed in water, which will preſerve them good."
——— To prepare the wood for burniſh gilding, it ſhould
firſt be well rubbed with fiſh-ſkin; and then with Dutch
ruſhes: but this can only be practiſed in the larger and
plainer parts of the work, otherwiſe it may damage the
carving, or render it leſs ſharp by wearing off the
points. It muſt then be primed with the glover's ſize,
mixed with as much whiting as will give it a tolerable
body of colour: which mixture muſt be made by melting the ſize, and ſtrewing the whiting in a powdered
ſtate gradually into it, ſtirring them well together, that
they may be thoroughly incorporated. Of this priming ſeven or eight coats ſhould be given, time being
allowed for the drying of each before the other part be
put on; and care ſhould be taken in doing this, to work
the priming well with the bruſh, into all the cavities or
hollows there may be in the carved work. After the
laſt coat is laid on, and before it be quite dry, a bruſh
pencil dipt in water ſhould be paſſed over the whole, to
ſmooth it and take away any lumps or inequalities that
may have been formed: and when it is dry, the parts
which admit of it ſhould be again bruſhed over till they
be perfectly even. The work ſhould then be repaired,
by freeing all the cavities and hollow parts from the
priming, which may choak them, or injure the relief of
the carving: after which a water poliſh ſhould be giv-
en to the parts deſigned to be burniſhed, by rubbing
them gently with a fine linen rag moiſtened with water.
The work being thus prepared, when it is to be gilt,
dilute the compoſition of bole, &c. with warm ſize
mix'd with two thirds of water; and with a bruſh
ſpread it over the whole of the work, and then ſuffer
it to dry; and go over it again with the mixture, in the
ſame manner, at leaſt once more. After the laſt coat,
rub it in the parts to be burniſhed with a ſoft cloth,
till it be perfectly even. Some add a little vermillion
to the gilding ſize, and others colour the work, if carved, before it be laid on, with yellow and the glover's
ſize; to which a little vermillion, or red lead, ſhould
be added. This laſt method is to give the appearance

of gilding to the deeper and obfcure parts of the carving, where the gold cannot, or is not thought neceffary to be laid on. But this practice is at prefent much
difufed ; and inftead of it fuch parts of the work are
coloured after the gilding ; which treatment 's called
matting. The work being thus properly prepared, fet
it in a pofition almoft perpendicular, but declining a
little from you : and having the gilding fize, place all
the neceffary inftruments above defcribed ready, as alfo
a bafon of clean water ready at hand : wet then the
uppermoft part of the work, by means of a large
camel's hair pencil dipped in the water ; and then lay
on the gold upon the part fo wet, in the manner above
directed for the gilding in oil, till it be completely covered, or become too dry to take the gold. Proceed
afterwards to wet the next part of the work, or the
fame over again if neceffary, and gild it as the firft ;
repeating the fame method till the whole be finifhed.
Some wet the work with brandy, or fpirit of wine,
inftead of water ; but I do not conceive any advantage
can arife from it, that may not be equally obtained by
a judicious ufe of water. This manner is moreover
much more troublefome and difficult, as well as expenfive. For only a fmall part muft be wet at one time,
and the gold laid inftantly upon it, or the brandy or
fpirits will fly off, and leave the ground too dry to take
the gold. The work being thus gone over with the
gilding, muft be then examined ; and fuch parts as require it repaired, by wetting them with the camel's hair
pencil, and covering them with the gold ; but as little
as poffible of the perfect part of the gilding fhould be
wet, as the gold is very apt to turn black in this ftate.
When the repaired part alfo is dry, the work may be
matted, if it require it ; that is, the hollow parts muft
be covered with a colour the neareft in appearance to
gold. For this purpofe fome recommend red lead,
with a little vermillion ground up with the white of an
egg : but I think yellow oker, or Dutch pink, with
red lead, would better anfwer the end : or the *terra di
Sienna* very flightly burnt or mixed with a little red lead

:uch better effect; and be more durable
· mixture fo near the colour of gold in
fs fize will likewife equally well fupply
e whites of eggs in the compofition for
 work being thus gilt, it muft remain
our hours; and then the parts of it that
 be burnifhed, muft be polifhed with the
 r with the burnifhers of agate or flint
purpofe. But it fhould be previoufly
it be of the proper temper as to drynefs.
wenty-four hours be the moft general
 in which it becomes fit, yet the diff-
ou, or the degree of wet given to the
he drying irregular, with regard to any
The way of diftinguifhing the fitnefs of
ake the burnifh, is to try two or three
s at a diftance from each other; which,
e polifh in a kindly manner, the whole
ded fit. But if the gold peel off, or be
the rubbing, the work muft be deemed
nough: and if the gold abide well the
 yet receives the polifh flowly, it is a
:ing too dry: which fhould be always
 watching the proper time. For the
o dry, both requires much more labour
ind fails at laft of taking fo fine a polifh.
s gilding.] The japanners gilding is
means of gold powder, or imitations of
o the ground by a kind of gold fize much
 drying oil: for the making which, there
pes followed by different perfons. I fhall,
 give one of the more compound, that
ed; and another very fimple, but which,
i equally good for the purpofe with the
The more compound gold fize may be
Take of gum animi and afphaltum each
read lead, litharge of gold and umbre,
and a half. Reduce the groffer ingredi-
powder; and having mix'd them, put
· with a pound of linfeed oil, into a pro-

per veſſ.l, and boil them gently ; conſ
them, with a ſtick or tobacco-pipe, till
pear to be incorporated. Continue the boi
ly ſtirring them, till, on taking out a ſt
it appear thick like tar, as it grows col
mixture then through flannel ; and kee
ſtopt up in a bottle having a wide mouth,
when it is wanted, it muſt be ground wit
million, as will give it an opake body ; a
time diluted with oil of turpentine, ſo as
a conſiſtence proper for working freely wi
——The aſphaltum does not, I concei
to the intention of gold ſize : and the li
and read lead, are both the ſame thing
to this purpoſe, under different names
they nor the umbre neceſſary, but cloggi
to the compoſition. This gold ſize ma
equally well, or perhaps better prepared,
ing manner.—" Take of linſeed oil one ¡
gum animi four ounces. Set the oil to ſ
veſſel ; and then add the gum animi gra
der ; ſtirring each quantity about in the
pear to be diſſolved ; and then putting ĩ
the whole become mixed with the oil. I
continue to boil, till on taking a ſmall q
appear of a thicker conſiſtence than ſ
ſtrain the whole thro' a coarſe cloth, and
But it muſt, when applied, be mixed ·
and oil of turpentine, in the manner d
foregoing."—This gold ſize may be ʋ
wood, or any other ground whatever.
enter on the particular manner of gildi
preparation of the true and counterfeit
are neceſſary to be ſhown. The true go
be well and eaſily made by the followin¡
" Take any quantity of leaf gold ; and gr
gin honey, on a ſtone, till the texture o
perfeᵭly broken ; and their parts divic
nuteſt degree. Then take the mixture c
ney from off the ſtone, and put it into a

uch bafon, with water; and ftir it well about, that
he honey may be melted; and the gold by that means
reed from it. Let the bafon afterwards ftand at reft,
ill the gold be fubfided; and when it is fo, pour off
he water from it; and add frefh quantities till the ho-
ey be entirely wafhed away; after which the gold may
e put on paper, and dried for ufe."——A gold pow-
ler of a more intenfe yellow colour, brighter than this,
nay be made by a precipitation from gold diffolved in
iqua regia, by means of either green or Roman vitriol,
n this manner.——" Take a folution of gold in *aqua
regia*; and add to it gradually, a folution of green
vitriol or copperas in water, till it appear that no fur-
her precipitation of the gold be made, on adding a
refh quantity. The folution of the copperas may be
nade, by putting one drachm of it powdered into an
unce of water, and fhaking them till the whole appear
o be diffolved. After which the folution muft ftand;
nd the clear part be poured off from the fediment, if
ny be found. The fluid muft be poured off from the
precipitated gold, as foon as it is perfectly fubfided:
nd the precipitation muft be well wafhed, by pouring
on it feveral fuccefive quantities of water. Roman or
lue vitriol may be employed for this purpofe inftead of
he green, but it is fomewhat dearer, and has no ad-
antage over the other. The gold precipitate thus ob-
ained is very bright and fhining. A fimilar kind may
e prepared, by putting flat bars or plates of copper
nto the folution of the gold in *aqua regia:* but
he precipitate is of a brown colour, without any
luftre or fhining appearance."—The German gold
powder, which is the kind moft generally ufed, and,
where it is well fecured with varnifh, will equally an-
wer the end in this kind of gilding with the genuine,
nay be prepared from the fort of l af gold, called the
Dutch gold, exactly in the fame manner as the true.
The *aurum Mofaicum*, which is tin coloured, and rendered of a flaky or pulverine texture, by a chemical
procefs, fo as greatly to refemble gold powder, may be
likewife ufed in this kind of gilding; and prepared in

the following manner—"Take of tin one pound, of flowers of fulphur feven ounces, and of *fal Ammoniacus* and purified quickfilver each half a pound. Melt the tin ; and add the quickfilver to it in that flate : and when the mixture is become cold, powder it, and grind it with the *fal Ammoniacus* and fulphur, till the whole be thoroughly commixt. Calcine them then in a mattrafs ; and the other ingredients fubliming, the tin will be converted into the *aurum Mofaicum ;* and will be found in the bottom of the glafs like a mafs of bright flafky gold powder : but if any black or difcoloured parts appear in it, they muft be carefully pick'd or cut out."— The *fal Ammoniacus* employed ought to be perfectly white and clean ; and care fhould be taken that the quickfilver be not fuch as is unadulterate with lead ; which may be known, by putting a fmall quantity in a crucible into the fire, and obferving, when it is taken out, whether it be wholly fublimed away, or have left any lead behind it. The calcination may be beft performed in a coated glafs body, hung in the naked fire ; and the body fhould be of a long figure, that the other ingredients may rife fo as to leave the coloured tin clear of them. The quickfilver, tho' it be formed into cinnabar along with the fulphur, need not be wafted ; but may be revived by diftilling it with the addition of quick-lime ; for which a very cheap and commodious method and apparatus may be found in a late treatife on practical chemiftry, intitled, *The Elaboratory laid open. &c.* There are fome other coarfer powders in imitation of gold, which are formed of precipitations of copper. But as they are feldom ufed now for gilding, I fhall defer fhowing the manner of preparing them, till I come to fpeak of bronzing, where they more properly occur. Befides thefe powders, the genuine leaf or Dutch gold may be ufed with the japanners gold fize, where a more fhining and gloffy effect is defired in the gilding. But in that kind of gilding which is intended to be varnifhed over, or to be mixed with other japan work or paintings in varnifh, the powders are moft frequently employed. The gilding with japanners gold

fize may be practifed on almoft any fubftance whatever,
whether wood, metal, leather, or paper: and there is
no further preparation of the work neceffary to its being gilt, than the having the furface even and perfectly
clean. The manner of ufing the jappanners fize, is
this. Put then a proper quantity of it, prepared as
above directed, and mixed with the due proportion of
oil of turpentine and vermillion, into a fmall gally-pot,
or one of thofe tin veffels above defcribed, for containing the colours when ufed for in painting varnifh. Then
either fpread it with a brufh over the work, where the
whole furface is to be gilt; or draw with it, by means
of a pencil, the proper figure defired, avoiding carefully to let it touch any other parts. Suffer it afterwards to reft till it be fit to receive the gold: which
muft be diftinguifhed by the finger, in the fame manner
as with the fat oil; the having a proper clamminefs or
fticky quality, without being fo fluid as to take to the
finger, being alike the criteriton in both cafes. Being
found of a proper drynefs, when the gold powders are
to be ufed, a piece of the foft leather, called *wafhlea-
ther*, wrapt round the fore finger, muft be dipt in the
powder, and then rubbed very lightly over the fized
work; or, what is much better, the powder may be
fpread by a foft camel's hair pencil. The whole being
covered, it muft be left to dry; and the loofe powder
may then be cleared away from the gilded part, and
collected, by means of a foft camel's hair brufh. When
leaf gold is ufed, the method of fizing muft be the fame
as for the powders: but the point of due drynefs is very
nice and delicate in thefe cafes. For the leaves muft be
laid on while the matter is in a due ftate, otherwife the
whole of what is done muft be fized and gilt over again.
When more gold fize is mixed up with the oil of turpentine and vermillion, than can be ufed at one time,
it may be kept, by immerfing it under water till it be
again wanted: which is indeed a general method of
preferving all kind of paint, or other fuch compofitions
as contain oily fubftances.

Of gilding paper, vellum or parchment.] There are

a variety of methods ufed for gilding paper, according
to the feveral ends it is defigned to anfwer; but for the
moft part fize, properly fo called, and gum water, are
ufed as the cements; and the powders are more generally employed than the leaf gold. As I have given
the preparation of thefe feveral fubftances before, it is
needlefs to repeat them here; and I fhall therefore only
point out thofe circumftances in the manner of their ufe,
which are peculiar to the application of them to this
purpofe.

*Of the gildings on paper proper to be ufed along with
paintings in water colours, or frefco.*] The gilding proper to be ufed with water colours may be either with
the leaf gold, or powder; which laft, when mixed
with the proper vehicle, is called *fhell gold*. The leaf
gold is neceffary in all cafes, where a metalline and fhining appearance is wanted: and it may be laid on the
defigned ground, by means either of gum water, or
ifinglafs fize. The gum water or fize fhould be of the
weaker kind, and not laid too freely on the ground;
and proper time fhould likewife be given for it to dry;
the judgment on which muft be formed, in this cafe, as
in the other kinds of gilding, by touching with the
finger. The management of the gold alfo is much the
fame in this as in the former: and where a polifhed appearance is wanting, the dog's tooth or other kind of
burnifher may be ufed. In the gilding larger furfaces,
it will be found advantageous to colour the ground
with the gall ftone: and where colours are to be laid
on the gilding, the brufhing the gold over with the gall
of any beaft will make it take them in a much more
kindly manner. When the gold powders are ufed
along with paintings in water colours, it is previoufly
formed into *fhell gold*, (as it is called, from its being
ufually put into mufcle fhells, in the fame manner as the
colours.) This fhell gold is prepared, by tempering the
gold powder with very weak gum water; to which a little foap-fuds may be put, to make the gold work more
eafily and freely. The preparation of the gold powders is before given, p. 12, and that of the gum

: thus prepared.——" Take three quar-
ice of gum Arabic, and a quarter of
gum Senegal. Powder them, and then
in a linen rag; leaving fo much un-
n the bag, as to admit its being flat-
reffure of the hand. Having fqueezed the
: flat, put it into a quart of hot water;
it continue, moving it fometimes about,
the water for about twenty-four hours.
I then be diffolved; and the bag muft be
he fluid being divided into two parts, to
add a quarter of an ounce of white fu-
dered, and keep the other in its pure ftate.
is, a ftrong and weak gum water, each
ir particular purpofes, will be obtained."
ig proper for the coloured paper for binding
r fuch purpofes.] This kind of gilding is
nuch the fame manner as that for mixing
; in water colours; except with regard
ng particulars. Firft, in this cafe, the
intended generally to form fome figure or
m water or fize, inftead of being laid on
>r pencil, is moft generally conveyed to
means of a wooden plate, or print, and
ly by an engraved roller, which make an
he figure or defign intended. Secondly,
the gold from the furface of the ground
:age in this kind of gilding, as it is in
h paintings, the gum water or fize may
:er; which will contribute both to bind
r, and to give it a fort of emboffed ap-
improves the effect. In this kind of
panners gold fize may be alfo commodi-
. For, as the paper muft be moiftened
nted, there is no inconvenience liable to
he running of the gold fize thus ufed.
>uffed appearance is wanted in the great-
gold fize fhould indeed always be ufed:
: fhould be thickened with yellow oker,
nuch read lead, as the proper working

of the print will admit. The wooden plates or prints
ufed for gilding in this manner, are worked by the hand,
and are to be charged with the gum water or fize, of
whatever kind it be, by letting it gently and evenly
down on a cufhion on which the gum water or fize has
been copioufly fpread by means of a proper brufh ; and
then preffing it on the paper prepared by moiftening
it with water, and laid horizontally with fome fheets of
other paper under it. Where the rolling print is employed, the gum water or fize muft be laid on it by a
proper brufh, immediately out of the pot or veffel which
contains it : but too copious an ufe muft be avoided,
for fear of fpreading it beyond the lines of the defign
or pattern. The fubfequent management of the gold,
whether leaf or powder, muft be the fame as in the
foregoing kinds of gilding. It rarely anfwers to ufe
the leaf gold in this kind of painting, nor even the true
gold powder : but the German powder, or that formed of the leaves called *Dutch gold*, is moftly employed,
and anfwers well enough the purpofe. The manufactures of the gilt and marbled papers have not been fo
much cultivated in our own country, as it were to be
wifhed, fince very great fums have been always annual-
ly paid, both to Germany and Genoa, on this account.
The improvement of this manufacture is, therefore, a
very fit object of attention to that moft laudable fociety
for the eftablifhment and encouragement of ufeful arts,
who have offered premiums to thofe who would give
proofs of their endeavours or fuccefs in parallel inftances.
This fociety has accordingly given lately a bounty
to Mr. Moor, of New-ftreet, who has eftablifhed a
manufacture of gilt and flowered paper ; which exceeds
greatly the foreign in beauty, and is fold at a cheaper
rate than that can be afforded, even when the duty on
importation is not paid.

*Of gilding proper for letters of gold on paper, and the
embellifhment of manufcripts.*] The moft eafy and neat
method of forming letters of gold on paper, and for
ornaments of writings, is, by the *gold ammoniac*, as it
was formerly called : the method of managing which is

s follows.—"Take gum Ammoniacum, and powder
t, and then diffolve it in water previoufly impregnated
with a little gum Arabic, and fome juice of garlic. The
gum Ammoniacum will not diffolve in water, fo as to
orm a tranfparent fluid, but produces a milky appear-
ince; from whence the mixture is called in medicine
he *lac Ammoniacum*. With the lac Ammoniacum thus
prepared, draw with a pencil, or write with a pen on
paper, or vellum, the intended figure or letters of the
gilding. Suffer the paper to dry; and then, or any
time afterwards, breathe on it till it be moiftened;
and immediately lay leaves of gold, or parts of leaves
cut in the moft advantageous manner to fave the gold,
over the parts drawn or written upon with the lac Ammoniacum; and prefs them gently to the paper with a
ball of cotton or foft leather. When the paper becomes
dry, which a fhort time or gentle heat will foon effect,
brufh off, with a foft pencil, or rub off by a fine linen
rag, the redundant gold which covered the parts between
the lines of the drawing or writing; and the fineft hair
ftrokes of the pencil or pen, as well as the broader, will
appear perfectly gilt."— It is ufual to fee in old manufcripts, that are highly ornamented, letters of gold
which rife confiderably from the furface of the paper or
parchment containing them, in the manner of emboffed
work; and of thefe fome are lefs fhining, and others
have a very high polifh. The method of producing
thefe letters is of two kinds; the one by friction on a
proper body with a folid piece of gold: the other by
leaf gold. The method of making thefe letters by means
of folid gold is as follows.——" Take cryftal, and
reduce it to powder. Temper it then with ftrong gum
water, till it be of the confiftence of pafte; and with
this, form the letters. When they are dry, rub them
with a piece of gold of good colour, as in the manner
of polifhing; and the letters will appear as if gilt with
burnifhed gold."—Kunckel has, in his fifty curious
experiments, given this recipe: but omitted to take
the leaft notice of the manner how thefe letters are to
be formed; though the moft difficult circumftance in

the production of them. It may, however, be done by means of a ftamp in this manner. Let the emboffed figure, either of the feparate letters or of the whole words be cut in fteel ; and, when the ftamps are to be ufed, anoint each letter carefully with the end of a large feather dipped in oil ; but not fo wet as to leave drops in the hollows of the ftamps. Fill thefe concave letters, in the ftamps, with the above mixture of powdered cryftal and gum water; and, wiping the other parts of them perfectly clean, place them then on the paper or vellum, laid over fome fheets of paper ; taking care that the letters may be in the exact pofition where they ought to lie : ftrike then the ftamp in a perpendicular direction, but not too forcibly ; and take it off in the fame direction. The letters will be left in their proper places by this means, and will have the fame proportions as their archetypes in the ftamps. Where leaf gold is ufed for making emboffed letters in-manufcripts, the above compofition cannot be ufed ; but there are feveral others which will very well fupply its place : of which the following has been given as very excellent.—" Take the whites of eggs, and beat them to an oily confiftence ; then take as much vermillion as will be required to thicken the whites of the eggs to the confiftence of pafte. Form the letters of this pafte, by means of the ftamps, in the manner before directed ; and when they are become dry, moiften them by a fmall pencil with ftrong gum water ; obferving not to let it run beyond the bounds of the letters. When the gum water is of a proper drynefs, which muft be judged of by the rule before given, cover the letters with leaf gold, and prefs it clofe to every part of them, by cotton or foft leather. After the gilding is dry, it may be polifhed by the dog's tooth, or the other proper burnifhers."

Of gilding proper for the edges of books and paper.] There are feveral various methods with refpect to the cement ufed, by which the edges of books or paper may be gilt : as ftrong gum water, or ifinglafs fize, or glovers fize, may be employed : but as the gum water, and weaker fizes are apt to run beyond the edge, and

stick the leaves together, isinglass melted with the addition of some common proof spirit of wine, and a sixth
part of honey or sugar candy is greatly preferable : but
a third of bole ammoniac well powdered must be added.
The following composition has been likewise approved
of for this purpose.——" Take bole ammoniac and
sugar candy well powdered, each equal parts : mix
them with the whites of eggs beaten to an oily consistence ; and the cement will be fit for use."—In order to
the using any of these cements, the paper, whether it
be in quires or books, should be well cut, and polished
on the edges to be gilt ; and then strongly screwed
down by a press : in which state, it is to be brushed
over, first with a little of the cement without the sugar-
candy or the bole ; and when that is dry, either with
the cement above given, or any other solution of gum
or size, with the proper proportion of the bole : after
which it may be suffered to dry ; and then water polished, by rubbing it with a fine linen rag slightly
moistened. It is then in a state fit for receiving the
gold ; only it must be again gently moistened at that
time : and the leaves may then be laid on, being cut
according to the breadth they are to cover, and pressed
closely down by a cotton ball : and after the gilding is
thoroughly dry and firm, it may be polished in the manner of the foregoing kinds.

Of gilding leather.] Leather may be gilded for common occasions by all the same methods which have
been given for gilding paper or velum ; except, that
where the gold size is used, there is no occasion to wet
the leather, to prevent the running of the oil out of
the bounds. Either leaf gold or the powders may
therefore be employed as well for leather as paper.
But, unless, in some fine work, or for very particular
purposes, the German gold powder would answer as
well as the true gold. It is needless consequently to repeat here the methods above shown with respect to the
gilding paper for covers to books, &c. which equally
well suit for this purpose in general : but as there is a
manner of gilding leather peculiar to the book-binders,

it is requifite to explain it. The method of gilding
ufed by the book-binder, is to have the letters or co
partments, fcrolls, or other ornaments, cut in flee
ftamps ; not by finking, as in moft other cafes, but by
the projection of the figure from the ground. Thefe
ftamps are made hot ; and leaves of gold being laid on
the parts accommodated to the pattern or defign of the
gilding, the hot ftamps are preffed ftrongly on the
gold and leather ; and bind the gold to it in the hollows formed by the ftamp: the other redundant part
of the gold being afterwards brufhed or rubbed off
The manner practifed by the profeffed leather gilders
for the making hangings for rooms, fkreens, &c. is
not properly *gilding*, but *laquering*, being done by
means of leaf filver, coloured by a yellow varnifh, or
the fame principle with the laquered frames of pictures,
&c. which were formerly in ufe. It is an important
manufacture, as the leather ornamented in this manner
not only admits of great variety of defigns in emboffed
work, refembling either gilding or filver ; but alfo of
the addition of paintings of almoft every fort. The
manner of performing this kind of leather gilding is as
follows. The fkins are firft procured in a dry ftate, after the common dreffing and tanning. Thofe moft proper for this purpofe, are fuch as are of a firm clofe texture ; on which account, calf, or goat fkins are preferable to fheep. But in that condition they are too
hard and ftiff for gilding in this way. In order
therefore to foften them, they are firft put for fome
hours in a tub of water, where they are, during
fuch time, to be frequently ftirred about with a ftrong
ftick. They are then taken out ; and, being held by
one corner, beaten againft a flat ftone. They are next
made fmooth, by fpreading them on the ftone, and rubbing them ftrongly over by an iron inftrument refembling a blade, but with the lower edge formed round,
and the upper edge fet in a wooden handle, paffing horizontally the whole length of the blade. This inftrument the workman flides on the furface of the fkin as
it lies on the ftone, at the fame time preffing and lean-

l his weight. When one of the skins
ner is laid over it, and treated in the
d the others over that. The skins being
re joined together, to form pieces of
for any particular purpose. In order
properly, they are cut into a square,
square form. To which end, a ruler
, or the skins are placed on a table or
ding in size and figure to a wooden
we shall have occasion to speak of be-
h of the skin is taken off, as leaves it ·
dimensions of the table or block. Any
or holes in the skin, are then to be
ich is done by paring away with a pen-
thickness of the skin for some little
: hole, or defective part; putting a
pondent piece of the same kind of skin
patch, or piece, is to have a margin
ie thickness, to suit the pared part of
then to be fixed in its place, by means
parchment, or glovers cuttings, in the
i before. After the skins are thus pre-
operation is the sizing them, which is
of a kind of soft glue, or stiff size,
the gold size, used in other kinds of
ng, prepared from parchment, or glo-
This is, in fact, the same with that di-
·d for joining the pieces; only it must
onger boiling to a thicker consistence,
: that of a very stiff jelly. To size a
ie workman takes a piece of the size of
a nut; which, however, he does not
:uts into two parts. With one of these
ll the skin, or piece of leather, strong-
t is, by this means, spread over the
the leather, he rubs it with the palm
lisperse it more equally, and uniformly
. To the effecting this end, the heat
itributes as well as the motion : as it
ia certain degree of fluidity, and ren-

ders it confequently more capable of being diffufed
over the whole furface. The workman then leaves the
fkin for fome time to dry, and afterwards fpreads the
other part of the fize on it, in the fame manner as the
firft ; which finifhes the operation of fizing. It is neceffary to allow fome fpace of time betwixt the laying
on the two parts of the fize. For if the whole was
laid on together ; or the firft part before the other was
dry to a certain degree, the whole would diffolve, and
be forced forwards before the hand, inftead of being
fpread by it. In the profecution of this bufinefs, the
workman therefore, as foon as he has fpread the firft
part of the fize, takes another fkin, and treats it in
the fame manner : which filling up the interval of time,
proper for drying the firft, he returns then to that, and
puts on the other parts of the fize, and by this alter-
native treatment of them, employs the whole of his
time, without any lofs, by waiting till either be dry.
The fide of the fkin on which the hair grew, or what
is called the *grain* of the leather, is always chofen for
receiving the fize and filver. This is neceffary to be
obferved : becaufe that fide is evener, and of a clofer
texture than the other. The fkins, being thus fized,
are ready for receiving the leaves of filver : which are
thus laid on. The workman, who filvers them, ftands
before a table ; on which he fpreads two fkins before
they are dry after the fizing. On the fame table, on
the right hand, he puts alfo a large book of leaf filver
on a board, which near one end of it has a peg fufficiently long to raife it in fuch manner, as to make it flope
like a writing defk. The book being thus placed, he
takes out one by one the leaves of filver, and lays them
on the fkin previoufly fized as above. This he does by
means of a fmall pair of pincers, formed by two little
rods of wood faftened together at one end, and glued
to a fmall piece of wood cut into the form of a trian-
gle, intended to keep the ends of the two rods at a
diftance from each other ; and to make them anfwer
the purpofe, when preffed by the fingers, of taking
hold of the leaves of filver. On the fide of the piece

toon, larger than the leaf, of a figure nearly square ; and which has the corners of the end, that is to be placed in the hand of the workman, bent. This piece of cartoon is called a pallet. The workman takes it in his left hand, and, having put on it a leaf of silver, he turns it downward ; and lets the leaf fall on the skin, spreading it as much as he can, and bringing, as near as possible, the sides of it, to be parallel to those of the square of leather, or skin. If it happen, that any part of it gets double, or is not duly spread, he sets it right ; raises it sometimes, and puts it in its place, or rubs it gently with the kind of brush, or hair pencil which is at the end of the pincers. But most generally, the workman only lets the leaf fall in its place, spread out on the surface of the leather, without either touching or pressing it ; except in the case we shall mention below. After he has done with this leaf, he lays a new one in the same line, and continues the same till such line be complete. He then begins close to the edge of this row of leaves, and forms another in the same manner ; and goes on thus, till the whole skin be entirely covered with the leaf silver. This work is very easily and readily performed ; as the leaves which are of a square form, are put on a plain surface, which is also rectangular. The skin being thus covered with the silver, the workman, takes a fox's tail, made into the form of a ball at the end, and uses it to settle the leaves, by pressing and striking them, to make them adhere to the size, and adopt themselves exactly to the places they are to cover. He afterwards rubs the whole surface gently with the tail, without striking, which is done to take off the loose and redundant parts of the silver, and at the same time to move them to those places of the surface, where there was before any defect of the

D

filver; and where, confequently, the fize being bare, thefe will now take. The reft of the loofe filver is brufhed forwards to the end of the table, where a bag, or linen cloth is placed to receive it.

The skins, when they are thus filvered, are hung to dry on cords, fixed by the ends to oppofite walls, at fuch height as to fufpend the skins out of the way of the workman. To hang them on thefe cords, a kind of crofs is ufed, formed of a ftrong ftick, with a fhorter piece of the fame fixed croffwife at the end of it; over which theskin being hung without any doubling and with the filvered fide outwards, it is conveyed and tranf-ferred to the cord in the fame ftate. The skins are to dry in this condition, a longer or fhorter time, according to the feafon and the weather. In fummer, four or five hours is fufficient; or thofe skins which have been filvered in the morning, may remain till the even-ing, and thofe in the evening, till next morning. But in winter a longer time is required, according to the ftate of the weather. There is no occafion, neverthelefs, to wait till they be entirely dry. As they may be put in any back yard or garden expofed to the wind, and the heat of the fun. For this purpofe they fhould be put over two boards joined together, where they muft be kept ftretched out by means of fome nails. But in this cafe, the filvered fide muft be next the boards, in order to prevent any dirt from falling on it, and fticking to the fize, which would hinder their taking well the burnifh, that will be mentioned below. The heat, and the drynefs of the air, muft determine, alfo, the time of their hanging in this ftate: but experience alone can teach how to judge of this point. It is proper the fkin fhould be free from moifture; but yet, they fhould retain all their foftnefs: in fummer this will happen in a few hours, and they will be then in a condition to be burnifhed. The burnifher which is ufed for this purpofe, is a flint, of which various figures may be allowed, and which muft be mounted differently with a handle, according to the difference of the figure. A cylindrical form is often chofen, in which cafe, one

of the ends fhould be of a round figure, of about an
inch and a half diameter, and have the furface extremely fmooth ; as the polifhing is performed with this furface. The flint is fixed in the middle of a piece of
wood of a foot length, the whole of which length is
neceffary to its ferving as a handle; or the workman
takes hold of it at each end, with each of his hands,
thofe parts being roundifh, and the middle being left of
a greater thicknefs, in order to admit of a hole of a
proper depth for receiving the flint, fo as to keep it
quite firm and fteady. All the art required in the manner of burnifhing is, to rub the leaf filver ftrongly ;
for which purpofe, the workman applies both hands to
to the burnifher, dwelling longer on thofe parts which
appear moft dull. In order to perform this operation,
the fkin is put and fpread even on a fmooth ftone of
a requifite fize, placed on a table, where it may be fo
firm and fteady, as to bear all the force of preffure the
workman can give in fliding the burnifher backwards
and forwards over every part of the fkin. It would
fave a great deal of labour to employ, inftead of this
method of burnifhing, that ufed by the polifhers
of glafs, and alfo by the card makers. This method confifts in fixing the burnifher at the end of a
ftrong crooked ftick, of which, the other end is faftened to the ceiling. The ftick being fo difpofed, as to
act as a fpring, of which the force bears on the fkin,
it exempts the workman from this part of the labour,
and leaves him only that of fliding the burnifhers along
the fkin, in the directions the polifhing requires. The
objections to this method are, that fome parts of the
fkin require a greater preffure than others, and that
fometimes dirt fticking to the fize, which paffes through
the joining of the filver, will fcratch the work, if the
workman in going along did not fee and remove it,
which he cannot fo well do in ufing the fpring burnifher. But certainly, thefe inconveniencies have obvious
remedies, when they are underftood. The ufing the
fpring burnifher for the greateft part of the work, does
not prevent taking the aid of the common one for

finifhing, if any parts, that appear imperfectly polifhed,
fhall render it neceffary; and the workman may well
afford the trouble of examining the fkin, and cleanfing
it thoroughly, by the labour he will fave in this way;
or, perhaps, it is always beft to do this office, before
any kind of polifhing be begun, rather than to leave
it to be done during the polifhing. In fome manufactures, the burnifhing is performed, by paffing the filvered fkins betwixt two cylindrical rollers of fteel,
with polifhed faces. If this be well executed, it muft
give a confiderable brilliance to the filver, and take
away all thofe warpings and inequalities in the leather,
which tend to render the filvered furface lefs equal and
fhining. The fkins or leather, being thus filvered and
burnifhed, are now prepared to receive the yellow
laquer or varnifh, which gives the appearance of gilding.
The perfection of this work depends, obvioufly, in a
great degree, on the colour, and other qualities of the
compofition ufed as fuch varnifh: for which different
artifts in this way have different recipes; each pretend-
ing, in general, that his own is beft, and making confequently a fecret of it. The following is, however,
at leaft equal to any hitherto ufed; and may be
prepared without any difficulty, except fome little nicety in the boiling.——"Take of fine white refin four
pounds and a half; of common refin the fame quantity; of gum fandarac two pounds and a half, and of
aloes two pounds. Mix them together, after having
bruifed thofe which are in great pieces; and put them
into an earthen pot, over a good fire made of charcoal,
or over any other fire where there is no flame. Melt
all the ingredients in this manner, ftirring them well
with a fpatula, that they may be throughly mixed
together, and be prevented alfo from fticking to the
bottom of the pot. When they are perfectly melted
and mixed, add gradually to them, feven pints of linfeed oil, and ftir the whole well together with the
fpatula. Make the whole boil, ftirring it all the time,
to prevent a kind of fediment, that will form, from
fticking to the bottom of the veffel. When the var-

nifh is almoft fufficiently boiled, add gradually, half an
ounce of litharge, or half an ounce of read lead ; and
when they are diffolved, pafs the varnifh through a
linen cloth, or flannel bag."

The time of boiling fuch a quantity of varnifh, may
be in general about feven or eight hours. But as the
force of the heat, and other circumftances, may vary,
it does not permit of any precife rule. The means of
judging of this, is by taking a little quantity out of
the pot, with a filver fpoon, or other fuch inftrument,
and touching it with the finger ; when, if the varnifh
appear, on cooling, of the confiftence of a thick fyrup,
become foon after ropy, and then drying, glue the fingers together, and give a fhining appearance ; it may be
concluded, the time of boiling is fufficient. But if thefe
figns are found wanting, the contrary muft be inferred ;
and the boiling muft be continued till they do arife.
When the quantity of ingredients is diminifhed, the
time of boiling may be alfo contracted. A pint of oil,
and a correfpondent proportion of fine refin and aloes,
has produced a varnifh perfectly good in an hour and a
half. In this procefs, it is very neceffary to have a pot,
that will not be half filled with all the ingredients ; and
alfo to guard with the greateft caution againft any flame
coming near the top of the pot, or the vapour, which
rifes from it during the boiling. For it is of fo combuftible a nature, it would immediately take fire ; and
the ingredients themfelves would burn in fuch a manner,
as would not only defeat the operation, but occafion the
hazard of other inconveniencies. The varnifh thus prepared, attains a brown appearance ; but, when fpread
on filver, gives it a colour greatly fimilar to that of gold.
If, however, it fhould not be found, after this proceed-
ing, that the force of yellow was fufficiently ftrong, an
addition of more aloes muft be made before the boiling
be difcontinued. Care muft be taken, neverthelefs, in
doing this, not to throw in a large lump at once ; becaufe fuch an effervefcence is excited, in that cafe, as
would endanger the varnifh rifing over the edge of the

veſſel, and producing a flame, that would inſtantly make
the whole take fire. On the other hand, if the varniſh
ſeem too ſtrong of the colour, ſandaric muſt be added
with the ſame precaution, which increaſing the quantity
of varniſh, will dilute the colour. The laying the laquer, or varniſh on the filvered leather, is performed in
the open air : and ſhould be done in ſummer, when it
is hot and dry. It is thus performed : The ſkins are
again to be ſtretched and faſtened with nails to the ſame
boards on which they were before fixed to complete the
drying after the filvering : but with this difference, that
the filvered ſide muſt be outwards. Eighty or twenty
ſkins may be treated thus at the ſame time : there being
two or three on each board. All the boards ſhould be
then ranged on treſſels parallel to each other, in ſuch
manner, that all, both of them and the ſkins, may be
cloſe to each other. Every thing being thus prepared,
the principal workman ſpreads ſome of the white of eggs
over each ſkin. The uſe of this is to fill up ſmall inequalities in the ſurface of the ſkin ; and to prevent the
varniſh paſſing through the interſtices of the filver, and
being abſorbed by the leather. Some omit this : and
with advantage, if theſe inconveniencies could be avoided
without it : as it renders the varniſh more apt to crack
and peel off the filver. But where it is omitted, the
varniſh ſhould be of a thicker conſiſtence ; the ſurface
of the leather of a firm denſe texture ; and the leaves
of filver of a greater thickneſs than the common. When
the white of eggs is dry, the workman who lays on the
varniſh ſets it on the table before him in a pot ; being,
as before directed, pretty near the conſiſtence of a thick
ſyrup. He then dips the four fingers of one of his
hands in the varniſh ; and uſes them as a pencil to ſpread
it on the ſkin. In doing this, he holds the fingers at a
ſmall but equal diſtance from each other, and putting
the ends of them on the ſkin near one of the edges of it ;
and he then moves his hands ſo, that each finger paints
a kind of S with the varniſh, from one end of the ſkin
to the other. He afterwards dips his fingers again in
the varniſh, and repeats the ſame operation again on the

e fkin, till the whole be gone over in the
This might be done with a pencil or
but the workman finds the ufing the fing-
: the readieft method for diftributing the
over the fkin. After the varnifh is thus
1, it is to be fpread: which is ftill done
lely. The method is, to rub the flat of
over every part of the fkin on which the
n put by the fingers, and by that means
/ over every part. After this, it is to be
aten by ftrokes of the palms of the hands,
e frequently repeated on every part in ge-
greater degree on thofe places where the
to lie thicker than on the reft : and in
th hands are, for difpatch, employed at
When this operation is finifhed, the
:o be left on the boards where they were
nailed ; and thofe boards are, therefore,
:d till that time on the treffels where the
t on the fkin ; or, if they be wanted for
:en off, and fixed up againft the wall of
any other proper fupport. The time of
s of courfe on the heat of the fun and
at a feafonable time does not exceed a few
o be known, as to each particular parcel
kamining them with the finger. If on
l, they be found free from any ftickinefs,
of workmen, tackinefs, or that the finger
reffion on the varnifh, they may be con-
ntly dry ; and the contrary, when they
e otherwife. This coat of varnifh being
are to be again put on the treffels as be-
her coat laid on exactly in the fame man-
ft. In doing this, examination muft be
:r any of the fkins appear ftronger or
ed than the others ; in order that the de-
ow remedied, by making this coat thicker
may appear neceffary. When this coat
rnifhing for producing the appearance of
pleted ; and if it has been well performed,

the leather will have a very fine gold colour, with a
confiderable degree of polifh or brightnefs. When
there is an intention to have one part of the leatber
filver, and the other gold, a pattern is formed on the
furface, by printing, calking, or ftamping a defign on
the furface after the filvering. The fkin is then to be
varnifhed, as if the whole were intended to be gold ; but
after the laft coat, inftead of drying the varnifh, it is to
be immediately taken off that part which is intended to
be filver, according to the defign printed or calked upon
it, by a knife ; with which the workman fcrapes off all
that he can without injuring the filver, and afterwards
by a linen cloth, with which all that remains is endeavoured to be wiped or rubbed off. The skins, being
thus filvered and varnifhed, are made the ground of various defigns for emboffed work and painting. The emboffed work or relief is raifed by means of printing with
a rolling prefs, fuch as is ufed for copper plates ; but
the defign is here to be engraved on wood. The painting may be of any kind : but oil is principally ufed, as
being durable and moft eafily performed. There is nothing more neceffary in this cafe, than in painting on
other grounds, except that, where varnifh or water is
ufed, the furface be clean from any oily or greafy matter.

Of gilding of glafs without annealing or burning.]
Glafs may be gilt, by applying as a cement, any gold
fize, or other fize, gum water or varnifh ; and, when
it is of a proper degreè of drynefs, laying on the gold,
as in the other methods of gilding. The work may
alfo be polifhed afterwards in the fame manner, if the
burnifhed appearance be defired : but where that is intended, it is proper to add bole ammoniac, chalk, or
other fuch fubftance, to the cement. When drinking-
glaffes are to be gilt, without burning, the cement fhould
be either fome gold fize formed of oil, or fome kind of
varnifh compounded of the gum refins, that will not
diffolve in water ; but require either fpirit of wine or
oil of turpentine for their folution. At prefent, neverthelefs, this is not only negleſted by thofe who gild

drinking-glaffes for fale ; but glaffes gilded with gum
arabic, or the fizes which will diffolve in water, are im-
pofed upon the public for the German glaffes gilt with
the annealed gold ; and fold at the dear rate under that
pretence ; though after they have been ufed for a very
fhort time, the gold peels and rubs off in fpots when the
glaffes are cleaned ; and renders them very unfightly.
As the glaffes with gilt edges are at prefent much in
fafhion, and the true kind are brought from Germany,
or elfewhere, the incitement of the cultivating this
branch of gilding here, would not be an unfit object of
the premiums of the worthy fociety for the encouragement of arts. Since for the doing this work in perfection, there is nothing more wanting, than that dexterity
of the manœuvre, which arifes from a little practice in
matters of this kind.

Of filvering.] Silvering may be practifed on the fame
fubftances ; and all by the fame methods, either with
leaf or powder, as we have before pointed out with regard to gilding ; variation being made in a few circumftances below mentioned. It is, neverthelefs, but feldom
ufed, notwithftanding the effect would be very beautiful
and proper in many cafes ; and there is an extreme good
reafon for fuch a neglect of it. This reafon is, its tarnifhing in a very fhort time ; and acquiring frequently,
befides the general depravity of the whitenefs, fuch fpots
of various colours, as render it very unfightly : and this
tarnifh and fpecking is not only the conftant refult of
time, but will be often produced inftantly by any extraordinary moifture in the air, or dampnefs, as well as
by the fumes and effluvia of many bodies which may
happen to approach it. Wherever, therefore, filvering
is admitted, a ftrong varnifh ought to be put over it :
and this even is not fufficient wholly to fecure it from
this deftructive confequence. The varnifh muft be fome
of the compofitions of maftic, fanderac, the gums animi
or copal, and white refin ; (the particular treatment of
which in the forming varnifhes will be found in other
parts of this work) for the other fubftances ufed for
compounding varnifhes are too yellow. Some put a

for this purpofe, and the kind before given, p. 28, under
that head, may be applied to other purpofes. The
methods of making the filver powders, is alfo the fame
as thofe of gold, except with regard to one of the German powders, which is correfpondent both in its appearance and ufe, abating the difference of colour, to
aurum Mofaicum or *mufivum:* whence it has been indeed, though improperly, called the *argentum mufivum.*
The procefs for this being, therefore, different from any
before given, it is proper to infert it fully, as follows:
——" Take of very pure tin one pound : put it into a
crucible, and fet it on a fire to melt : when it begins to
run into fufion, add to it an equal proportion of bif-
muth or tin glafs : and ftir the mixture with an iron rod,
or the fmall end of a tobacco-pipe, till the whole be
intirely melted, and incorporated. Take the crucible
then from the fire ; and, after the melted compofition
is become a little cooler, but while it is yet in a fluid
ftate, pour into it a pound of quickfilver gradually;
ftirring it in the mean time, that the mercury may be
thoroughly conjoined with the other ingredients. When
the whole is thus commixt, pour the mafs out of the
crucible on the ftone ; where, as it cools, it will take
the form of an amalgama or metalline pafte ; which will
be eafily bruifed into a flafky powder ; and is then fit
for ufe."—This powder may be either tempered, in the
manner of the fhell gold, with gum water ; or rubbed
over a ground properly fized, according to any of the
methods above directed for gold powder; and it will
take a very good polifh from the dog's tooth or burnifhers, and hold its colour much better with a flight
coat of varnifh over it, than any true filver powder or
leaf. The fizes for filvering ought not to be mixed, as
in the cafe of gold, with yellow, or bole ammoniac :
but with fome white fubftance, whofe effect may prevent

r; or wherever the glover's or parchment
ome recommend tobacco pipe clay in the
ig ; and add a little lamp-black to give a
ifhnefs to the compofition.   Leather is
: who have the manufactures of hangings,
iough not fo frequently with a view to
:s own colour, as to produce the imita-
:, of which the whole procefs is before
In fome cafes, neverthelefs, the appear-
s retained ; and it is therefore proper to
:e of the manner of performing this work.
y in filvering the leather, is to be in all
ne, as when it is to have the appearance
which the particular manner has been
inder the article of gilding leather) till
he procefs where the varnifh or laquer,
: the yellow colour, is to be laid on.   In-
:llow varnifh, a clear colourlefs one is to
where the appearance of filver is to be
this is neceffary only, in order to pre-
and difcolouring, which of courfe hap-
time to filver expofed in a naked and un-
to the air.   The molt common varnifh
irpofe, is only parchment fize, prepared
ted, p. 7, which is preferred to others,
its cheapnefs.   This is made warm, in
it fluid, and then laid on with a fpunge
icil or brufh.   There is no reafon, how-
d of varnifh is liable to fuffer by moifture,
and difcoloured, that better kinds, fuch
rtin, or others, which are ufed for *papier*
&c. fhould not be employed here, pro-
:olourlefs.   The more hard and tranfpa-
oore they are of a refinous nature, the
nd white, and the more durable will be

the filvery, and polifhed appearance of the filver leather.
Some, inftead of parchment fize, ufe that made of
ifing'afs, which may be prepared according to the method laid down, p. 7. This refifts moifture, and will
keep its colour and tranfparency, better than the other
kinds of fize : but all of them grow yellow and cloudy
with time ; efpecially if any damper moifture have accefs to them. Indeed filver fecured even by the beft
varnifh, will ftill in time take a tarnifh, and lofe its
beauty : and therefore the giving the leaf filver on leather
the appearance of gold, even tho' attended with fome
additional expence, is preferable in moft cafes. Leather
filvered in this manner may be ornamented by printing
in relief, and by painting, in the fame manner as that
reprefenting gilding : though, on account of the want
of durability, this is much feldomer practifed. It is
poffible that fome amalgama of quickfilver, or other
compofition, might be found that would have the refemblance of filver, and yet refift tarnifhing : which
would not only be a great improvement, by the furnifh-
ing a durable kind of filvering for leather, paper, &c.
but alfo fave part of the expence of leaf filver for a
ground for gilded leather. This has been attempted in
France with fome fuccefs ; but not to the degree of
perfection wifhed for.

Of bronzing.] Bronzing is colouring, by metalline
powders, plafter, or other bufts and figures, in order
to make them appear as if caft of copper or other metals. This is fometimes done by means of cement, and
fometimes without, in the inftance of plafter figures :
but the bronzing is more durable and fecure when a cement is ufed. The gold powders, and the *aurum Mofaicum*, we have before given the preparation of, are frequently employed for this purpofe ; but the proper bronzing ought to be of a deeper and redder colour, more refembling copper ; which effect may be produced by
grinding a very fmall quantity of red lead with
thefe powders ; or the proper powder of copper may be
ufed : and may be prepared as follows——" Take filings of copper, or flips of copper-plates, and diffolve

them in any kind of *aquafortis* put into a glafs receiver, or other proper formed veffel. When the *aquafortis* is faturated with the copper, take out the flips of
the plates ; or, if filings were ufed, pour off the folution from what remains undiffolved, and put into it fmall
bars of iron : which will precipitate the copper from
the *aquafortis* in a powder of the proper appearance and
colour of copper. Pour off the water then from the powder ; and wafh it clean from the falts, by feveral fucceffive
quantities of frefh water."——Where the apearance of
brafs is defigned, the gold powders, or the *aurum Mô-
faicum*, may be mixed with a little of the powder called *argentum mufivum* ; of which the preparation is
above given. Where the appearance of filver is wanted, the *argentum mufivum* is the beft and cheapeft method ; particularly as it will hold its colour much longer
than the true filver ufed either in leaf or powder.
Where no cement is ufed in bronzing, the powder muft
be rubbed on the fubject intended to be bronzed, by
means of a piece of foft leather, or fine linen rag, till
the whole furface be coloured. The former method of
ufing a cement in bronzing was, to mix the powders
with ftrong gum water, or ifinglafs fize ; and then
with a brufh, or pencil, to lay them on the fubject.
But at prefent fome ufe the japanners gold fize : and
proceed in all refpects in the fame manner as in gilding
with the powders in other cafes : for which ample directions have been before given. This is the beft method hitherto practifed. For the japanners gold fize
binds the powders to the ground, without the leaft hazard of peeling or falling off ; which is liable to happen
when the gum water or glover's or ifinglafs fizes are ufed. Though, notwithftanding the authority of the old
practice for the contrary, even thefe cements will much
better fecure them when they are laid on the ground,
and the powders rubbed over them, than when both are
mixed together, and the effect, particularly of the *aurum Mofaicum*, will be much better in this way than the
other. The gold fize fhould be fuffered, in this cafe,
to approach much nearer to drynefs, than is proper in

E

the cafe of gilding with leaf gold, as the powders
would otherwife be rubbed amongft it in the laying
them on. The fictitious filver powder, called the *argentum mufivum*, may, as above-mentioned, be applied
in the manner of bronze, by thofé whofe caprice dif-
pofes them to filver figures or bufts. But it is the only
fort of filver powder that fhould be ufed in this way,
for the reafon above given : and all fuch kind of filvering is much better omitted. For the whitenefs itfelf
of plaifter in figures or bufts, and much more a gloffy
or fhining whitenefs, is injurious to their right effect ;
by its eluding the judgment of the eye, with refpect to the proper form and proportion of the parts
from the falfe and pointed reflections of the lights, and
the too faint force of the fhades. To remove which
inconvenience it is probable was the firft inducement to
bronzing.

Of japanning.] By japanning is to be here underftood the art of covering bodies by grounds of opake
colours in varnifh ; which may be either afterwards
decorated by paintings or gilding, or left in a plain
ftate. This is not at prefent practifed fo frequently on
chairs, tables, and other furniture of houfes, except
tea-waiters, as formerly. But the introduction of it
for ornamenting coaches, fnuff-boxes, and fkreens, in
which there is a rivalfhip betwixt ourfelves and the
French, renders the cultivation and propagation of this
art of great importance to commerce. I fhall therefore
be more explicit in fhowing the methods both now and
and formerly in ufe ; with the application of each to
the feveral purpofes to which they are beft adapted ; and
point out at the fame time feveral very material improvements, that are at prefent only enjoyed by particular perfons; or not at all hitherto brought into
practice. The fubftances which admit of being japanned are almoft every kind that are dry and rigid, or not
too flexible ; as wood, metals, leather, and paper prepared. Wood and metals do not require any other
preparation, but to have their furfaces perfectly even
and clean. But leather fhould be fecurely ftrained

either on frames or on boards; as its bending or forming folds would otherwife crack and force off the coats
of varnifh. Paper alfo fhould be treated in the fame
manner; and have a previous ftrong coat of fome kind
of fize; but it is rarely made the fubject of japanning
till it is converted into *papier mache*, or wrought, by
other means, into fuch form, that its original ftate,
particularly with refpect to flexibility, is loft. One
principal variation in the manner of japanning is, the
ufing or omitting any priming or undercoat on the
work to be japanned. In the older practice, fuch
priming was always ufed; and is at prefent retained in
the French manner of japanning coaches and fnuff
boxes of the *papier mache*. But in the Birmingham
manufacture here, it has been always rejected. The
advantage of ufing fuch priming or undercoat is, that
it makes a faving in the quantity of varnifh ufed; becaufe the matter of which the priming is compofed,
fills up the inequalities of the body to be varnifhed;
and makes it eafy, by means of rubbing and water-
polifhing, to gain an even furface for the varnifh.
This was therefore fuch a convenience in the cafe of
wood, as the giving a hardnefs and firmnefs to the
ground, was alfo in the cafe of leather, that it became
an eftablifhed method: and is therefore retained, even
in the inftance of the *papier mache*, by the French,
who applied the received method of japanning to that
kind of work on its introduction. There is neverthelefs this inconvenience always attending the ufe of an
undercoat of fize, that the japan coats of varnifh and
colour will be conftantly liable to be cracked and peel-
ed off, by any violence, and will not endure near fo
long as the bodies japanned in the fame manner, but
without any fuch priming. This may be eafily obferved in comparing the wear of the Paris and Ber-
mingham fnuff boxes; which latter, when good of
their kind, never peel or crack, or fuffer any damage,
unlefs by great violence, and fuch a continued rubbing,
as waftes away the fubftance of the varnifh: while the
japan coats of the Parifian boxes crack and fly off in

flakes, whenever any knock or fall, particularly near
the edges, expofes them to be injured. But the Birmingham manufacturers, who originally practifed the
japanning only on metals, to which the reafon above
given for the ufe of priming did not extend, and who
took up this art of themfelves as an invention, of
courfe omitted at firft the ufe of any fuch undercoat;
and not finding it more neceffary in the inftance of
papier mache, than on metals, continue ftill to reject it.
On which account the boxes of their manufacture are,
with regard to the wear, greatly better than the French.
The laying on the colours, in varnifh inftead of gum water,
is alfo another variâtion from the method of japanning
formerly practifed. But the much greater ftrength of
the work, where they are laid on in varnifh or oil,
has occafioned this way to be exploded, with the
greateft reafon, in all regular manufactures. However,
they who may practife japanning on cabinets, or other
fuch pieces, as are not expofed to much wear and violence, for their amufement only, and confequently may
not find it worth their while to encumber themfelves
with the preparations neceffary for the other methods,
may paint with water colours on an undercoat laid on
the wood, or other fubftance, of which the piece to
be japanned is formed ; and then finifh with the proper
coats of varnifh, according to the methods below
taught. If the colours are tempered with the ftrongeft
ifinglafs fize and honey, inftead of gum water, and
laid on very flat and even, the work will not be much
inferior in appearance to that done by the other method ; and will laft as long as the common old japan
work, except the beft kinds of the true japan. It is
practifed likewife, in imitation of what is fometimes
done in the Indian work, to paint with water colours
on grounds of gold ; in which cafe the ifinglafs fize,
with fugar-candy or honey, as above directed, is the
beft vehicle. Imitations are alfo made of japan work,
by colouring prints, gluing them to wood-work,
and giving them a fhining appearance, by the ufe of
fome white varnifh.

Of japan grounds.] The proper japan grounds are
either such as are formed by the varnish and colour,
where the whole is to remain of one simple colour;
or by the varnish either coloured or without colour, on
which some painting or other decoration, is afterwards
to be laid on. It is necessary, however, before I
proceed to speak of the particular grounds, to show the
manner of laying on the priming or undercoat, where any
such is used. This priming is of the same nature with
that called clear coating (or vulgarly clear coaling)
practised erroneously by house-painters; and consists
only in laying on, and drying in the most even manner,
a composition of size and whiting. The common size
has been generally used for this purpose: but where
the work is of a nicer kind, it is better to employ the
glover's or the parchment size; and if a third of isinglass be added, it will be still better; and if not laid
on too thick, much less liable to peel and crack. The
work should be prepared for this priming, by being
well smoothed with the fish skin, or glass shaver; and,
being made thoroughly clean, should be brushed over
once or twice with hot size, diluted with two thirds of
water, if it be of the common strength. The priming
should then be laid on with a brush as even as possible;
and should be formed of a size, whose consistence is betwixt the common kind and glue, mixed with a much
whiting as will give it a sufficient body of colour to
hide the surface of whatever it is laid upon, but not
more. If the surface be very even, on which the priming is used, two coats of it, laid on in this manner,
will be sufficient: but if, on trial with a fine rag wet,
it will not receive a proper water polish, on account of
any irregularities not sufficiently filled up and covered,
two or more coats must be given it: and whether a
greater or less number be used, the work should be
smoothed, after the last coat but one is dry, by rubbing it with the Dutch rushes. When the last coat is
dry, the water polish should be given, by passing over
every part of it with a fine rag gently moistened, till
the whole appear perfectly clean and even. The prim-

ing will then be completed, and the work ready to receive the painting, or coloured varnifh : the reft of the proceedings being the fame in this cafe, as where no priming is ufed.

Of common grounds of varnifh which are to be painted upon.] Where wood or leather is to be japanned, and no priming is ufed, the beft preparation is to lay two or three coats of coarfe varnifh compofed in the following manner.——" Take of rectified fpirit of wine one pint, and of coarfe feed-lac and refin, cach two ounces. Diffolve the feed-lac and refin in the fpirit : and then ftrain off the varnifh."— This varnifh, as well as all others formed of fpirit of wine, muft be laid on in a warm place ; and, if it can be conveniently managed, the piece of work to be varnifhed fhould be made warm likewife : and for the fame reafon, all dampnefs fhould be avoided ; for either cold or moifture chill this kind of varnifh ; and prevent its taking proper hold of the fubftance on which it is laid. When the work is fo prepared, or by the priming of the compofition of fize and whiting above defcribed, the proper japan ground muft be laid on, which is much the beft formed of fhell-lac varnifh, and the colour defired ; if white be not in queftion, which demands a peculiar treatment, as I fhall below explain ; or great brightnefs be not required, when alfo other means muft be purfued. The colours ufed with the fhell-lac varnifh, may be any pigments whatever which give the teint of the ground defired ; and they may be mixed together to form browns or any compound colours : but with refpect to fuch as require peculiar methods for the producing them of the firft degree of brightnefs, I fhall particularize them below. The colours for grounds may otherwife be mixed with the white varnifhes formed in oil of turpentine ; but thefe varnifhes have no advantages over the fhell-lac but in their whitenefs, that preferves the brightnefs of the colours ; and they are at the fame time greatly inferior in hardnefs to it. As metals never require to be under coated with whiting,

they may be treated in the fame manner as wood or leather when the under-coat is omitted, except in the inftances particularly fpoken of below.

Of white japan grounds.] The forming a ground perfectly white, and of the firft degree of hardnefs, remains hitherto a defideratum, or matter fought for in
the art of japanning. As there are no fubftances which
can be diffolved, fo as to form a very hard varnifh, but
what have too much colour not to deprave the whitenefs, when laid on of a due thicknefs over the work,
except fome very late difcoveries not hitherto brought
into practice. The neareft approach, however, to a
perfect white varnifh, by means already known to the
public, is made by the following compofition.——
" Take flake white, or white lead, wafhed over and
ground with a fixth of its weight of ftarch, and then
dried; and temper it properly for fpreading, with the
maftic varnifh, or compound them with the gum animi."—Lay thefe on the body to be japanned, prepared
either with or without the under-coat of whiting, in the
manner as above ordered: and then varnifh over it with
five or fix coats of the following varnifh.——" Pro-
vide any quantity of the beft feed lac; and pick out
of it all the cleareft and whiteft grains; referving the
more coloured and fouler parts for the coarfer varnifhes,
fuch as that above mentioned for priming or preparing wood or leather. Take of this picked feed lac
two ounces; and of gum animi three ounces; and diffolve them, being previoufly reduced to a grofs powder,
in about a quart of fpirit of wine; and ftrain off the
clear varnifh."——The feed lac will yet give a flight
tinge to this compofition; but cannot be omitted,
where the varnifh is wanted to be hard: though, where
a fofter will anfwer the end, the proportion may be diminifhed; and a little crude turpentine added to the gum
animi, to take off the brittlenefs. A very good varnifh, free entirely from all brittlenefs, may be formed,
by diffolving as much gum animi, as the oil will take,
in old nut or poppy oil; which muft be made to boil

gently, when the gum is put into it. The ground of white colour itfelf may be laid on in this varnifh; and then a coat or two of it may be put over the ground: but it muft be well diluted with oil of turpentine when it is ufed. This, though free from brittlenefs, is, neverthelefs, liable to fuffer; by being indented or bruifed by any flight ftrokes; and it will not well bear any polifh, but may be brought to a very fmooth furface without, if it be judicioufly managed in the laying it on. It is likewife fomewhat tedious in drying, and will require fome time where feveral coats are laid on, as the laft ought not to contain much oil of turpentine. It muft be obferved, likewife, that the gum refin, fuch as the animi, copal, &c. can never be diffolved in fubftantial oils, by the medium of heat, without a confiderable change in the colour of the oils, by the degree of heat neceffary to produce the folution. A method of diffolving gum copal in oil of turpentine is, however, now difcovered by a gentleman of great abilities in chemiftry; and he has alfo obtained a method of diffolving amber in the fame menftruum, fo that we may hope foon to fee the art of japanning carried to a confummate degree of perfection; when the public are put in poffeffion of thefe moft important inventions, or the fruits of them.

Of blue japan grounds.] Blue japan grounds may be formed of bright Pruffian blue; or of verditer glazed over by Pruffian blue; or of fmalt. The colour may be beft mixed with fhell-lac varnifh; and brought to a polifhing ftate by five or fix coats of varnifh of feed-lac. But the varnifh, neverthelefs, will fomewhat injure the colour, by giving to a true blue a caft of green; and fouling in fome degree a warm blue, by the yellow it contains. Where, therefore, a bright blue is required, and a lefs degree of hardnefs can be difpenfed with, the the method before directed, in the cafe of white grounds, muft be purfued.

Of red japan grounds.] For a fcarlet japan ground, vermillion may be ufed. But the vermillion alone has

a glaring effect, that renders it much lefs beautiful than
the crimfon produced by glazing it over with carmine
or fine lake ; or even with rofe pink, which has a very
good effect ufed for this purpofe. For a very bright
crimfon, neverthelefs, inftead of glazing with carmine,
the Indian lake, known in the fhops by the name of
fafflower, fhould be ufed, diffolved in the fpirit of which
the varnifh is compounded (which it readily admits of
when good). But in this cafe, inftead of glazing
with the fhell-lac varnifh, the upper or polifhing coats
need only be ufed ; as they will equally receive and
convey the tinge of the Indian lake, which may be actually diffolved by fpirit of wine : and this will be found a
much cheaper method than the ufing carmine. If, neverthelefs, the higheft degree of brightnefs be required, the white varnifhes muft be ufed. It is at prefent,
however, very difficult to obtain this kind of lake.
For it does not appear that more than one confiderable
quantity was ever brought over, and put into the hands
of colourmen : and this being now expended, they
have not the means of a frefh fupply : it, however,
may be eafily had from the fame place whence the
former quantity was procured, by any perfons who go
thither in the Eaft-India fhips.

Of yellow japan grounds.] For bright yellow grounds,
King's yellow, or turpeth mineral, fhould be employed,
either alone or mixed with fine Dutch pink. The effect may be ftill more heightened, by diffolving powdered turmeric root in the fpirit of wine, of which
the upper or polifhing coat is made ; which fpirit of
wine muft be ftrained from off the dregs, before the
feed-lac be added to it to form the varnifh. The feed-
lac varnifh is not equally injurious here, and with
greens, as in the cafe of other colours ; becaufe, being
only tinged with a reddifh yellow, it is little more than
an addition to the force of the colours. Yellow
grounds may be likewife formed of the Dutch pink
only, which, when good, will not be wanting in
brightnefs, though extremely cheap.

Of green japan grounds.] Green grounds may be produced by mixing King's yellow and bright Pruffian blue ; or rather, turpeth mineral and Pruffian blue. A cheap, but fouler kind, may be had from verdigrife, with a little of the above mentioned yellows, or Dutch pink. But where a very bright green is wanted, the cryſtals of verdigrife, (called *diſtilled verdigrife)* ſhould be employed ; and to heighten the effect, they ſhould be laid on a ground of leaf gold, which renders the colour extremely brilliant and pleaſing. They may any of them be uſed ſuccefsfully with good feed-lac varnifh, for the reaſon before given : but will be ſtill brighter with the white varnifh.

Of orange-coloured japan grounds.] Orange-coloured japan grounds may be formed, by mixing vermillion, or red lead, with King's yellow, or Dutch pink ; or the orange lake ; or red orpiment, will make a brighter orange ground than can be produced by any mixture.

Of purple japan grounds.] Purple japan grounds may be produced by the mixture of lake, and Pruffian blue ; or a fouler kind, by vermillion and Pruffian blue. They may be treated as the reſt, with reſpect to the varnifh.

Of black japan grounds, to be produced without heat.] Black grounds may be formed by either ivory-black, or lamp-black : but the former is preferable, where it is perfectly good. Theſe may be always laid on with the ſhell-lac varnifh : and have their upper or poliſhing coats of common feed-lac varnifh ; as the tinge or foulnefs of the varnifh can be here no injury.

Of common black japan grounds on iron or copper, produced by means of heat.] For forming the common black japan grounds by means of heat, the piece of work to be japanned muſt be painted over with drying oil : and when it is of a moderate drynefs, muſt be put into a ſtove of ſuch degree of heat, as will change the oil black, without burning it, ſo as to deſtroy or weaken its tenacity. The ſtove ſhould not be too hot when the work is put into it, nor the heat increaſed too faſt ; either of which errors would make it bliſter :' but the flower the heat is augmented, and the longer it is continued, provided it be reſtrained within the due degree, the harder will be the coat of japan. This kind of varniſh requires no poliſhing, having received, when properly managed, a ſufficient one from the heat.

Of the fine tortoiſe-ſhell japan ground, produced by means of heat.] The beſt kind of tortoiſe-ſhell ground produced by heat is not leſs valuable for its great hardneſs, and endured to be made hotter than boiling water without damage, than for its beautiful appearance. It is to be made by means of a varniſh prepared in the following manner.——"Take of good linſeed oil one gallon, and of umbre half a pound. Boil them together till the oil become very brown and thick : ſtrain it then through a coarſe cloth ; and ſet it again to boil ; in which ſtate it muſt be continued till it acquire a pitchy conſiſtence, when it will be fit for uſe."—— Having prepared thus the varniſh, clean well the iron or copper-plate, or other piece which is to be japanned ; and then lay vermillion tempered with ſhell-lac varniſh, or with drying oil diluted with oil of turpentine very thinly, on the places intended to imitate the more tranſparent parts of the tortoiſe-ſhell. When the vermillion is dry, bruſh over the whole with the black varniſh, tempered to a due conſiſtence with oil of turpentine ; and when it is ſet and firm, put the work into a ſtove, where it may undergo a very ſtrong heat ; and muſt be continued a conſiderable time, if even three weeks or a month, it will be the better. This was given amongſt other recipes by Kunckel ; but appears to have been neglected till it was revived with great ſucceſs in the Birmingham manufactures, where it was not only the ground of ſnuff-boxes, dreſſing-boxes, and other ſuch leſſer pieces, but of thoſe beautiful tea waiters, which have been ſo juſtly eſteemed and admired in ſeveral parts of Europe where they have been ſent. This ground may be decorated with painting and gilding, in the ſame manner as any other var-

nifhed furface, which had beft be done after the ground
has been duly hardened by the hot ftove : but it is well
to give a fecond annealing with a more gentle heat after it is finifhed.

Of painting japan work.] Japan work ought properly to be painted with colours in varnifh. But in order
for the greater difpatch, and, in fome very nice works
in fmall, for the freer ufe of the pencil, the colours
are now moft frequently tempered in oil: which fhould
previoufly have a fourth part of its weight of gum
animi diffolved in it ; or, in default of that, of the
gums fanderac or maftic, as I have likewife before intimated. When the oil is thus ufed, it fhould be well
diluted with fpirit of turpentine, that the colours may
be laid more evenly and thin : by which means, fewer
of the polifhing or upper coats of varnifh become neceffary. In fome inftances, water colours, as I before
mentioned, are laid on grounds of gold, in the other
paintings ; and are beft, when fo ufed, in their proper
appearance, without any varnifh over them ; and they
are alfo fometimes fo managed, as to have the effect of
emboffed work. The colours employed in this way
for painting, are (as I before intimated) beft prepared
by means of ifinglafs fize corrected with honey, or fugar-candy. The body of which the emboffed work is
raifed, need not, however, be tinged with the exterior
colour ; but may be beft formed of very ftrong gum
water, thickened to a proper confiftence by bole ammoniac and whiting in equal parts : which being laid
on in the proper figure, and repaired when dry, may
be then painted with the proper colours tempered in the
ifinglafs fize, or in the general manner with fhell lac
varnifh.

Of varnifhing japan work.] The laft, and finifhing
part of japanning, lies in the laying on and polifhing
the outer coats of varnifh ; which are neceffary, as
well in the pieces that have only one fimple ground of
colour ; as with thofe that are painted. This in general
is beft done with common feed-laq varnifh ; except in

the inftances, and on thofe occafions, where I have
already fhown other methods to be more expedient:
an { the fame reafous, which decide as to the fitnefs or
impropriety of the varnifhes, with refpeft to the colours
of the ground, hold equally well with regard to thofe
of the painting. For where brightnefs is the moft material point, and a tinge of yellow will injure it, feed-
lac muft give way to the whiter gums. But where
hard ı: fs, and a greater tenacity, are moft effential, it
muft be adhered to: and where both are fo neceffary,
t'at it is proper one fhould give way to the other,
in a certain degree reciprocally, a mixed varnifh muft
be adopted. This mixed varnifh, as I before obferved,
fhould be made of the pick'd feed-lac, as directed in
p. 43. The common feed-lac varnifh, which is the
moft ufeful preparation of the kind hitherto invented,
may be thus made. "Take of feed-lac three ounces,
and put into water to free it from the fticks and filth
that frequently are intermixed with it; and which
muft be done by ftirring it about, and then pouring
off the water and adding frefh quantities, in order
to repeat the operations till it be free from all impurities; as it very effectually may be by this means.
Dry it then, and powder it grofsly; and put it, with
a pint of rectified fpirit of wine, into a bottle, of
which it will not fill above two-thirds. Shake the mixture well together, and place the bottle in a gentle
heat, till the feed appear to be diffolved; the fhaking
being in the mean time repeated as often as may be
convenient; and then pour off all which can be obtained clear by that method: and ftrain the remainder
through a coarfe cloth. The varnifh thus prepared
muft be kept for ufe in a bottle well ftopt."——When
the fpirit of wine is very ftrong, it will diffolve a
greater proportion of the feed-lac: but this will fatu-
rate the common, which is feldom of a ftrength
fufficient for making varnifhes in perfection. As the
chilling, which is the moft inconvenient accident attending thofe of this kind, is prevented, or produced
more frequently, according to the ftrength of the

fpirit, I will take this opportunity of fhowing a method by which weaker rectified fpirits may with great eafe, at any time, be freed from the phlegm, and rendered of the firft degree of ftrength.——"Take a pint of the common rectified fpirit of wine, and put it into a bottle, of which it will not fill above three parts. Add to it half an ounce of pearl-afhes, falt of tartar, or any other alkaline falt, heated red-hot, and powdered, as well as it can be without much lofs of its heat. Shake the mixture frequently for the fpace of half an hour; before which time, a great part of the phlegm will be feparated from the fpirit; and will appear, together with the undiffolved part of the falts in the bottom of the bottle. Let the fpirit then be poured off, or freed from the phlegm and falts by means of a *tritorium*, or feparating funnel; and let half an ounce of the pearl-afhes, heated and powdered as before, be added to it, and the fame treatment repeated. This may be done a third time, if the quantity of phlegm feparated by the addition of the pearl-afhes appear confiderable. An ounce of alum reduced to powder and made hot, but not burned, muft then be put into the fpirit; and fuffered to remain fome hours; the bottle being frequently fhaken. After which, the fpirit, being poured off from it, will be fit for ufe."——The addition of the alum is neceffary, to neutralize the remains of the alkaline falt or pearl-afhes; which would otherwife greatly deprave the fpirit with refpect to varnifhes and laquers, where vegetable colours are concerned; and muft confequently render another diftillation neceffary. The manner of ufing the feed-lac, or white varnifhes, is the fame; except with regard to the fubftance ufed in polifhing; which where a pure white, or great clearnefs of other colours, is in queftion, fhould be itfelf white; whereas the browner forts of polifhing duft, as being cheaper, and doing their bufinefs with greater difpatch, may be ufed in other cafes. The pieces of work to be varnifhed fhould be placed near a fire, or in a room where there is a ftove; and made perfectly dry: and then the varnifh may be rubbed over them by the

proper brushes made for that purpose, beginning in the
middle, and passing the brush to one end; and then,
with another stroke from the middle, passing it to the
other. But no part should be crossed or twice passed
over, in forming one coat, where it can possibly be
avoided. When one coat is dry, another must be laid
over it; and this must be continued at least five or six
times, or more; if, on trial, there be not a sufficient
thickness of varnish to bear the polish, without laying
bare the painting, or the ground colour underneath.
When a sufficient number of coats is thus laid on, the
work is fit to be polished: which must be done, in
common cases, by rubbing it with a rag dipped in tripoli (commonly called *rotten stone*), finely powdered.
But towards the end of the rubbing, a little oil of any
kind should be used along with the powder; and when
the work appears sufficiently bright and glossy, it
should be well rubbed with the oil alone, to clean it
from the powder; and give it a still brighter lustre.
In the case of white grounds, instead of the tripoli,
fine putty or whiting must be used; both which should
be washed over, to prevent the danger of damaging
the work from any sand or other gritty matter,
that may happen to become mixed with them. It
is a great improvement of all kinds of japan work, to
harden the varnish by means of heat; which, in every
degree that it can be applied short of what would burn
or calcine the matter, tends to give it a more firm and
strong texture. Where metals form the body, therefore, a very hot stove may be used, and the pieces of
work may be continued in it a considerable time; especially if the heat be gradually increased. But where
wood is in question, heat must be sparingly used; as it
would otherwise warp or shrink the body, so as to injure the general figure.

Of gilding japan work.] All the methods of gilding,
which are applicable to the ornamenting japan work,
having been before taught under the article of gilding,
it is needless to repeat them here. I shall therefore only
again observe, that in gilding with gold size (which is

a'moft the only method now practifed in japan work) where it is defired to have the gold not to fhine, or ap proach in the leaft towards the burnifhing flate, the fize fhould be ufed either with oil of turpentine only, or with a very little fat oil. But where a greater luftre, and appearance of polifh, are wanting, without the trouble of burnifhing, and the preparation neceffary for it, fat oil alone, or mixed with a little gold fize, fhould be ufed; and the fame proportionable effect will be produced from a mean proportion of them.

Of laquering.] Laquering is the laying either coloured or tranfparent varnifhes on metals, in order to produce the appearance of a different colour in the metal; or to preferve it from ruft and the injuries of the weather. Laquering is therefore much of the fame nature with japanning, both with regard to the principles and practice; except that no opake colours, but tranfparent tinges alone, are to be employed. The occafions on which laquering is now in general ufed, are three: where brafs is to be made to have the appearance of being gilt: where tin is wanted to have the refemblance of yellow metals: and where brafs or copper locks, nails, or other fuch matters, are to be defended from the corrofion of the air or moifture. There was indeed formerly another very frequent application of laquering; which was colouring frames of pictures, &c. previoufly filvered, in order to give them the effect of gilding; but this is now greatly difufed. Thefe various intentions of laquering require different compofitions for the effectuating each kind; and as there is a multiplicity of ingredients which may be conducive to each purpofe, a proportionable number of recipes have been devifed, and introduced into practice; efpecially for the laquering brafs work to imitate gilding; which is a confiderable object in this kind of art; and has been improved to the greateft degree of perfection. I fhall, however, only give one or two recipes for each; as they are all which are neceffary; the others being either made too complex by ingredients not effential to the intention, or too coftly by the ufe of fuch as are expenfive; or inferior in goodnefs, from the im-

proper choice or proportion of the component substances. The principal body or matter of all good laquers used at present is seed-lac ; but, for coarser uses, resin or turpentine is added ; in order to make the laquer cheaper, than if the seed lac, which is a much dearer article, be used alone. Spirit of wine is also consequently the fluid or menstruum of which laquers is formed ; as the ethereal oils will not dissolve the seed-lac : and it is proper that the spirit should be highly rectified for this purpose. As it is seldom practicable, nevertheless, to procure such spirits from the shops, it will be found very advantageous to use the method above given for dephlegmating it by alkaline salts ; but the use of the alum, directed in that process, must not be forgotten on this occasion ; as the effect of the alkaline salt would otherwise be the turning the metal of a purplish, instead of a golden colour, by laying on the laquer. The following are excellent compositions for brass work which is to resemble gilding.—
" Take of turmeric ground, as it may be had at the dry salters, one ounce, and of saffron and Spanish annatto each two drachms. Put them into a proper bottle, with a pint of highly-rectified spirit of wine ; and place them in a moderate heat, if convenient, often shaking them, for several days. A very strong yellow tincture will then be obtained ; which must be strained off from the dregs through a coarse linen cloth : and then, being put back into the bottle, three ounces of good feed-lac powdered grosly must be added, and the mixture placed again in a moderate heat, and shaken, till the feed-lac be dissolved ; or at least such part of it as may. The laquer must then be strained as before ; and will be fit for use ; but must be kept in a bottle carefully stopt."——Where it is desired to have the laquer warmer or redder than this composition may prove, the proportion of the annato must be increased ; and where it is wanted cooler, or nearer a true yellow, it must be diminished. The above, properly managed, is an extreme good laquer ; and of moderate price ; but the following, which is cheaper, and may be made where the Spanish annatto cannot be procured good is not greatly inferior to it.——" Take a turmeric roo

ground one ounce, of the best dragon's blood half a drachm. Put them to a pint of spirit of wine, and proceed as with the above."—By diminishing the proportion of the dragon's blood, the varnish may be rendered of a redder, or truer yellow cast. Saffron is sometimes used to form the body of colour in this kind of laquer, instead of the turmeric ; but though it makes a warmer yellow, yet the dearness of it, and the advantage which turmeric has in forming a much stronger tinge in spirit of wine, not only than the saffron, but than any other vegetable matter hitherto known, gives it the preference. Tho' being a true yellow, and consequently not sufficiently warm to overcome the greenish cast of brass, it requires the addition of some orange coloured tinge to make a perfect laquer for this purpose. Aloes and gamboge are also sometimes used in laquers for brass : but the aloes is not necessary where turmeric or saffron are used ; and the gamboge, though a very strong milky yellow in water, affords only a very weak tinge in spirit of wine. The varnish for tin may be made as follows :——" Take of turmeric root one ounce, of dragon's blood two drachms, and of spirit of wine one pint. Proceed as in the former."—This may, like the former, have the red or yellow rendered more prevalent, by the increasing or diminishing the proportion of the dragon's blood. Where a coarser or cheaper kind is wanted, the quantity of seed-lac may be abated ; and the deficiency thence arising supplied by the same proportion of resin. The laquer for locks, nails, &c. where little or no colour is desired, may either be seed-lac varnish alone, as prepared above, or with a little dragon's blood : or a compound varnish of equal parts of seed-lac and resin, with or without the dragon's blood. The laquer for picture frames, &c. where the ground is silver, and the appearance of gilding is to be produced, may be the composition before given, p. 28, for gilding leather : the principle being exactly the same in this case and that. The manner of laying on the laquer is as follows : First let the pieces of work to be laquered, be made thoroughly clean; which, if they be new founded, must be done by means of *aqua-*

fortis. Being ready, they muſt be heated by a ſmall charcoal fire in a proper veſſel, or any way that may be moſt convenient : the degree muſt not be greater than will admit of their being taken hold of without burning the hand. The laquer muſt then be laid on by a proper bruſh in the manner of other varniſhes; and the pieces immediately ſet again in the ſame warm ſituation. After the laquer is thoroughly dry and firm, the ſame opera-tion muſt be renewed again for four or five times, or till the work appear of the colour and brightneſs intended. For very fine work, ſome uſe a leſs proportion of ſeed-lac; which occaſions the laquer to lie evener on the me-tal : but, in this caſe, a greater number of coats are re-quired; which multiplies the proportion of labour; though, where the price of the work will allow for ſuch additional trouble, it will be the more perfect for it. The laquering tin may be performed in the ſame manner, as is here directed for braſs : but being for coarſer pur-poſes, leſs nicety is obſerved; and fewer coats (or per-haps one only) are made to ſuffice; as the laquer is com-pounded very red, that the tinge may have the ſtronger effect. Locks, nails, &c. where laquer is only uſed in a defenſive view, to keep them from corroding, and not for the improvement of the colour, may be treated in the ſame manner : but one or two coats are generally thought ſufficient. Though where any regard is had to the wear, the coats of laquer or varniſh ſhould always be of a due thickneſs, when they are to be expoſed to the air; otherwiſe, the firſt moiſt weather makes them chill, and look grey and milly, in ſuch manner, that they are rather injurious than beneficial to the work they are laid upon. The laquering picture frames, &c. where the ground is leaf ſilver, may be performed in the ſame manner as was before directed in the caſe of gilding lea-ther; the circumſtances being nearly the ſame, except with relation to the texture of the ſubject; to ſuit which, the different manner of treatment may be eaſily adapted. But the laquer, as was before obſerved, may be the ſame.

Of ſtaining wood yellow.] Take any white wood, and

bruſh it over ſeveral times with the tincture of turmeric root, made by putting an ounce of the turmeric ground to powder, to a pint of ſpirit; and, after they have ſtood ſome days, ſtraining off the tincture. If the yellow co-lour be deſired to have a redder caſt, a little dragon's blood muſt be added, in the proportion that will produce the teint required. A cheaper, but leſs ſtrong and bright yellow, may be given to the wood, by rubbing it over ſeveral times with the tincture of the French berries, made boiling hot. After the wood is again dry, it ſhould be bruſhed over wi. h a weak alum water uſed cold. Leſ-ſer pieces of wood, inſtead of being bruſhed over with them, may be ſoaked in the decoctions or tinctures. Wood may be alſo ſtained yellow by means of *aquafortis*; which will ſometimes produce a very beautiful yellow co-lour, but at other times a browner. The wood ſhould be warm, when the *aquafortis* is laid on; and be held to the fire immediately afterwards; and care muſt be taken, that either the *aquafortis* be not too ſtrong, or that it be ſparingly uſed; otherwiſe a brown, ſometimes even a blackiſh colour, may be the reſult. In order to render any of theſe ſtains more beautiful and durable, the wood ſhould be bruſhed over after it is coloured; and then var-niſhed by the ſeed lac varniſh; or when deſired to be very ſtrong, and to take a high poliſh, with three or four coats of ſhell-lac varniſh.

Of ſtaining wood red.] For a bright red ſtain for wood, make a ſtrong infuſion of Braſil in ſtale urine, or water impregnated with pearl aſhes, in the proportion of an ounce to a gallon; to a gallon of either of which, the proportion of Braſil wood muſt be a pound: which being put to them, they muſt ſtand together two or three days, often ſtirring the mixture. With this infuſion ſtrained, and made boiling hot, bruſh over the wood to be ſtained, till it appear ſtrongly coloured; then, while yet wet, bruſh it over with alum-water made in the proportion of two ounces of alum to a quart of water. For a leſs bright red, diſſolve an ounce of dragon's blood in a pint of ſpirit of wine, and bruſh over the wood with the

e ſtain appear to be as ſtrong as is deſired.
aᤈ, rather laquering than ſtaining. For
ed, add to a gallon of the above infuſion
two additional ounces of the pearl aſhes,
s before directed : but it is neceſſary, in
uſh the wood over often with the alum-
reaſing the proportion of pearl-aſhes, the
dered yet paler : but it is proper, when
quantity is added, to make the alum-
Theſe reds, when it is neceſſary, may
the yellows.

vood blue.]   Wood may be ſtained blue,
r of copper or indigo : but the firſt will
r colour ; and is more generally practica-
ter.   Becauſe the indigo can be uſed only
which it is brought by the manner of pre-
y the dyers : of whom indeed it muſt be
ot be properly ſo prepared but in large
with a particular apparatus.   The me-
g blue with the copper is therefore as
Take a ſolution of copper, and bruſh it,
ral times over the wood.   Then make a
rl-aſhes, in the proportion of two ounces
ater ; and bruſh it hot over the wood,
e ſolution of copper, till it be of a per-
ur."   Wood ſtained green as above by
likewiſe be made blue, by uſing the ſo-
pearl aſhes in the ſame manner.   When
or ſtaining wood blue, it muſt be managed
'ake indigo prepared with ſoap lees as
he dyers ; and bruſh the wood with it.
Prepare then a ſolution of white tartar,
artar, which is to be made, by boiling
f the tartar, or cream, in a quart of wa-
this ſolution, uſed copiouſly, bruſh over
e the moiſture of the tincture of indigo
l out of it."——Theſe blues muſt be
niſhed as the reds, where there is occaſion.

wood of mahogany colour.]   Mahogany
oſt uſeful of any ſtain for wood (eſpeci-

ally fince the veneering with different colours is out of
fafhion) as it is much practifed at prefent for chairs
and other furniture made in imitation of mahogany; which, when well managed, may be brought
to a very near refemblance. This ftain may be
of different hues, as the natural wood varies greatly,
being of all the intermediate teints betwixt the red
brown and purple brown, according to the age, or
fometimes the original nature of different pieces. For
the light red brown, ufe a decoction of madder and
fuftic wood, ground in water; the proportion may be
half a pound of madder, and a quarter of a pound of
fuftic, to a gallon: or in default of fuftic, an ounce of
the yellow berries may be ufed. This muft be brufhed
over the wood to be ftained, while boiling hot, till the
due colour be obtained; and, if the wood be kindly
grained, it will have greatly the appearance of new
mahogany. The fame effect nearly may be produced
by the tincture of dragon's blood and turmeric root,
in fpirit of wine: by increafing or diminifhing the
proportion of each of which ingredients, the brown
ftain may be varied to a more red or yellow caft at
pleafure. This fucceeds better upon wood, which has
already fome tinge of brown, than upon whiter. For
the dark mahogany, take the infufion of madder made
as above, except the exchanging the fuftic for two
ounces of logwood: and when the wood to be ftained
has been feveral times brufhed over, and is again dry, it
muft be flightly brufhed over with water in which pearl-
afhes have been diffolved, in the proportion of about a
quarter of an ounce to a quart. Any ftains of the
intermediate colours may be made, by mixing thefe ingredients, or varying the proportion of them. Where
thefe ftains are ufed for better kind of work, the wood
fhould be afterwards varnifhed with three or four coats
of feed lac varnifh; but for coarfe work, the varnifh
of refin and feed lac may be employed, or they may
be only well rubbed over with drying oil.

Of ftaining wood green.] Diffolve verdigrife in vinegar, or cryftals of verdigrife in water; and, with

n, bruſh over the wood till it be duly
may be bruſhed and varniſhed, as the

ood purple.] Bruſh the wood to be ſtained
·ith a ſtrong decoction of logwood and
n the proportion of one pound of the
quarter of a pound of the Braſil, to a
er; and boiled for an hour or more.
l has been bruſhed over there will be a
of colour, let it dry; and then be
over by a ſolution of one drachm of
quart of water. This ſolution muſt be
as it will gradually change the colour
red, which it will be originally found to
due purple; and therefore its effect muſt
the due point for producing the colour
may be varniſhed as the reſt.
wood black.] Bruſh the wood ſeveral
·ot decoction of logwood made as above;
ie Braſil. Then having prepared an in-
·, by putting a quarter of a pound of
· to two quarts of water, and ſetting
unſhine, or any other gentle heat, for
ays, bruſh the wood three or four times
and then paſs over it again, while yet
lution of green vitriol in water, in the
wo ounces to a quart. The above is the
d: but a very fine black may be produ-
ng the wood ſeveral times over with a
per in *aquafortis*; and afterwards with
of logwood, which muſt be repeated til
of a ſufficient force; and the greens by
he ſolution of the copper, wholly over-
blacks may be varniſhed as the colours.
· ſtains are deſired to be very ſtrong, and
vood intended to be uſed for veneering,
·neceſſary, they ſhould be ſoaked, and
to render which the more practicable,
be previouſly ſlit or ſawed into pieces of
·eſs for inlaying. It is to be underſtood

alfo, that when the wood is above ordered to be brufhed
feveral times over with the tinging fubftances, it fhould
be fuffered to dry betwixt each time.

Of ftaining ivory, bone, or horn, yellow.] Boil them
firft in a folution of alum, in the proportion of one
pound to two quarts of water: and then prepare a
tincture of the French berries, by boiling half a
pound of the berries, pounded, in a gallon of water
with a quarter of a pound of pearl-afhes. After this
tincture has boiled about an hour, put the ivory, &c.
previoufly boiled in the alum water, into it; and let
them remain there half an hour. If turmeric root be ufed
inftead of the French berries, a brighter yellow may be
obtained; but the ivory, &c. muft in that cafe be
again dipped in alum-water after it is taken out of
the tincture; otherwife an orange colour, not a yellow,
will be produced from the effect of the pearl-afhes on
the turmeric.

Of ftaining ivory, bone and horn, green.] They muft
be boiled in a folution of verdigrife in vinegar; or of
copper in *aquafortis,* prepared as above directed, (a
veffel of glafs or earthen ware being employed for this
purpofe) till they be of the colour defired.

Of ftaining ivory, bone and horn, red.] Take ftrong
lime water, prepared as for other purpofes; and the
rafpings of Brafil wood, in the proportion of half a
pound to a gallon. Let them boil for an hour; and
then put in the ivory, &c. prepared by boiling in alum
water in the manner above directed for the yellow; and
continue it there till it be fufficiently colqured. If it
be too crimfon, or verge towards the purple, it may
be rendered more fcarlet, by dipping again in the alum
water.

Of ftaining ivory, bone and horn, blue.] Stain the ivory, &c. firft green, according to the manner above directed; and then dip it in a folution of pearl-afhes
made ftrong and boiling hot; but it muft not be continued longer, nor dipped oftener than is neceffary to con-
vert the green to blue. The ivory, &c. may otherwife be boiled in the tincture of indigo prepared as by

the dyers; and afterwards in the folution of tartar made as is directed for the ftaining wood.

Of ftaining ivory, bone and horn, purple.] Treat them in the fame manner as. was directed for red; except that logwood muft be fubftituted in the place of Brafil wood; and the ufe of the alum water muft be omitted wholly. If a redder purple be wanted, a mixture of the logwood and Brafil muft be employed, inftead of the logwood alone. The proportion may be equal parts; or any lefs proportion of the Brafil, according to the colour defired.

Of ftaining horn to imitate tortoife-fhell.] The horn to be ftained muft be firft preffed into proper plates or fcales, or other flat form. The following mixture muft then be prepared——" Take of quicklime two parts, and of litharge one; and temper them to the confiftence of a foft pafte with foap lye."——Put this pafte over all the parts of the horn, except fuch as are proper to be left tranfparent, in order to the greater refemblance of the tortoife-fhell. The horn muft then remain thus covered with the pafte till it be thoroughly dry: when the pafte being brufhed off, the horn will be found partly opake, and partly tranfparent, in the manner of tortoife fhell; and when put over a foil, of the kind of latten called *affidae*, will be fcarcely diftinguifhable from it. It requires fome degree of fancy, and judgment, to difpofe of the pafte in fuch a manner, as to form a variety of tranfparent parts of different magnitude and figure, to look like the effect of nature; and it will be an improvement to add femi tranfparent parts. This may be done by mixing whiting with fome of the pafte to weaken its operation in particular places; by which fpots of a reddifh brown will be produced; that, if properly interfperfed, efpecially on the edges of the dark parts, will greatly increafe as well the beauty of the work, as its fimilitude with the real tortoife fhell.

To ftain ivory, bone and horn, black.] Proceed in the fame manner as is above directed for wood.

Of ftaining paper or parchment, yellow.] Paper may

be ftained yellow by the tincture of French berries; but a much more beautiful colour may be obtained by ufing the tincture of turmeric formed by infufing an ounce or more of the root powdered in a pint of fpirit of wine. This may be made to give any teint of yellow, from the lighteft ftraw to the full colour, called French yellow; and will be equal in brightnefs even to the beft dyed filks. If yellow be wanted of a warmer or redder caft, annatto, or dragon's blood, muft be added to the tincture. The beft manner of ufing thefe and the following tinctures, is to fpread them even on the paper or parchment by means of a broad brufh in the manner of varnifhing.

Of ftaining paper or parchment, red.] Paper or parchment, may be ftained red, by treating it in the fame manner as is directed for wood, p. 56; or by red ink. It may alfo be ftained of a fcarlet hue by the tincture of dragon's blood in fpirit of wine: but this will not be bright. A very fine crimfon ftain may be given to paper, by a tincture of the Indian lake, which may be made, by infufing the lake fome days in fpirit of wine; and then pouring off the tincture from the dregs.

Of ftaining paper or parchment, green.] Paper or parchment, may be ftained green, by the folution of verdigrefe in vinegar; or by the cryftals of verdigrife diffolved in water. As alfo by the folution of copper in *aquafortis* made by adding filings of copper gradually to the *aquafortis* till no ebullition enfues: or fpirit of falt may be ufed in the place of the *aquafortis*.

Of ftaining paper or parchment, blue.] A blue colour may be given to paper or parchment, by ftaining it green by any of the above-mentioned methods; and treating it afterwards as is directed for the ftaining wood blue, by the fame means, or by indigo, in the manner there explained likewife.

Of ftaining paper or parchment, orange.] Stain the paper or parchment, firft of a full yellow, by means of the tincture of turmeric, as above directed. Then brufh it over with a folution of fixed alkaline falt, made by diffolving half an ounce of pearl afhes, or falt of tartar, in a quart of water, and filtering the folution.

Of staining paper on parchment purple.]. Paper or
parchment, may be stained purple by archal, or by the
tincture of logwood, according to the method above
directed for staining wood. The juice of ripe privet
berries expressed, will likewise give a purple dye to paper or parchment.

*Of staining alabaster, marble, and other stones, of va-
rious colours.*] Alabaster, marble, and other stones,
may be stained of a yellow, red, green, blue, purple,
black, or any of the compound colours, by the means
above given for staining wood. But it is better, when
a strong tinge is wanted, to pour the tincture, if made
in water, boiling hot, on the alabaster, &c. spreading
it equally on every part, then to brush it over only;
though that may be sufficient where a slighter dye will
suffice. When tinctures in spirit of wine are used, they
must not be heated; as the spirit would evaporate, and
leave the tinging gums in an undissolved state. Where
stones are not perfectly white, but partake of brown-
ness or greyness, the colour produced by the tinges will
be proportionably wanting in brightness. Because the
natural colour of the stone is not hid or covered by these
tinges; but combines with them: and, for the same
reason, if the stone be of any of the pure colours, the
result will be a compound of such colour and that of
the tinge.

Of the method of preparing and colouring marbled paper.]
There are several kinds of marbled paper; but the principal difference of them lies, in the forms in which the
colours are laid on the ground: some being disposed in
whirles or circumvolutions; some in waving jagged
lengths; and others only in spots of a roundish or oval
figure. The general manner of managing each kind is,
nevertheless, the same: being the dipping the paper in
a solution of gum dragacanth (or, as it is commonly
called, gum dragon); over which the colours, previously prepared with ox-gall and spirit of wine, are first
spread. The peculiar apparatus necessary for this purpose is, a trough for containing the gum dragacanth
and the colours; a comb or quill for disposing them in

the figure ufually chofen; and a burniſhing ſtone for poliſhing the paper. The trough may be of any kind of wood: and muſt be fomewhat larger than the ſheets of paper, for marbling which it is to be employed: but the ſides of it need only rife about two inches above the bottom: for, by making it thus ſhallow, a leſs quantity of the folution of the gum will ferve to fill it. The comb may be alſo of wood, and five inches in length: but ſhould have braſs teeth, which may be about two inches long, and placed at about a quarter of an inch diſtance from each other. The burniſhing ſtone may be of jafper, or agate: but as thofe ſtones are very dear, when of fufficient largenefs, marble or glafs may be ufed, provided their furface be poliſhed to a great degree of fmoothnefs. Thefe implements being prepared, the folution of gum dragacanth muſt be made, by putting a fufficient proportion of the gum, which ſhould be white, and clear from all foulneffes, into clean water; and letting it remain there a day or two; frequently breaking the lumps and ſtirring it, till the whole ſhall appear diffolved, and equally mixed with the water. The confiſtence of the folution ſhould be nearly that of ſtrong gum water, ufed in miniature painting: and, if it appear thicker, water muſt be added; or, if thinner, more of the gum. When the folution is thus brought to a due ſtate, it muſt be paffed through a linen cloth, and being then put into the trough, it will be ready to receive the colours. The colours employed for red are carmine, lake, rofe-pink, vermillion and red-lead: but the two laſt are too hard and glaring; unlefs they be mixed with rofe pink, or lake, to bring them to a fofter caſt: and with refpect to the carmine and lake, they are too dear for common purpofes;—for blue, Pruffian blue and verditer, may be ufed:—for yellow, Dutch pink and yellow ochre, may be employed:—for green, verdigrife, a mixture of Dutch pink and Pruffian blue, or verditer, in different proportions:——for orange, the orange lake, or a mixture of vermillion, or red-lead, with Dutch pink:—for purple, rofe-pink and Pruffian blue. Thefe feveral colours

should be ground with spirit of wine, till they be of a
proper fineness ; and then at the time of using them, a
little fish gall, or, in default of it, the gall of a beast
should be added, by grinding them over again with it.
The proper proportion of the gall must be found by
trying them ; for there must be just so much as will suffer the spots of colour, when sprinkled on the solution
of the gum dragacanth, to join together, without inter-
mixing or running into each other. When every thing
is thus prepared, the solution of the gum dragacanth
must be poured into the trough ; and the colours, being
in a separate pot, with a pencil appropriated to each,
must be sprinkled on the surface of the solution, by
shaking the pencil, charged with its proper colour, over
it : and this must be done with the several kinds of colour desired, till the surface be wholly covered. Where
the marbling is proposed to be in spots of a simple form,
nothing more is necessary : but where the whirles or
snail shell figures are wanted, they must be made by
means of a goose quill ; which must be put among the
spots to turn them about, till the effect be produced.
The waving jagged lengths must be made by means of
the comb above described, which must be passed through
the colours from one end of the trough to the other ;
and will give them that appearance. But if they be
desired to be pointed both ways, the comb must be
again passed through the trough in a contrary direction ;
or if some of the whirles or snail shell figures be required
to be added, they may be yet made by the means before directed. The paper should be previously prepared for receiving the colours, by dipping it over night
in water ; and laying the sheets on each other, with a
weight over them, in the case of paper to be imprinted
by copper plates. The whole being thus ready, the
paper must be held by two corners, and laid in the

pended near at hand for that purpofe : and in that ftate
it muft continue, till it be perfectly dry. It then remains only to give the paper a proper polifh ; in order
to which it is firft rubbed with a little foap ; and then
muft be thoroughly fmoothed by the glafs polifhers,
fuch as are ufed for linen, and called the calender glaffes.
After which it fhould be again rubbed by a burnifher
of jafper or agate, or, in default of them, of glafs
ground to the higheft polifh : for on the perfect polifh
of the paper depends in a great degree its beauty and
value. Gold or filver powders may be ufed, where defired, along with the colours ; and require only the
fame treatment as them : except that they muft be firft
tempered with gum water.

*The original recipe for the making Pruffian blue, as
publifhed by Dr. Woodward.*] " Take any quantity of
blood, and evaporate it to drynefs ; continuing the
heat till it becomes black ; but avoiding the burning
any part of it to afhes. Powder the dry matter, and
mix it thoroughly with an equal weight of pearl afhes ;
and calcine the mixture in an iron pot or crucible, on
which a cover is put. The calcination muft be continued fo long as the matter emits any flame ; the fire
being raifed to a confiderable degree of heat at the end
of the operation ; and the matter muft be then powdered ; and put, while yet hot, into twelve times its
weight of water ; which muft be again fet on the fire
to boil for the fpace of three quarters of an hour, or
more. The fluid muft then be filtered off through a
thin flannel bag, from the part remaining undiffolved :
through which remaining part frefh water fhould be
paffed, before it be taken out of the filtering bag, to
extract as much as poffible of the folution : and the
water thus paffed through fhould be added to the quantity before filtered : after which, what is retained in
the bag may be thrown away. In the mean time a folution fhould be made of alum, and copperas calcined
to whitenefs, in the proportion of two pounds of the
alum, and two ounces of the calcined vitriol, to each
pound of the pearl afhes ufed with the blood, which fo-

lution muſt be made by boiling the alum and copperas
in five times their weight of water, and then filtering
them through flannel or paper, where great nicety is
required. When the ſolution of the alum and copperas
is thus prepared; it muſt be added to the lixivium filtered off from the calcined blood and pearl-aſhes; from
which mixture, the precipitation of a blackiſh green
matter will ſoon enſue. After the precipitated matter
has ſubſided to the bottom of the veſſel, and the fluid
appears clear over it, ſeparate it from the green ſediment, firſt by pouring off all that will run clear out of
the veſſel, and afterwards by ſtraining off the remainder;
and then put the green matter again into a veſſel, that
will contain as much fluid as it was before mixed with.
Add ſpirit of ſalt to it afterwards, in the proportion of
ſix ounces to every pound of the pearl-aſhes uſed; and
the green matter will then ſoon appear to be converted
into a beautiful blue. Water muſt then be added, to
waſh off the ſpirit of ſalt; which muſt be renewed ſeveral times, till it come off perfectly ſweet; and the
laſt quantity muſt then be ſtrained off; and the blue
ſediment dried in lumps of a moderate ſize. The produce will be about three ounces for every pound of the
pearl-aſhes employed."——If the produce be deſired
to be made either of a lighter or darker hue, it may
be done by increaſing the proportion of the pearl-aſhes
to the blood, to give a lighter kind; or the ſpirit of
ſalt to the pearl-aſhes, to give a deeper kind: but the
quantity will in the latter caſe be proportionably dimi-
niſhed. The ſtraining or filtering the lixivium through
flannel is not ſo good a method as the doing it thro'
paper; eſpecially where the colour is wanted of a very
great brightneſs and purity; and the water is beſt ſeparated from the great ſediment firſt produced, and afterwards from the blue one, by the ſame means: but in
theſe caſes a fine linen cloth much worn, though whole,
ſhould be laid over the paper. The colour, when reduced to a proper conſiſtence, may be laid on chalk
ſtones to dry: and a moderate heat may be alſo uſed
for greater diſpedition, when required; but great care

fhould be taken not to burn the matter. The calcination may be performed in a reverberatory furnace, fuch as is ufed by the chemifts; or in the furnaces where metals are melted; for the crucible or pot, containing the matter, may either be furrounded by the coals, or placed over them, provided a fufficient heat be given to it. But where larger quantities are to be calcined, they may be very cheaply and commodioufly managed in the potters or the tobacco-pipe-makers furnaces; being put into them along with the earthen-ware and pipes.

The Englifh Fifty Pounds Premium Receipt for either taking or deftroying Rats, or Mice, without Poifon.] There is no better place of fecurity to decoy thefe vermin into than a large round wire cage, made in form of the common moufe traps, about fixteen inches wide, with feveral places for entrance: thofe for receiving mice fhould be much fmaller, and fo fhould the holes they enter at. It will be neceffary, firft, to obferve the places they moft frequent, and to difcover the holes they make for paffing and repaffing. The traps are to be fet within four or five yards of thefe holes, and from which, quite to thofe traps, the floor is to be rubbed (in a ftrait line about four inches wide) with a piece of ftrong rich cheefe toafted, on which a few drops of oil of annifeed has been dropped, and the trap fhould be well rubbed likewife. *Baits for the traps are to be made thus:* Of ftrong cheefe eight ounces; oatmeal the like quantity; feven or eight drops of oil of annifeed; Indian berries one ounce; featherfew half an ounce; droppings of fweet oil fufficient to make it up into a pafte: then form it into many little balls, and this will moft affuredly decoy them into the cage, though many people were prefent. I advife the ufe of traps, otherwife they would retire to their private haunts, and expire, which would prove very offenfive for fome time to all near them, efpecially in warm weather.

The following is likewife by a Candidate for the Fifty Pound's Premium.] Procure an earthen veffel, well glazed in the infide, near two feet high, and full one broad fill it to the middle with water, and hang a very smooth board to the top by two strong pins, and so even that the least weight will trip it up on either side; this board is to be well daubed over with the greasy composition before mentioned, (only he leaves out the featherfew) which entices the vermin on the board, and that slides them into the water, from whence there is no escaping.

Discovery of the true reason of burning sulphur in hogsheads for preserving wine, by a new and curious experiment.] If two or three drops of the oil of tartar are poured into half a glass of very fine red wine, the wine will lose its red colour, and become opaque and yellowish, is turned and pricked wine; but if two or three drops of the spirit of sulphur, which is a very strong acid, are afterwards poured into the glass, the same wine will entirely resume its beautiful red colour; whence the reason is easily perceived, why sulphur is burnt in hogsheads in order to preserve wine, since it is not the inflammable part of sulphur that causes this effect, but its acid spirit, that enters and permeates the wood of the vessel.

The manner of silvering Looking-glasses, as done in London and Birmingham.] First spread a paper on an even board or stone (a stone is best) on that sprinkle a little fine chalk, over which lay the leaf of tin: then dip a piece of cotton in quicksilver, and rub gently over the tin leaf (where the glass is to cover) till it looks bright. You are now to pour on the quicksilver as long as it will lie. Lay slips of paper, three double on each side, to support the glass, and then gently move it forward, keeping your hand pressing on it, to force out the superfluous quicksilver; let it be removed to another flat board, or stone, or lay a weight on it on the same, and in a day or two it will be dry. Note, for large plate glasses, a screw answers much better than a weight laid on.

For softening Crystal.] It must be left some time in the milk of a goat which has been made to feed during forty six days on ivy leaves. The use of this milk has been proved to be of singular service to those troubled with the gravel.

The useful Alarm-Bell.] This is originally a Dutch invention, and by which a person may be enabled to rise at any time of the night ; or know how time goes as well as by a clock, or watch, by observing the following directions.

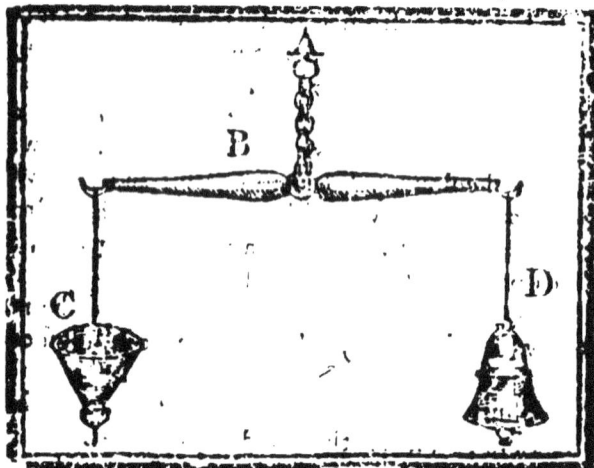

A is a small chain in the middle of a beam, and by which it hangs. B is a kind of a beam, like those belonging to scales. C a vessel made of either glass or tin, in the form described, which is to be filled with fine dry sand, the quantity to be more or less, according to the time you would rise : the vessel C is to have a small hole at the bottom, as in an hour glass, thro' which the sand is to pass. D is along at the opposite end of the beam B. When the vessel C is empty, the bell D is to be a very little heavier than C, by which means, after the sand is all discharged, the bell D becoming more weighty than C, the ballance instantly falls on that side, and the bell continues ringing for some time, and by which noise the person is called at the time required. The way to proportion the sand to the time is thus : Suppose a person required to be called in four hours after going to rest : if, on trial, half a pound of sand will run four hours, then that is to be the quantity ; if in six hours, then

12 ounces are to be put into the veſſel; if in eight hours, one pound, and ſo in proportion to the time it is to run.

For ſoftening Ivory and Bones.] Take ſage, boil it in ſtrong vinegar, ſtrain the decoction through a piece of cloſe cloth; and, when you have a mind to ſoften bones or ivory, ſteep them in this liquor, and the longer they remain in it, the ſofter they will grow.

Another preparation for ſoftening bones.] Take roman-vitriol and common ſalt, of each one pound; bruiſe and reduce them into an impalpable powder; put them into an alembic: the diſtilled water will have the virtue of ſoftening bones; and, to ſucceed therein, they need only be left to ſteep in it for half a day.

For ſoftening glaſs.] Take the blood of a he-goat and a duck, ſome dregs of oil and vinegar; mix theſe things together, and put them into a varniſhed earthen pot; let the whole be warmed a little, and afterwards, having put ſome glaſs in, let it there remain till it becomes ſoft.

A ready way for melting iron.] Take ſulphur, mix it with a little ſalt, and dilute the mixture with a child's urine, till it becomes white: beſmear the iron with it, and you will ſoon ſee it liquefy. As to the more compact and harder metals, fire alone can make them liquefy.

The virtues of Succinum.] Mizaldus ſays, that faſtened about the neck, it radically and ſurpriſingly cures the fiſtula lachrymalis and ſoreneſs of the eyes. A woman of Copenhagen, being tormented with a continual pain of the head, was adviſed to wear an amber necklace, whereupon the pain ſoon vaniſhed. This induced her to leave it off but ſeldom, and only when ſhe was apprehenſive it cauſed too great a dryneſs, by diſſipating too great a quantity of her humours. This obſervation is ſupported by that of Caſpard Scholler, a magiſtrate of the ſame city, who is laviſh of his commendations of ſuccinum, having himſelf found very good effects by it.

A remarkable circumſtance concerning ale; with an unerring method of brewing malt liquor, that will ſoon be fine and fit for drinking; and far more palatable and

wholefome than what is procured from the too common
errineous way many brewers follow.] Whoever brews
and expects to have either good ale or beer, will b
fure to be difappointed, if care is not taken to provid
good malt and hops ; nor is the water made ufe of fi
very immaterial an article as fome imagine, for a grea
deal depends upon it. What I have above advanced
may very likely be credited by many ; but when I com
to tell them, there is more malt liquor fpoiled by higl
boiling, than by all mifmanagements put together, it i
eafy to perceive I fhall have many obftinate infatuatec
people to encounter with, who very fimply imagine
that ale or beer, cannot poffibly be bad which has hac
a four hours boiling. It is well known there are man)
parts of England remarkable for fine malt liquors ; anc
I as well know, that not one of the counties that hav
excelled in either ale or beer, ever boiled above half ai
hour at moft. There is, indeed, a town in Devonfhire
that is faid to have conftantly good ale. I am well acquainted with it ; Barnftable, no doubt, has a ftrong
glutinous ale, that pleafes many people ; and thofe whc
brew, I dare fay, moft fcandaloufly boil it, at leaft foui
hours. But what is the confequence ? Why there is
fcarce a houfe in that place but affords a pair or two oi
crutches, and unhappy cripples to make ufe of them,
I muft own people in England have not followed this
pernicious cuftom fo much of late years. They find
they are gainers by their reformation ; and many have
owned, they never had fuch valuable ale or beer, as fince
they left off the old miftaken way of boiling for three
or four hours, and acknowledge they have reduced it to
lefs than a quarter of that time. There are others
again, who declare, to their cuftomers, that they actually boil four hours : when in fact, a quarter of an
hour is the moft they have boiled for five or fix years
paft. I believe this reformation is chiefly owing to
fome treatifes publifhed concerning brewing, in which
the pernicious confequence of high boiling is fufficiently difplayed and exploded. I will beg leave to give an
inftance of the bad confequences of long boiling, than

will be fufficient to fatisfy any perfon who practifes it,
of their error. A gentleman of my acquaintance, in
Chefter, often complained to me, that he bought the
beft of malt and hops ; that they had fine water from
the river Dee, and he had it conftantly boiled full four
hours ; and yet notwithftanding all this, he could not
have either good ale or beer. His lady too joined in
the complaint, and faid, it would be a great fatisfaction if a remedy could be found, as many of the gentle-
men who vifited there preferred a glafs of fine beer to
any liquor whatever. I then told him, if he would
have a brewing after my direction, I would be anfwer-
able, that it would prove fatisfactory. Accordingly
good malt and hops were provided, and the water was
fetched from the river Dee, as ufual. I muft own it was
with the utmoft difficulty I prevailed on the man who
brewed to boil it fo fhort a time, who protefted it would
be good for nothing However, I at length prevailed,
and he proceeded in the following manner : the quantity of liquor was fixty gallons ; and to put the thing
quite out of difpute, and to prove that boiling long
was erroneous, the firft twenty gallons were boiled
twenty fix minutes ; the fecond twenty gallons one hour
and a quarter : and the third and laft twenty gallons
full two hours. In about a month, the three cafks
were examined : that which was boiled twenty-fix minutes, proved extremely fine and well tafted, and gave
a general fatisfaction. But the cafk which contained
the liquor of the fecond boiling, was very far from being either fo fine or pleafant. And the third cafk which
contained the laft and long boiled liquor, proved very
foul, and quite difagreeable in many other refpects.
Now as there was no difference in the management of
the fixty gallons of ale I have been fpeaking of, boiling only excepted, how will the advocates for long
boiling malt liquors account for this : the fame malt,
hops and water, tunned at the fame time, and in cafks
of the fame fize, and placed in the fame good cellar.
I have to add to this account, that at the two months
end, the fecond boiling was foul and ill tafted, and was

made fine with great difficulty. The laſt boiling was very foul and bad ; at the end of ſix months it was cloudy, ropy, and ill taſted ; ſome attempts were made in vain, to fine it ; but at about ten months old, it was far worſe. The gentleman, who, indeed, was too fond of long boiling, for many years before, as it had been often inſinuated to him, that drink could not be boiled too much, was greatly pleaſed to find the firſt caſk prove ſo exceeding good, with little boiling ; he then gave orders to the man who brewed for him, never for the future, to boil his liquor above twenty minutes, which directions were ſtrictly obſerved : and it is now as uncommon to find any malt liquor that is bad in his cellars, as it was before to have any that was good. I would fain know what it is boiled for the length of four hours ? Some tell you, 'tis to get the goodneſs out of the hops. To which I anſwer, it is a ſad thing ſo many thouſand gallons of malt liquor ſhould be ſpoiled every year, only to get goodneſs (as they are pleaſed to call it) out of the hops, when many other means might be uſed to do it in a few minutes. In one word, the long boiling malt-liquor has many bad properties attending it, without having any thing in its favour : for it renders ſuch ale too gummy and fray to be wholeſome, and is the cauſe of many becoming cripples, who make a too frequent uſe of thoſe pernicious long boiled liquors : for the blood, by this means, becomes too glutinous to paſs the fine blood veſſels : hence ariſe thoſe various diſorders ! thoſe pains ! thoſe aches ! that render the unhappy cripples not only a fatigue to themſelves, but introduce diſorders that are felt by future generations. Nor does the miſchief ſtop here (though I muſt own this is the moſt melancholy part of it) for whenever ſuch ale or beer proves foul, which is too commonly the caſe, it is with great difficulty made fine, and fit for drinking. In ſhort, thoſe who once experience the great advantage that will reſult from boiling their liquor not longer than twenty-five or thirty minutes, will be ſure to have this ſatisfaction, that their ale will be much better, plea-

fanter, and more wholefome, than thofe that are long
boiled ; by which they will not only preferve the health
of thofe who drink it, but alfo have more liquor from
the fame quantity of malt ; which very likely may be
a means of prevailing, as intereft is in the cafe, more
than any other arguments. It is to be remarked that
all liquor fhould be boiled as nimbly as poffible (fo as
not to make it run out of the boiler) and alfo that the
long ftupid way of boiling for the goodnefs of the hop,
is of the utmoft prejudice ; for its fine flavour will be
foon extracted : what comes after, by length of ftew-
ing, is only an earthy, heavy, pernicious quality, that
will be fure to render the ale difagreeable, and prove
prejudicial to thofe who drink it.——Thus much I have
prefumed to fay, in order to prevent the pernicious cuftom, that has too long prevailed : perfons of reafon
will very likely try the experiment : 'tis on thofe I rely
and on whom it will chiefly depend to decide, which
method is beft to purfue, that guided by reafon, long
experience, and the refult of many years practice ; or
the method obftinately purfued by unreafonable bigots,
and a fet of infatuated old women.

The benefits arifing from drinking Tar-water.] Tar-
water has been lately recommended to the world as a
certain, fafe, and almoft infallible medicine in almoft all
difeafes ; a flow, yet effectual alterative in cachexies, fcurvies, chlorotic, hyfterical, hypochondrical, and other chronical complaints : and a fudden remedy in acute diftempers
which demand immediate relief, as pleurifies, peripneumo-
nies, the fmall pox, and all kinds of fevers in general : yet,
though it may fall fhort, in fome cafes, of the charac-
ter given it ; it is, doubtlefs, in a multitude of cafes,
of great utility : it fenfibly raifes the pulfe, and occafions fome confiderable evacuations, generally by perfpi-
ration, or urine, though fometimes by ftool or vomit :
hence it is fuppofed to act by increafing the vis vitæ,
and enabling nature to expel the morbific humours.
We fhall here infert, from the firft public recommen-
der of this liquor (Bifhop Berkeley) fome obfervations
on the manner of ufing it. Tar-water, when right, is

not paler than French, nor deeper coloured than Spa-
niſh white wine, and full as clear : if there be not a
ſpirit very ſenſibly perceiv:d in drinking, you may con-
clude the tar-water is not good. It may be drank either cold or warm ; in cholicks, I take it to be beſt
warm. As to the quantity in common chronical diſpo-
ſitions, a pint a day may be ſufficient, taken on an
empty ſtomach, at two, or four times, to wit, night
and morning, and about two hours after dinner and
breakfaſt : more may be taken by ſtrong ſtomachs. But
thoſe who labour under great and inveterate maladics,
muſt drink a greater quantity ; at leaſt a quart every
twenty four hours ; all of this claſs muſt have much patience and pe.ſeverance in the uſe of this, as well as of
all other medicines, which, though ſure, muſt yet, in
the nature of things, be flow in the cure of inveterate
chronical diſorders. In acute caſes, fevers of all kinds,
it muſt be drank in bed warm, and in great quantity,
(the fever ſtill enabling the patient to drink) perhaps
a pint every hour, which I have known to work ſurpriſing cures. But it works ſo quick and gives ſuch ſpirits, that the patients often think themſelves cured, before the fever hath quite left them.

Biſhop BERKLEY's *manner of preparing Tar-water.*]
Tar, two pounds ; water, one gallon. Stir them
ſtrongly together with a wooden rod : and after ſtand-
ing to ſettle for two days, pour off the water for uſe.
It muſt be acknowledged the tar water prepared after
the directions here given, has done great ſervice in the
multitude of diſorders, after many other medicines had
been tried, to very little purpoſe : particularly in the
ſmall-pox, fevers, ſcurvy, &c. though of the moſt inveterate kind.

How to take off ſuperfluous hair.] This is often adverti-
ſed in the news-papers, and is ſold at ſo high a price,
that a perſon has acquired a fortune by the ſale of it ;
the preparation is both eaſy and cheap, being only
quick-lime and orpiment, made into a paſte with com
mon river water ; but thoſe who uſe this compoſition,

ought to be cautious how they put it on the part, and not
fuffer it to remain above a minute or two.

To turn acid Cider into Vinegar.] Cream of tartar
half a pound, boil it in a quart of ſtrong white wine
vinegar, and put it hot into twenty gallons of cider,
which you are to ſet in the ſun a few days, and it will
be excellent vinegar. The bung muſt be off.

To make Vinegar of Beer.] Boil a quart of ſharp beer-
vinegar about eight minutes ; take off the ſcum, and
put therein two ounces of bay-ſalt, four of cream of
tartar, and two of alum ; then put it to twenty gallons of beer, and let it ſtand in the hot ſun as the cider is directed.

*The celebrated Bath Liquid for taking out Spots,
Stains, &c.*] Put half a pound of ſoap boiler's aſhes
into three pints of river water; let it ſtand four days
(often ſtirring it), then pour off the clear water, and
mix it, as you uſe it, with fuller's earth, in which a
few drops of ſpirits of turpentine have been mixed :
this you are to lay hot on the place, and it will ſurely
take out either ſpot or ſtain.

To clean Jewels, Pearl, &c.] There is nothing
cleans any kind of jewels like fine ſmalt and emery mixed together. Rub them well with a fine ſoft bruſh dip-
ed in the powder. Pearls are to be waſhed with a ſtrong
lee of burnt tartar.

To boil up Plate, to look like new.] Of unſlacked
lime and alum one pound each ; beer grounds two
quarts : boil the plate in theſe about a quarter of an
hour.

A ſafe and ſure cure for an intermitting Fever.]
Drink plentifully of warm lemonade in the beginning
of every fit, and in a few days the fever will ceaſe.
Or, take twenty grains of ſal almoniac in a cup of tea,
an hour or two before the fit comes on.

How to prevent the ſmoaking of lamp oil.] Soak
your match, or cotton, in vinegar, and dry it well before you uſe it ; it will then burn both ſweet and pleaſant, and give abundance of ſatisfaction for the trifling trouble you have in preparing it.

How to make Homberg's black Phofphorus, which takes fire immediately on being expofed to the open air.] This article, which may be made ufeful on fundry occafions, either at home, or abroad, is prepared with alum and wheat floor (five parts of the former to one of the latter) calcined together to a brownifh, or black mafs; which being powdered and fet in a phial loofely ftopped, in a fand heat, fo as to continue glowing for fome time; then removing the whole from the fire, and fuffering it to cool gradually, and at laft ftopping the bottle clofe, it fhould be kept in a dark and dry place. A little of this powder being expof.d to the open air, it at once takes fire, and appears like a glowing coal; and it is remarkable, that it may be made of any animal or vegetable fubftance, inftead of wheat flour; but that no falt can be fubftituted inftead of alum. This is very neceffary in a family, as it conftantly affords light on any occafion, day or night, when a tinder-box is not to be had.

Another Phofphorus, by Mr. Homberg.] This is made of one part of fal ammoniac, and two parts of lime, flacked in the air; mix thefe well together, and fill a fmall crucible with them fet this in a fmall fire of fufion, and as foon as the crucible is red hot, the mixture will melt, and fhould be ftirred with an iron rod to prevent its running over. When the matter is entirely fufed, pour it into a brafs mortar, and, when cold, it will appear of a grey colour, and as if vitrified; if now it be ftruck upon with any hard body, it appears as on fire in the whole extent of the ftroke; but the matter being brittle, it is proper, for the experiment's fake, to dip little bars of iron, or copper, in the melted matter in the crucible, for thus they will be enamelled as it were with the matter; and thefe bars being ftruck upon, will give the fame fire, and the experiment may be feveral times repeated before all the matter falls off. Thefe bars muft be kept in a dry place, to prevent the phofphorus upon them from running, by the moiflure of the air. Both thefe phofphori were difcovered by accident; the firft, in fearching for a lim-

pid oil from the common ftercoracious matter that
fhould fix quickfilver; and the fecond, by endeavouring
to calcine fal ammoniac with lime, fo as to render it
fufible like wax: which end was obtained, but not the
other.

Phofphorus, in phyfiology, is a denomination given
to all bodies which fhine, and feem to burn, without
having any degree of heat: and that thefe bodies owe
their lucidity to the motion of the parts, feems evident
for the following reafons. 1. Several phofphori are
undoubtedly owing to putrefaction, as rotten wood,
very ftale meat, efpecially veal, fome forts of fifh long
kept, as oyfters, lobfters, flounders, whitings, &c.
which putrefaction is the effect of a flow and gentle
fermentation, or inteftine motion of the parts. 2. Moft
phofphori have their light fo weak as to fhine only in
the dark, which feems to argue a leffer degree of velocity
in the parts than what is neceffary to produce heat; becaufe
this laft degree of velocity will caufe bodies to fhine in open
day-light. 3. Some phofphori are the parts of animated bodies, as the cicindela or glow-worm; but all the parts of an
animal are undoubtedly in motion. 4. Other phofphori put on the appearance of flame, as the ignis fa-
tuus, the writing of common phofphorus made from
urine, flafhes of lightning, &c. but all flame is nothing but a kindled vapour, whofe parts are all in motion, which may be too weak to caufe burning, or even
a fenfible degree of heat. 5. Several of thofe inno-
cent lambent flames may have their matter fo agitated,
or the velocity of their motion fo increafed, as actually
to produce heat, and burn: thus, the writing of phofphorus on blue paper, fufficiently rubbed, will kindle
into an ardent flame, and burn the paper. 6. Phofphori feem to have the effential nature of fire, becaufe
they are fo eafily fufceptible of a burning quality from
fire: thus, common phofphorus is immediately kindled into a moft ardent and inextinguifhable flame, by
common fire. 7. By ftroking the back of a black horfe,
or cat, in the dark, we produce innumerable fcintillæ,
or lucid fparks; in the fame manner, the rubbing a

piece of black cloth, which has hung in the fun to dry, will caufe it to throw out the particles of light which it had imbibed from the fun ; whereas, a white piece of cloth, which reflects moft of the fun's rays, emits no fuch lucid fparks in the dark. Many other reafons might be urged to fhow, that light of every kind is owing to one and the fame caufe in a greater or leffer degree, viz: the velocity of the parts of the lucid body. Phofphori in general fays Lemeri, may be confidered as fo many fpunges full of the matter of light, which is fo flightly retained therein, that a fmall external force is fufficient to put it in motion, and caufe it to exhale in a lucid form. Thus the phofphori is made of human urine, and other chemical preparations, receive fo large a proportion of fire in their preparation, and retain it fo well in their unctuous fubftance, that it may be kept there in water, for twenty years ; fo as upon the firft laying them open to the air, they fhall take fire, and exhale in lucid flames. Not that the fire is fuppofed to be fixed and quiefcent all the while in the body of the phofphorus ; for that it has a real motion all the time is evident hence, that it is feen in any dark place, in the fummer feafon, fulminating and emitting flames (though, with all this, it fcarce lofes any thing of the fire) fo that the fire is not fixed in the phofphorus, but in a continual undulatory motion. Chemiftry, fays Dr. Snaw, hath fcarce afforded any thing more furprifing than the common phofphorus. To fee letters traced with this matter become luminous in the dark, images and the bodies of men to blaze with light, and abundance of the like experiments, performed by means of phofphorus, muft awaken the curiofity of thofe who have feen thefe experiments, and render them defirous of being acquainted with the method of preparing it. The preparation, even to this day, is kept as a fecret in few hands, and the matter fold at a very great price.——Whence we apprehend it would be no unacceptable prefent to the world, to render this commodity cheaper, and difcover its further ufes.

*The fuccefsful method of preparing the Phofphorus of
urine is this.*] Evaporate any quantity of frefh urine
over a gentle fire, to a black and almoft dry fubftance ;
then with two pounds thereof, thoroughly mix twice its
weight of fine fand ; put this mixture into a ftrong
coated ftone long neck ; and having poured a quart or
two of clear water into a large receiver, join it to the
long neck, and work it in a naked fire : let the heat be
fmall for the firft two hours ; then increafe it gradually
to the utmoft violence ; and continue this for three or
four hours fucceffively : at the expiration of which
time, there will pafs into the receiver a little phlegm
and volatile falt, much black and fœtid oil, and, laftly,
the matter of phofphorus, in form of white clouds,
which either ftick to the fides of the receiver, like a
fine yellow fkin, or fall to the bottom in form of fmall
fand. Now let the fire go out, but let the receiver
continue till all be cold, left the phofphorus take fire
on the admiffion of the air. To reduce thefe fmall
grains into one piece, put them into a little tin ingot-
mould, with water ; heat the ingot to make the grains
melt together ; then add cold water, till the matter is
congealed into one folid ftick, like bees-wax ; which
being cut into fmall pieces, fit to enter the mouth of a
vial, may be preferved by water, and keeping the glafs
clofe ftopped. If the glafs were not to be ftopped,
the phofphorus would turn black on its furface, and at
length be fpoiled. The cautions required to make
this procefs fucceed, are, 1. To evaporate the urine,
while it is recent. 2. To prevent its boiling over and
by that means lofing the moft unctuous part. 3. To
et the matter afterwards ferment in the cold. 4. To
mix the black matter with the fand, to prevent its
melting and running over. 5. To ufe a ftone long
neck, thofe of earth being too porous, and fuffering
he phofphorus to tranfude fooner than pafs into the
receiver. 6. To have the receiver very large, and
with a very long neck, to prevent its breaking and over
heating, which would either evaporate the white vapour
wherein the phofphorus confifts, or elfe prevent its co-

agulating. 7. To pat water into the receiver, foi
keeping it cool, and quenching the phofphorus as il
falls to the bottom. 8. To make the fire fmall al
firft, that the long neck may be preferved, and the
black matter gradually dried; which would otherwife
fwell and run over in a black froth. 9. Laftly, it is
found necellary, that the urine for the operation be oi
fuch as drink malt liquors, rather than wine. Al
thefe circumftances being required for obtaining the
phofphorus to advantage, it is no wonder that fo many
of thofe who attempted it, mifcarried. This operation may be greatly fhortened, by freezing and concen-
trating frefh urine; afterwards evaporating it with
eare; then digefting it in the manner above mentioned
When thoroughly digefted, commit the matter, in a
large quantity, to an iron pot, with an earthen head
as the chemifts ufually do for making fpirit of harts-
horn, or the fpirit and falt of urine : and when, by thi
method, all the falt and oil are obtained, let the capu
mortuum be taken out, and mixed with twice its owi
weight of alum. The matter may now be put into
well-coated long-necks, and worked with care in a re
verberatory furnace, into large receivers filled with wa
ter, and connected to the long-necks by adopters, th
lower ends whereof may enter the water, as in diftilling
of quickfilver; the operation being continued eight o
ten hours. And this is apprehended to be the beft wa'
hitherto known of procuring phofphorus to advantage
This phofphorus has been feveral ways difguifed, fo a
to make it appear under various forms; fometimes as
folid, fometimes as a liquid, fometimes as an ointment
and fometimes as a running mercury. Dr Wall in
forms us, that Mr. Boyle, being concerned to fin
how fmall a proportion of phofphorus was afforded b
urine, defired him to look out for another fubject tha
might afford it in greater plenty. The doctor afterward
caufing a piece of dry matter to be dug up in th
fields where night-men emptied their carts, he ob
ferved a great number of fmall particles of phofphoru
therein. This matter the doctor immediately carrie

to Mr. Boyle, who set Bilgar, the chemist, to work
upon it; but he could obtain very little phofphorus
from it, till another material was added to it in diftillation; and then he procured phofphorus in fuch plenty,
that, felling large quantities at fix guineas the ounce,
he foon became rich, and left England. The matter
which thus fixes and increafes the phofphorus is apprehended to be alum, which is itfelf not only in fome
meafure prepared from urine, but appears to afford the
fame kind of acid that phofphorus yields by burning;
for, upon its analyfis, phofphorus appears to be a compofition of a ftrong acid and inflammable matter, exactly in the manner of common brimftone, whence it
may not improperly be called an animal fulphur: and
accordingly, like common brimftone, it will burn under a glafs bell, and afford flowers that become an acid
liquor, like oleum fulphurus per campanam, by attract-
ing the moifture of the air. This phofphorus has
been employed for making curious experiments, a few
whereof we fhall here exhibit from Dr. Shaw. 1.
The light of this phofphorus appears greater in vacuo
than in the open air. 2. In hot weather it is obferved
to dart flafhes of light through the water wherein it is
contained, fo as exactly to refemble lightning; which
thus darts unextinguifhed through watry clouds and vapours. 3. Thefe flafhes of light are not apt to kindle or burn any combuftible matter, in which they refemble the harmlefs kind of lightning; but in a con-
denfed ftate this phofphorus burns very furioufly, and
with a moft penetrating fire, fo as to melt and diffolve
metals; in which refpect it again refembles the more
deftructive kinds of lightning, which are found to
have the fame effects. 4. If a little piece of this
phofphorus be viewed through a microfcope, the inter-
nal parts appear in a conftant ebullition. 5. Though
the phofphorus appears to be a kind of fulphur, yet it
it does not diffolve in highly rectified fpirit of wine,
but communicates fome fulphureous parts thereto; for,
if this fpirit be poured into water in the dark, it yields
a faint degree of light. 6. This phofphorus, being

mixed with a large quantity of pomatum, makes a
ſhining unguent, which may be rubbed on the hand
and face, without danger of burning, ſo as to rende
them luminous in the dark.   Many other ſurpriſing ex
periments may be made with this phoſphorus, which i
a ſubſtance that ſeems in chemiſtry to be much ſuch a
thing as the loadſtone in natural philoſophy ; and it
effects almoſt as odd and difficult to explain, for wan
of knowing the latent properties of bodies.

*To make a varniſh for Braſs, that will cauſe it to loo
like Gold.*]   Take two quarts of ſpirit of wine, an
put them into a retort glaſs ; then add to it an ounc
of gumbuge, two ounces of lacca, and two ounces o
maſtic : ſet this in a ſand-heat for ſix days, or elſe nea
a fire, or you may put the body of the bolt-head fre
quently into warm water, and ſhake it two or thre
times a day. : then ſet it over a pan of warm ſaw duſt
But before this varniſh is laid over the metal, let it b
well cleaned.   This is a good varniſh to mix with an
colours that incline to red, and the amber-varniſh fo
thoſe that are pale.

*To make a varniſh for any thing covered with Lea
Silver.*]   Firſt paint the thing over with ſize, an
ground chalk or whiting ; let them ſtand till they ar
thoroughly dry, and then do them over with very goo
gold ſize, of a bright colour (for there is much dif
ference in the colour of it, ſome being yellow, an
others almoſt white : the firſt is proper for gold, an
the laſt for ſilver) when this ſize is ſo dry, as that i
will juſt ſtick a little to the touch, lay on the leaf ſil
ver, and cloſe it well to the fire.

END OF THE FIRST PART.

THE

GOLDEN CABINET:

BEING THE

LABORATORY,

OR

HANDMAID to the ARTS.

CONTAINING

Such *Branches* of *Useful Knowledge,*

As nearly concerns all Kinds of People,

From the S q u i r e to the P e a s a n t :

AND WILL AFFORD BOTH

P r o f i t and D e l i g h t.

PART THE SECOND.

PHILADELPHIA:

PRINTED AND SOLD BY WILLIAM SPOTSWOOD,

AND H. AND P. RICE, MARKET-STREET.

1793.

SCHOOL of ARTS.

PART the SECOND.

Of Drawing in General.

OF all the polite arts, none have had fo large a fhare of admirers as that of Drawing, the number of them including almoft all mankind : and no wonder, fince it reprefents objects to us in fuch pleafant refemblances, that we are apt to imagine we fee things which we really do not. It likewife teaches us to imitate all the works of the Creation : it brings to our remembrance things long fince paft, the deeds of people and nations long fince dead, and reprefents to us the features and refemblances of our anceftors for feveral generations. There are few arts or profeffions to which if drawing be not the parent, fhe muft, at leaft, be acknowledged a kind of affiftant ; all defigns and models being executed by drawing; mathematicians, architects, and navigators, daily practife it ; it is ufed in moft ftations of life, from the general who commands an army, to the common mechanic. Nor have the ladies been lefs fond of this moft excellent art ; feveral of whom have acquired a great degree of perfection. The public are greatly obliged to Mrs. Mariana, as well as to Mifs Smyth, and Mifs St. Laurence : the

I 2

two fair ladies have even excelled Heckel, in the flower way; and Mrs. Mariana's moſt ſurpriſing genius has excited our utmoſt admiration. To this lady we are remarkably obliged for the invention of a fine blue co- lour, little inferior to that of ultramarine (of which more will be ſaid in its proper place) and only remark here, that I ſhall endeavour to find a colour to anſwer that of carmine; by which means thoſe two extrava- gantly expenſive articles will be leſs called for, and the worthy fraternity of colourmen have leſs to anſwer for; as they have for many years impoſed, what they are pleaſed to call ultramarine on the public, at the very modeſt price of four, five, ſix or ſeven pounds per ounce; when, in fact, a better blue might have been produced for leſs than five ſhillings. And, in- deed, much the ſame may be ſaid of carmine; it ge- nerally ſells from three to four pounds per ounce: I know the French carmine (which is the worſt made uſe of) at this time fetches two guineas and half the ounce. I am ſorry to ſay this laſt article is too often made an improper uſe of; which, indeed, occaſions the great demand for it; and though the fair ſex have ſpent many hours very agreeably in the polite art of painting; yet I cannot help obſerving, that it is the greateſt abſurdity to endeavour to mend the works of the Creator, by laying on a pernicious colour, that will very aſſuredly ſoon render the moſt beautiful object dull and diſagree- able. But this is too tender a point to touch ſeverely; and ſhall only add, in this place, the words of Shakeſ- peare's Polonius;

'Tis true, 'tis pity!—pity it is, 'tis true! Humbly hoping, that the ladies of North America will diſdain European faſhions; but, above all, abandon and abhor their vices *.

Rules to be obſerved in Drawing.] Drawing is the repreſenting, by lines or ſhades, the form or appear-

* The Ladies in ſeveral parts of Europe are ſo fond of painting their faces, that it is even done publicly; the mother teaches her daughter this pernicious art; and the men do it as frequent as the women.

ance of any thing in nature or art, the imitation of
another draught, or the expressing, by lines and shades,
any designs conceived in the mind. And as in imitating nature, or any draught, the mind is first impressed
with the form or shape of the figures; which by the
operation of the hand, is afterwards expressed by lines,
it will appear how neceffary it is, that the mind should
be frequently used in a curious observance of what is
propofed to it, by which ufe it will conceive more fully
and juftly of objects, and the hand will delineate, with
the greater cafe and exactnefs, what is thus ftrongly
imprelt on the memory. In order to arrive at perfection, it is neceffary to underftand what is good and
beautiful in a draught; in which knowledge the mind
will make a quick progrefs, by comparing prints and
draughts together. 'Tis a rock on which many painters
have fplit, they have fatisfied themfelves with a bare
imitation of bad pieces, without improving their genius,
or acquiring a capacity to difcover what are beauties,
and what defects. Our ideas, in fome meafure, ought
to ferve us for a model, and if we would improve thefe,
we muft frequently view the performances of others;
we ought to be nice and critical in obferving fuch as
are correct and good; we fhould meditate on every print
and draught we fee, make neceffary reflections on them,
and labour to fix in our minds a remembrance of their
beauties, the freedom and boldnefs of the out-line, and
the proportion of the feveral parts. If the judgment
be well formed, the young practitioner will be enabled
to make a much greater improvement than he can poffibly do, if he proceeds in practice, without increafing
in judgment. The labour of the hand muft fecond and
fupport that of the brain; 'tis impoffible to become an
able artift, without making the art habitual, and a perfect habit is not to be gained, without a great number
of acts, and without conftant practice. In all arts, the
rules of them are to be learned in a fhort time; but
the perfection of them is not acquired without practice
and diligence. It is a true maxim, that lazinefs never
produced any thing that was excellent; to be perfect

in drawing, 'tis neceſſary that the hand ſhould be improved in practice, and the mind in judgment every
day. Morning is the beſt and proper part of the day
for buſineſs; employ it therefore in the ſtudy and exerciſe of thoſe things which require the greateſt pains
and application. The firſt care ſhould be employed in
in imitating ſtraight and curved lines, ſquare, round,
regular, irregular, and inanimate figures, alſo parts of
out-lines of flowers, &c. &c. This will be a good
platform on which to erect the building; for by this
labour you will attain a facility of hand, a freedom
and exactneſs of drawing lines, and a cuſtomary exerciſe
of patience; qualifications, without which no one can
apply himſelf with pleaſure and diligence in the exact
imitation of the moſt difficult objects, which will require
a longer time, and more art in copying. The circum-
ferent ſtrokes are called out-lines; and the excellency
of a good out-line conſiſts in freedom, boldneſs, and
the exact proportion of all its parts. Always begin
your copy at the top; and draw the right ſide of the
figure firſt, for by that means the ſtrokes are always
expoſed to the eye; the reſt will follow more naturally,
and give leſs trouble. Be content for ſome time, to
practiſe after a good out-line, without attempting at
finiſhed pieces, or even without ſhading your own
draught: ſketch your out-line at firſt with ſlight touches,
and faint, that the amendment of it, when neceſſary,
may be the better performed, without appearing to be
re-touched: endeavour after the moſt exact imitation
in every ſtroke; and when you correct the out-line, by
taking away a little of ſome parts, and ſwelling others,
mind that you loſe nothing in the freedom and boldneſs
of it. Compare your copy frequently with the original,
carefully obſerving what is amiſs, that a fault may not
eſcape you without correction, and that in the next
draught you make after the ſame original, you may
avoid thoſe errors; for you are not to make new tran-
ſitions from one original to another, till you have obtained in ſome meaſure a proficiency in the firſt. Many
ſketches of the ſame figure, in every one endeavouring

to exceed the former, is the fureft way of practice. Be
flow in your firft operations; a conftancy of practice
will be fure to make your hand expeditious; learners
muft overcome their paffions by the exercife of patience;
they muft proceed flowly and prudently in their firft
attempts, and make it their care rather to perform well,
and to fecure every ftroke, and by that means make
one good draught, than in a heedlefs manner to hurry
over a number of bad ones. The fame may be faid with
regard to moft other arts. Before you begin your work,
and whilft you are at it, view your original with clofe
attention; divide it in your mind in feveral parts; obferve the length, the breadth, and the fimilitude of
each part; confider their proportion to each other, and
to the whole; the diftances from one part to the other,
and what parts lie parallel to each other. After you
have done your copy, and your mind perhaps been
employed about other affairs, you fhould view them
afrefh, for many faults will then appear, that were not
difcovered before; and whatfoever pains you beftow on
frequent reviewing and comparing the original with
your own copy, will not only ferve to perfect you in
that particular draught, but will alfo improve you in
the knowledge of lines, draughts, and proportions,
and by practifing in that method, you will be the fooner
qualified for the more nice and neareft imitations. The
out-lines muft be drawn in a flowing, gliding manner,
large and fmooth, for when they are too ftraight, they
appear ftiff; but, when performed in the manner here
directed, they have the refemblance of life and motion.
What other inftruments are neceffary, will be found in
the following pages; and fhall now direct to the

Proper Materials for Drawing.] Thefe are either
black-lead pencils, or black-lead fixed in a portcrayon,
charcoal, red, black, or white chalk, paftils or crayons,
pens, or hair-pencils, and Indian-ink. Black-lead is
as proper, in the beginning, to practife after the plain
lines, &c. as any other material: the ftroke it makes
being fmooth, will be more pleafing than what is effected
by charcoal or crayons. It muft have a fine point, and

accuftom yourfelf to hold it long in your hand, that the
end of your fingers may be at a much greater diftance
from the point, than they are from the nip of a pen
in writing, and form your ftrokes with light gentle
touches, by which means you will obtain a greater
command of hand, and your out-line will be more free
and bold. Pens are fometimes ufed in fhading draughts,
by hatching them with crofs ftrokes : but this is better
done with hair pencils and Indian-ink, which is ufed in
the fame manner as water-colours. The fhades in
hatching are effected by lines, and appear like the
ftrokes which fhade an engraved print : but contrary to
this, is ufing the hair-pencil and Indian-ink, there do
not appear any lines, but the fhades look like thofe in
a mezzotinto print.

Of Lights and Shadows.] It is the artful management of lights and fhades that gives the appearance of
fubftance, roundnefs, and diftance, to whatever bodies
we reprefent. Imagine you draw a circle on a piece
of paper ; confider this circle, when it is firft formed,
or fill it up with any even colour whatever, and it will
appear to be a body with a round circumference, and
flat fides : but, if you let the ftrongeft of the colour
remain in the middle, and gradually weaken it towards
the circumference, it will, by this means, pleafingly
deceive the fight, and receive a convex appearance like
a ball or globe. Wherever the vivacity of colour is
ftrongeft, that part of the object catches the light firft,
and appears neareft to it : whereas its weaknefs and
goings off are more and more broken and faint, and
feem to fly farther from the fight. In rounding the
parts of any object, the extremities in turning muft
lofe themfelves infenfibly and gradually, without preci-
pitating the light all of a fudden into the fhadows, or
the fhadows into the light ; but the paffage of the one
into the other muft be eafy and imperceptible ; that is,
the fhadow muft be foftened gradually, till it lofes itfelf in light. Objects that are painted light, muft have
a fufficient breadth of fhadow to fuftain them : and
dark bodies muft have a fudden light behind, to detach

them from the ground, or from those objects that are placed behind them, otherwise they will confusedly appear, as sticking upon each other; whereas the oppofition of shade to a light object, and of light to a dark one, gives a projection, and separates them from other bodies. The nearer any object is to the eye, it is seen so much the stronger and plainer; the sight is weakened by, distances; and the more remote any object is, 'tis seen in a more imperfect manner; therefore these objects that are placed foremost to the view, ought to be more finished than those that are cast behind; and they should have such a relative dominion over each other, that as the object, by its heightenings, causes others to retire more backward, so the same object must be chafed, and made to appear farther from the sight, than others which are more strongly illuminated. It is not sufficient that remote objects be only coloured in a more faint and languid manner, but, according to their distance and parts, must appear more or less confused; the eye does not minutely difcover what is feparated from it. At the length of a field or street, we defcry human figures, but the features of their faces, and the folds of their garments, are imperceptible to us; and fo the innumerable leaves that grow on distant plantations, appear to the sight but one mafs.

Directions for mixing and making Colours.

YELLOW. GUMBUGE is a moft beautiful yellow; by putting water to a lump of this, it foon diffolves, and is made paler or deeper to your liking: but no gum-water is to be ufed, it being a gum itfelf; nor fhould this yellow be ufed on prints defigned to be varnifhed. for the varnifh takes this colour quite off. This is fold cheap, and may be had at any druggift's.

Gall-flone is a fine tranfparent colour of an orange tinge, very fit to glaze with, or to fhade the yellow with.

Dutch-pink is another yellow, and fhould be ufed when prints are defigned for varnifhing.

GREEN. *Diſtilled-verdigriſe* is a bright ſhining green, to be uſed very ſparingly, and with judgment : but the addition of a little gumbuge makes it look far pleaſanter. This is bought in phials, ready prepared : the colourmen tell you, it is very troubleſome to make : and no doubt, ſell it dear.—But more of this in its proper place.

Sap Green is a lump diſſolved in water : and is uſed with moſt advantage when plenty of water is put to it : otherwiſe it is very dark and unpleaſant.

French-Berries, are to be diſſolved in water, and afford but an odd kind of green, unleſs mixed with ſome other article. Gum water is not to be uſed with theſe berries : or with the Sap-green above-mentioned.

Indigo and Gumbuge, mixed together, make a very agreeable green : and you may ſuit it to your liking, as you put more or leſs of the gumbuge : but judgment and fancy muſt direct what tinge is moſt agreeable in this and all other colours.

BLUE. *Ultramarine*, is the fineſt of all blues ; it is ſold extravagantly dear ; but indeed a very little goes a great way, when it can be procured of the right ſort : which is indeed rarely to be met with, notwithſtanding the high price it bears.

Smalt, if very fine, is a good blue : of itſelf it is but a heavy colour, difficult to lay ſmooth and be tranſparent : on which account care and judgment are required in uſing it.

Indigo, a deep heavy blue, proper for a dark ſhade, &c.

Verditer, a fine ſky-blue ; but it is to be uſed ſparingly, and with diſcretion.

Pruſſian Blue, is a fine blue, if laid on very thin, and proper to ſhade other blues with : but it is beſt when uſed in oil-colours.

CRIMSON and RED. *Carmine*, is the fineſt of all reds ; it affords a bright and beautiful colour, when good, and flows eaſily in the pencil ; and with the ſame colour, or lake, you may make the ſhades as ſtrong as you pleaſe.

Lake, is likewife a fine tranfparent colour, and is, when of a good kind, preferable to fome carmine.

Red-Lead, a powder, if fine, affords a good colour ; but it being of a heavy nature, care muft be taken that it be not laid on too thick, which would prevent its being tranfparent : it is likewife apt to turn blackifh, unlefs it be well cleanfed and refined. See wafhed red-lead.

Vermillion, we may fay the fame of as of the red-lead.

ORANGE. Lay firft a tint of gumbuge, and over that fome red lead, or carmine, or lake, either will do.

PURPLE. *Carmine and Ultramarine*, mixed together, make the fineft of all purples.

The above colours, by blending two together, may be altered to quite another tint : though in doing this, no certain rule can be laid down, but fancy, with judgment, muft direct. In ufing the colours, great care fhould be taken to lay the firft colour on very thin, or pale, by which means the fhade will appear ftronger, and the whole more beautiful. In moft cafes, if the white paper was left in the lights of the object, whether flower or figure, and only the fhades to be coloured, would be beft : or, fhould the white paper be thought to appear in too glaring a light, then (afterwards) a very thin tint may be laid on. And this caution I would advife to be univerfally obferved, to lay on all colours very thin at firft, it being eafy to make the light parts deeper ; but the damage is not eafily repaired, when the colour is laid on too thick at firft.

Some neceffary Remarks on Colours, &c.] As the the preparation of diftilled verdigrife is pretended to be both tedious and troublefome, I will here put it in the practioner's power to make his own ; which, if my directions are followed, I will anfwer for its being full as good, if not better, than what is fold at the colour-fhops.

Diftilled verdigrife, ufed in colouring prints, and in the prefent mode of painting, is a liquid, and which I have before mentioned, as fuch, under the article of

greens. You are to procure an ounce of diſtilled verdigriſe, in the lump, which will coſt about eight pence ;
this you are to bruiſe ſmall, and then put it into twelve
ounces of the beſt white wine vinegar, which muſt not
only be ſtrong, but very fine ; ſhake it well in the bottle, at firſt putting in, and ſet it ſtand in the ſun, or
ſome place that is warm, for a day or two, often ſhaking
it, and it will then be fit for uſe. This is the very extraordinary trouble of making the liquid diſtilled verdigriſe, and for which the venders are ſo well paid. They,
indeed, add about a ſpoonful of brandy to the above
quantity ; which can only be to diſguiſe it, as it cannot
be the leaſt ſervice : in common writing ink, brandy is
ſaid to prevent its turning mouldy, &c. but I have uſed
the article above mentioned both with and without the
brandy, and kept it many months, and could not perceive the difference ; but that is the preparation of the
ſhops. You are, however, to remark, that this liquid
is beſt kept on the fine powder that you will perceive at
the bottom of the bottle, being no way troubleſome,
and will ſoon precipitate, and be fine for uſe : it being
beſt to pour off a very ſmall quantity into a bottle or
gallipot, when you are uſing it. A little of this goes
a great way : it flows well in the pencil, and may be uſed
with a pen, even as well as common writing ink, if required. It is a very ſhining green, but may be made
pleaſant and agreeable, by mixing more or leſs gumbuge
with it, according as your fancy directs, or circumſtances require.

I ſhould have mentioned ſaffron among the yellows,
as being the higheſt of all, and appearing fine and delightful ; but as this colour is very apt to fly, I muſt
own, I make very little uſe of it ; and not at all, without being well loaded with gum ; nor will it bear varniſh
by any means.

As a good blue is the moſt difficult to procure, eſpecially at an eaſy price, I will here inſert a very valuable
one ; I don't give it as an invention of my own, but
acknowledge we are indebted to the ingenious Mrs. Ma-

riana for it, as I have before hinted ; and it is thus prepared, according to her directions.

" Take, says she, half an ounce of the finest Litmus :
it must be powdered very fine ; Pruſſian-blue half a
drachm, powdered very fine likewiſe : eight ounces of
the cleareſt ſmall beer wort, while it is running : the
above articles are to be thrown into the wort while
warm ; they are then to be put into a new earthen veſſel,
that is extremely well glazed, and remarkably ſweet and
clean : to be ſet over a moderate fire till it boils, then
to be taken off, ſtand till cold, and it is to be kept for
uſe. N. B. If this is made in ſummer time, when corn
is near ripe, throw in, when cold, half a ſcruple of
thoſe fine blue flowers that are often to be found a-
mong wheat, as it grows in the fields : it will be a moſt
heavenly blue ; but great care muſt be taken that it
touches not the leaſt acid, for that ſpoils all."

Mrs. Mariana gives great caution, to beware that acid
interferes not in the above curious colour : but the
greateſt difficulty ſeems to me to know how to prevent
it.——For, ſuppoſing that the wort in itſelf had no
acid property when firſt made uſe of ; yet in a hot ſeaſon
it would no doubt be not only acid, but even very ſour,
a few days after making, and thereby become uſeleſs, if
ſo very trifling an acid, as ſhe obſerves, would deprive
it of its beauty ; and which I myſelf have often expe-
rienced, and found to be true. In fact, the colour is
truly beautiful, and I have generally ſucceeded in the
preparation when I obſerved the following cautions, viz.
Firſt, that the earthen veſſel (for no other will anſwer
the end) be well glazed and clean ; I then throw in a
large lump of fine ſoft chalk, add as much water thereto
as will fill the veſſel, and then ſet it on a ſlow fire 'till
it is very hot ; I afterwards cover it up and let it remain
three or four hours, and then clean it very well. Secondly, I procure my new wort after the following manner : having obtained about four ounces of the fineſt
pale malt, I put this into a tea-pot, without being
either ground or even bruiſed ; and put about twelve

K

ounces (three quarters of a pint) of fine soft river water, boiling hot, thereto; I let this stand near the fire,
so as to keep it warm, an hour, afterwards I pour it off,
and it will be fit for the use according to the directions
of Mrs. Mariana. It is to be observed, that the water,
of which the wort is made, ought to be of the most
pure kind, very soft, and extremely fine; for much depends on it. And 'tis not to be wondered at, that
many have miscarried in making this curious article,
since they all procure the wort from any one that hap-
pens to be brewing. I must own I have made an extreme good blue with only the Litmus (it is best known
by the name of Lacmus, and sells for about four-pence
the ounce) being powdered and gently boiled in the
fine wort above-mentioned; it will soon jelly and grow
hard, and will keep in that manner for a year, or more;
it is made liquid immediately, by only dipping the pencil in fair soft water, and touching it as you do Indian-
ink.

I am not in this place going to treat of the common
black writing ink; perhaps it might well answer the
end of those who make and deal in it, to be better acquainted with the easy preparation of wort and litmus
boiled together. This, without much care, trouble or
expence, will make a good blue, that will flow in the
pen better than the ink commonly made use of; and as
to its growing soon hard (and more so, if long boiled,
and left to cool in very small quantities) it is a property
that makes it far more valuable, especially for those
who travel; because it will keep, in a dry place, a long
time, and soon liquefy as fin. In one word, it will
make the best black writing ink in the universe, with
the addition of some bruised galls, &c. but in this case
no gum is to be used.—It may be remembered, that all
good blacks should be raised from blues.

Mariana's fine blue has got discredit by some, from a
circumstance little thought of. I remember lady Fer
rers, after saying a great deal in its favour, complained
that it would not hold its colour. Know then, that
great part of the fine writing paper has what the mak

ers call an alum fize laid on it, which intirely fpoils this fine tender blue; and fo it does a fort of mixture—too often fold for ultramarine. But paper, fized after this manner, is foon known, by only putting the tongue thereto.

I make a blue that I find of good fervice after the following manner : having procured fome of the fineft Pruffian blue, I powder it, and grind it well with a ftrong gum water, made of the cleareft fort of gum-arabic. After it is fufficiently fine, I add fome flake white thereto, which I alfo grind well in ; and by adding more or lefs of the white, I make it lighter or darker, to my fancy. But, indeed, I generally keep three or four degrees, which I make up into fmall fquares, and ufe it in the fame manner I do the Indian-ink.

There is a fort of brown, much ufed by thofe who colour prints, which is quite tranfparent, and to be had in all places : procure a fmall quantity of the moft mild pale tobacco ; put a very little of this to a fpoonful of common water in a cup or gallipot, and in a few minutes you will have a good brown colour, that fuits on many occafions; and it may be made quite dark, by adding more of the leaf, or by putting hot water to it. Gum-water is not to be ufed with this article, unlefs it be very weak. I know an objection will be made againft the tobacco on account of its fmell ; but it is a miftake, for the fmell goes off immediately : indeed the colour-men don't approve of it ; and I well know the reafon of their diflike ; it would be the beft of browns, if they could contrive to difguife it, and fell it a great price, as they do many of their other articles, which in them-felves are very trifling.——Pray how does their Gall-ftone, &c. fmell ?

Rofe pink is no bad colour, if of a good fort : this I manage as I do the Pruffian-blue, and keep it dry in a cake ; two forts will be fufficient, one lighter than the other; which is made by the addition of the flake-white, as directed in the blue.

Black fhould never be mixed with any colour, becaufe it makes it look difagreeable and dirty. Indeed I fel- dom ufe any other black than Indian-ink, nor other white than flake-white, though I know white-lead is often ufed ; but the other is beft.

Wafhed red-lead is a fine colour, and comes reafonable; nor is the trouble much to prepare it. You are to pro- cure half a pound of the fineft red-lead, which muft be finely powdered : put this into a mug, and ftir it about well in near a quart of clear foft water ; pour the water off into another mug, ftir it about, and again pour it off ; ftir it, and pour it off again, and do in this man- ner fix or feven times, always obferving to pour as long as it will run, and leave the powder that precipitates to the bottom of each mug (which will grow lefs and lefs) to dry ; and though, in the whole, you will not have above half a drachm ; yet, if the red-lead was good, you are fure of a fine colour left at the bottom of each mug, which will foon dry, and may be ground with gum-water, and kept in fhells for ufe.

Vermillion may fometimes be improved in the fame manner; but as there are different preparations of it, and fome of them will not anfwer this operation, I would by no means advife it.

Logwood boiled in clear ftale beer, and a little fine Brazil-wood added thereto, makes a tolerable purple, which remains liquid.

But a good purple, intended for keeping, is to be made thus : new wort one pint, litmus one ounce, fine Brazil, bruifed, one ounce, let thefe boil over a flow fire, about half an hour, in a clean new mug, well glazed. When cold, ftrain it off, and keep it for ufe. If this is left in fmall quantities, it will be apt to jelly and grow dry : but, if defigned to be kept liquid, add a little fpirits of wine thereto, and keep it in a large bottle.

A delightful red, not inferior to carmine, is made thus ; fpirits of wine eight ounces, of the fineft lake one drachm, ripe barberries half an ounce, dragon's- blood, of the reddeft fort, one drachm, fine Brazil- wood a quarter of an ounce ; this is to remain feven or eight days in the sun, or moderate heat, in a phial well corked; you are to shake the bottle often; and after you see the colour very high and delightful, which it will be in little more than a week, let it settle, and pour it off for use. It should be in a clear flint glass bottle, that you may the better observe the colour. After standing some time, and you find it very fine, you may put a few drops into a shell, or on a Dutch-tile, smooth glass, &c. which will soon dry: you may then rub into it a little clear gum water, which gives it a better body, or it may be used liquid in many cases.

The colours I have already mentioned, are sufficient, by being blended together, to form a sufficient variety for most purposes, and for doing which I can lay down no certain rule, but must leave it to the fancy and judgment of the practitioner.

To make a Varnish for Silver.] Melt, in a well gla-zed pipkin, some fine turpentine, and put in three oun-ces of white amber, finely powdered (more or less, according to the quantity your work will require) put it in by little and little, keeping it continually stirring, adding by degrees, some spirit of turpentine, till all the amber is dissolved: then add to it an ounce of Sarcocolla well beaten, and an ounce of gum elemi well levigated, adding now and then a little spirit of turpentine, till all is dissolved: do this over a gen-tle fire, and keep it constantly stirring. This varnish is to be used warm, and hardened by degrees in an oven, whereby it will look like polished silver.

Manner of Engraving on Copper, &c.] This is per-formed with a graver on a plate of copper, which be-ing well polished, is covered over thinly with virgin-wax, and then smoothed while warm, with a feather, so that the wax be of an equal thickness on the plate: on this the draught or design, done in blacklead, red chalk, or ungummed ink, is laid with the face of the drawing on the wax: then they rub the back side, which will cause the whole design of the drawing to appear on the wax. The design, thus transferred, is traced through the cop-per, with a point, or needle: then beating the plate, and taking off. the wax, the ſtrokes remain to be followed, heightened, &c. according to the tenor of the deſign, with the graver, which muſt be very ſharp, and well pointed. In the conduct of the graver conſiſts almoſt all the art, which depends not ſo much upon rules, as upon practice, the habitude, diſpoſition, and genius of the artiſt, the principles of engraving being the ſame with thoſe of painting ; for if the engraver be not a perfect maſter of deſign, he can never hope to arrive at any degree of perfection in this art. In conducting the ſtrokes or cuts of the graver, he muſt obſerve the action of the fingers, and of all their parts, with their out-lines ; and remark how they advance towards, or fall back from his ſight, and then conduct his graver, according to the riſings or cavities of the muſcles or folds, widening the ſtrokes in the light, and contracting them in the ſhades : as alſo at the extremity of the out-lines, to which he ought to conduct the cuts of the graver, that the figures or objects repreſented, may not appear as if they yawn ; and lightening his hand, that the out-lines may be perfectly ſound, without appearing cut or ſlit : and altho' his ſtrokes neceſſarily break off where a muſcle begins, yet they ought always to have a certain connection with each other, ſo that the firſt ſtroke ſhould often ſerve to make the ſecond, becauſe this will ſhow the freedom of the graver. If hair be the ſubject, let the engraver begin his work by making the out lines of the principal locks, and ſketch them out in a careleſs manner, which may be finiſhed at leiſure with finer and thinner ſtrokes to the very extremity. The engraver muſt avoid making very acute angles, eſpecially in repreſenting fleſh, when he croſſes the firſt ſtrokes with the ſecond, becauſe it will form a very diſagreeable piece of tabby like lattice work, except in the repreſentation of ſome clouds, in tempeſts, the waves of the ſea, and in repreſentations of ſkins of hairy animals, and leaves of trees. So that the medium between ſquare and acute ſeems to be the beſt and moſt agreeable to the eye. He that would repreſent ſculpture, muſt remember that, as ſtatues, &c. are moſt

commonly made of white marble, or stone, whose colour does not produce such dark shades as other matters
do, have no black to their eyes, nor hair of the head,
and beard flying in the air. If the engraver would
preserve one quality and harmony in his works, he
should always sketch out the principal objects of his
piece before any part of them are finished. The instruments necessary for this sort of engraving are, besides
a graver, a cushion, or sand bag, made of leather, to
lay the plate on, in order to give it the necessary turns
and motions; a burnisher made of iron or steel, round
at one end, and usually flattish at the other, to rub out
slips and failures, soften the strokes, &c. a scraper, to
pare off the surface, on occasion; and a rubber of a
black hat, or cloth rolled up, to fill up the strokes, that
they may appear the more visible.

Method of Etching on Copper, &c.] Etching,
method of engraving on copper, in which the lines,
or strokes, instead of being cut with a tool or graver,
are eaten in with aquafortis: and this is done with
more ease and expedition than engraving; it requires
fewer instruments, and represents most kind of subjects
better and more agreeable, to nature, as landscapes,
ruins, grounds, and all small faint, loose, remote objects, buildings, &c. The method of etching is as
follows: choose the copper plate as directed for grav-
ing, and furnish yourself with a piece of ground, tied
up in a bit of thin silk, kept very clean, to be laid
upon the plate when both have been warmed; proper
needles to hatch with on the ground; a pencil or brush
to wipe away the bits of ground which rise after
hatching; a polisher; two or three gravers; a pair of
compasses, to measure distances and draw circles; a
ruler, to hatch straight lines; green wax, to make the
wall round the edges of the plate, to contain the aquafortis; an oil stone; a bottle of aquafortis; some red-
lead, to colour the back side of the copy; a stift, and
a hand-vice, to hold the plate over the candle. To
make the ground, take three ounces of asphaltum,
two ounces of clean rosin, half an ounce of burgundy-

pitch, three ounces of black wax, and three ounces of virgin's wax : let all thefe be melted in a clean earthen pipkin over a flow fire, ftirring it all the time with a fmall ftick : if it burn to the bottom, it is fpoiled. After the ingredients are well melted, and it boils up, put it into a pan of fair water : and before it be quite cold, take it out, and roll it into fmall lumps to be kept from duft : this ground is what others call the varnifh. The next thing is to clean the plate to receive the ground : take a piece of killing, roll it up as big as an egg, tie it very tight, fo as to make it a rubber, and having dropt a fmall quantity of fweet oil, and added a little powder of rotten ftone on the plate, rub it with this ball, till it will almoft fhow your face. Then wipe it all off with a clean rag, and after that, make it quite dry with another clean rag, and a little fine whiting. The next thing is to lay on the varnifh : to do which aright you muft take a hand-vice, and fix it at the middle of one part of the plate, with a piece of paper between the teeth of the hand vice and the plate, to prevent the marks of the teeth : then laying the plate on a chafing difh, with a fmall charcoal fire in it, till the plate be fo hot, that by fpitting on the backfide, the wet will fly off ; rub the plate with the ground tied up in filk, till it be covered all over ; and after that daub the plate, with a piece of cotton wrapped up in filk till the ground be quite fmooth, keeping the plate a little warm all the time. The varnifh being thus fmoothed upon the plate, it muft be blacked in the following manner : take a thick tallow candle that burns clear, with a fhort fnuff, and having driven two nails into the wall, to let it reft upon, place the plate againft the wall with the varnifh fide downward, and take care not to touch the ground with your fingers : then taking the candle, apply the flame to the varnifh as clofe as poffible, without touching the varnifh with the fnuff of the candle, and guide the flame all over it, till it becomes perfectly black. After this is done, and the plate dry, the defign is traced with a needle through the varnifh, and a rim or border of wax is raifed round

,ce of the plate ; and then the artift has
,f common varnifh and lamp-black, made
rewith he covers the parts that are not
)y means of a hair pencil. And he is
then covering or uncovering this or that
ign, as occafion may require ; the con-
uafortis being the principal concern, on
t of the print very much depends. The
)e attentive to the ground, that it does
part, and where it does, to ftop up the
above compofition. The plate is de-
e aquafortis every where, but in the lines
t through it with the needle, through
:r eats into the copper to the depth requiring to keep it ftirring with a feather all
ich done, it is to be poured off again.
tis is moft commonly ufed ; and if it be
x it with vinegar, otherwife it will make
1ard, and fometimes break up the ground :
having done its parts, the ground is
the plate wafhed and dried ; after which
ns for the artift but to examine the work
r, to touch it up, and heighten it where
has miffed. And laftly, it is to be re-
at a frefh dip of aquafortis is never given,
vafhing out the plate in fair water, and
e fire.

ays of making Carmine.] It is extracted
il, by means of water, wherein chouan
ave been infufed : fome add rocou, but
) much of the oval caft. Others make
brazil-wood, fernambouc and leaf gold,
tar, and fteeped in white-wine vinegar :
ig from this mixture, upon boiling, when
carmine : but this kind is vaftly inferior
r. There is another carmine, made of
nd fernambouc. But a fort, that is too
:h, is prepared from fhreds of fuperfine
infufed in fpirits of wine.

tion of Ultramarine.] This is prepared

from lapis lazuli, by calcination : but the German la
pis lazuli does not anfwer well in this procefs, and dif
covers itfelf by calcining eafier than the African or Afi
atic, and turning greenifh. The oriental kind calcine
to a finer blue than it naturally has, and retains the co
lour for ever. After calcining the ftone in a clear fir
of charcoal, they grind it to an impalpable powder or
a porphyry, and then mixing it up in a pafte, compofe
of pitch, wax, and oil, they work it about with th
hands: and finally, kneading this in a veffel of clea
water, as the powder feparates from the vifcid matter
it finks to the bottom : when all that is perfectly fine i
this is worked out, they let the water be drained of
and dry the powder for ufe. What remains embodie
in the pafte is afterwards feparated, and makes a wor
kind than the former. Ultramarine muft be chofen of
high colour, and well ground, which may be known b
putting it between the teeth, and if it feel gritty, i
is a fign it has not been well ground. To know whether i
be pure and unmixed, put a little of it into a crucible
and fo heat it red hot; and if the powder has no
changed its colour after this trial, it is certainly pure
on the contrary, if there be any change, or any blac
fpecks in it, then it has been adulterated. There i
alfo a fpurious fort, commonly called Dutch ultrama
rine, which is only fine fmalt well ground and pulveri
fed : and this fort is too often fold at a moft extravagan
price.

To foften Ivory and other Bones.] Lay them fo
twelve hours in aquafortis, and then three days in th
juice of beets, and they may be worked into any form
To harden them again, lay them in ftrong vinega
Diofcorides fays, that by boiling ivory for the fpace o
fix hours with the root of mandragoras, it will becom
fo foft, that it may be managed as one pleafer.

To whiten Ivory.] Lay it in quick lime, and pou
a little water over it, but not too much that the he
may not be too great, left it fcale and become brittl

Staining and marbling of Ivory.] 1. Of a fine cor
red : make a lye of wood-afhes, of which take tw

into a pan upon one pound of brazil;
)ound of alum ; boil it for half an hour:
)ff, and put in the ivory or bone, and
er of thefe continue in the liquor, the
ll be. 2. Of a fine green : take two
)fe, and one part of fal ammoniac : grind
ther, pour ftrong white wine vinegar on
)our ivory into this mixture, let it be co-
)lour has penetrated, and as deep as you
f you would have it fpotted with white,
wax ; or if you would have it marbled,
ax, and fcrape it off in veins, having all
)ered which you defire to have ftained.
)ake litharge and quick-lime, of each an
) ; put them in rain water over the
)s to boil, and in this put the bone or
hem well about with a ftick ; and after-
)u fee the ivory receive the colour, take
he fire, ftirring the ivory all the while
) is cold. 4. Marbling upon ivory is
) : melt bees-wax and tallow together,
r the ivory, and with an ivory bodkin
)s that are to imitate marbling : pour the
)e metal on them, and when it has ftood
)our it off : when it is dry, cover the
)ith the wax, and open fome other veins
in for another metallic folution ; and this
)umber of colours you defign to give it.
of gold gives it a purple ; of copper, a
r, a bad black ; of iron, a yellow and
)is method you may alfo imitate tortoife-
ral other fubftances on ivory.
thod of making Sealing-wax, &c.] Take
)ees-wax, three ounces of fine turpentine,
)fin (finely powdered) of each one ounce :
)well melted, and drofs taken off, put in
a half of vermillion, or red lead, finely
ir them together till they are well incor-
) this mixture grows a little cool, roll it
in any other form you would have it.

If you would have it black, inftead of vermillion, or
red-lead, put into it lamp-black—The foft, red, and
green wax, ufed in large feals to fome of our law writings, are thus made: melt bees wax over a gentle heat;
with fuch a proportion of Venice turpentine as, when
cold, will give it the due confiftence : this is determined
by repeated trials ; firft putting in but little turpentine,
and afterwards more and more, till by dropping a piece
upon a marble to cool, it is found of the true confiftence.
They then colour it with vermillion, or red-lead, or
with verditer, or whatever colour they pleafe, the mixture in this ftate, receiving any.

To imitate Fruit in Wax.] Take the fruit, and bury
it half way in clay ; oil its edges, and that part of the
fruit which is uncovered : then nimbly throw on it tempered alabafter, or plaifter of Paris, to a confiderable
thicknefs. When this is grown dry and hard, it makes
the half mould ; the fecond half of which may be obtained in the fame manner. The two parts of the mould
being joined together, a little bees wax melted and
brought to a due heat, being poured through a hole
made in a convenient part of the mould, and prefently
fhook therein, will reprefent the original fruit.

How to reprefent the Face, &c. in Wax] The reprefentation of the face, &c. of perfons living, or dead,
is done by applying plaifter of Paris in a kind of pafte,
and thus forming a mould containing the exact reprefentation of the features. Into this mould melted wax
is poured, and thus a kind of mafks are formed ; which
being painted and fet with glafs eyes, and the figures
dreffed in their proper habits, they bear fuch a refemblance, that it is difficult to diftinguifh between the copy
and the original.

Of Varnifhes in general.] There are feveral kinds
of varnifhes in ufe ; as the ficcative or drying varnifh,
made of oil of afpin, turpentine and fandarach melted
together. White varnifh, called alfo Venetian varnifh,
made of oil of turpentine, fine turpentine and maftic.
Spirit of wine varnifh, made of fandarach, white amber,
gum elemi and maftic ; ferving to gild leather, picture

frames, &c. withal. Also the gilt varnish, china varnish, common varnish, &c.

To make white Varnish.] Take gum sandarach, of the clearest and whitest sort, eight ounces; gum mastic, of the clearest sort, half an ounce; of sarcocolla, the whitest, three quarters of an ounce; Venice turpentine, an ounce, and a half; benzoin, the clearest, one quarter of an ounce; gum animæ, three quarters of an ounce; let all these be dissolved, and mixed in the manner following: Put the sarcocolla and rosin into a little more spirits than will cover them to dissolve: then add the benzoin, gum animæ, and Venice turpentine, into either a glass or glazed earthen vessel, and pour on as much spirits as will cover them an inch: then put the gum mastic into a glass or glazed vessel, and pour strong spirits upon it, covering it also about an inch thick, to dissolve it rightly: then put your gum elemi in a distinct vessel as before, and cover it with spirits to dissolve. For this purpose, you need only break the rosin a little, and powder the gum animæ, sarcocolla, and benzoin. Let all stand three or four days to dissolve, shaking the glasses, &c. two or three times a day, and afterwards put them all together into a glazed vessel, stirring them well, and strain the liquor and gums gently, beginning with the gums, through a linen cloth. Then put it into a bottle, and let it stand a week before you use it, and pour off as much of the clear only, as you think sufficient for present use.

The white Amber Varnish, according to Mr. Boyle.] Take white rosin four drachms, melt it over the fire in a clean glazed pipkin; then put into it two ounces of the whitest amber you can get, finely powdered. This is to be put in by a little and little, gradually, keeping it stirring all the while with a small stick, over a gentle fire, till it dissolves, pouring in now and then a little oil of turpentine, as you find it growing stiff; and continue so to do till all your amber is melted. But great care must be taken not to set the house on fire, for the very vapours of the oil of turpentine will take fire by heat only; but if it should happen so to do, immediately

L.

put a flat board or wet blanket over the fiery pot, and by keeping the air from it, you will put it out, or suffocate it. Therefore it will be beft to melt the rofin, in a glafs of cylindric figure, in a bed of hot fand, after the glafs has been well annealed, or warm'd by degrees in the fand, under which you muft keep a gentle fire. When the varnifh has been thus made, pour it into a coarfe linen bag, and prefs it between two hot boards of oak or flat plates of iron; after which it may be ufed with any colours in painting, and alfo for varnifhing them over when painted. But for covering gold, you muft ufe the following varnifh; mean time, it is to be obferved, that when you have varnifhed with white varnifh, you may put the things varnifhed into a declining oven, which will harden the varnifh.

A hard Varnifh, that will bear the Muffle.] Take of colophony, an ounce; fet it over the fire in a well glazed earthen veffel, till it is melted; then by little and little, ftrew in two ounces of powder of amber, keeping it ftirring all the while with a ftick; and when you perceive it begin to harden or refift the ftick, then put in a little turpentine oil, which will thin and foften it immediately: then put in two ounces of gum copal, finely powdered, fprinkling it in as you did the amber, now and then pouring in a little oil of turpentine; and when it is done, ftrain it as before directed. This is proper to varnifh over gold; and the things done with it muft be fet into a declining oven, three or four days fucceffively, and then it will refift even the fire itfelf.

To make a Varnifh for Gold, or Metals made in imitation of Gold.] Take colophony, and, having melted it, put in two ounces of amber finely powdered, and fome fpirit of turpentine, and, as the amber thickens, keep it well ftirring; then put in an ounce of gum elemi, well pulverifed, and more fpirit of turpentine; conftantly ftirring the liquor till all is well mixed and incorporated: but take care, however, to ufe as little turpentine as you can, becaufe, the thicker the varnifh is made, the harder it will be. Let this be done over a fand heat, in an open glafs; then ftrain it, as is directed for the preceding varnish. This varnish is to be used alone, first warming the vessels made of paper paste; and lay it on with a painting brush before the fire, but not near, left the fire raise it into blisters. After this has been done, harden it three several times in an oven; first with a flack heat, the next with a warmer, and the third with a very hot one; and the vessels will look like polished gold. And as for such vessels, &c. as shall be made with faw duft and gums, the varnish may be made of the same ingredients as above-mentioned, except the gum elemi; and this will dry in the fun, or in a gentle warmth.

Laying on of Varnishes.] 1. If you varnish wood, let your wood be very smooth, close grained, free from grease, and rubbed with rushes. 2. Lay on your colours as smooth as possible; and, if the varnish has any blisters in it, take them off by a polish of rushes. 3. While you are varnishing, keep your work warm but not too hot. 4. In laying on your varnish, begin in the middle, and stroke the brush to the outside; then to another extreme part, and so on till all be covered; for if you begin at the edges, the brush will leave the blots there, and make the work unequal. 5. In fine works use the finest tripoli in polishing: do not polish it at one time only; but, after the first time, let it dry for two or three days, and polish it again for the last time. 6. In the first polishing you must use a good deal of tripoli, but in the next a very little will serve; when you have done, wash off your tripoli with a sponge and water; dry the varnish with a dry linen rag; and clear the work, if a white ground, with oil and whiting; or if black, with oil and lamp black.

Painting in Oil.] The whole secret of painting in oil consists in grinding the colours with nut-oil, or linfeed-oil; but the manner of working is very different from that in frescoe, or in water, by reason the oil does not dry near so fast, which gives the painter an opportunity of touching and re-touching all the parts of his figures as often as he pleases; which in the other methods of painting is a thing impracticable. The figures done

in oil, are alfo capable of more force and boldnefs ; info-
much, that the black becomes blacker, when ground
with oil, than with water ; befides, all the colou:s 'mixing better together, makes the colouring the fweeter,
more delicate and agreeable, and gives an union and
tendernefs to the whole, inimitable in any of the other
manners. Painting in oil is performed on canvas, on
walls, wood, ftone, and all other forts of medals.

Painting on Cloth or Canvas is done as follows.] The
canvas being ftretched on a frame, give it a layer of fize,
or pafte-water, and then go over it with a pumice-ftone,
to fmooth off the knots. By means of the fize, the
little threads and hairs are all laid clofe on the cloth,
and the little holes filled up, fo that no colour can pafs
through. When the cloth is dry, lay on okre in oil,
which may be mixed with white-lead to make it dry
the fooner. When dry, go over it again with the pu-
mice ftone, to make it fmooth. After this a fecond
couch is fometimes applied, compofed of white-lead
and a little charcoal-black, to render the ground of
an afh colour. Others prime the canvas in the following
manner ; they firft fmooth the canvas with a pumice-
ftone, fize it over with good fize, and a little honey,
and let it ftand to dry ; after which they lay it over
with whiting and fize, mixed with a little honey : the
ufe of the honey is to prevent it from cracking, peeling,
and breaking out ; on this they firft draw the picture
with a coal, and then lay on the colours.

Painting on Walls.] When the wall is dry, they
give it two or three wafhes with boiling oil, till the
plaifter remains quite greafy, and will imbibe no more ;
upon this they lay drying colours, fuch as white chalk,
red okre, or other chalks beaten pretty ftiff. When
this couch or layer is well dried, the fubject, or defign,
is fketched out, and afterwards painted over, mixing
a little varnifh with their colours, to fave the varnifhing
afterwards. In order the better to fortify the walls
againft moifture, fome cover it with a plaifter of lime,
marble duft, or cement made of beaten tiles foaked in
linfeed-oil ; and at laft prepare a compofition of Greek

pitch, maftic, and thick varnifh boiled together, which they apply hot over the former plaifter; and when dry, lay on, the colours as before. Others, in fine, make their plaifter with lime-mortar, tile cement, and fand; and this being dry, they apply another of lime, cement and iron-fcoriæ; which being well beaten, and incorporated with linfeed-oil, and whites of eggs, make an excellent plaifter. When this is dry, the colours are laid on as before.

In Painting on Wood.] They ufually give their ground a couch or layer of white tempered with fize, and then proceed as in painting on walls.

In Painting on Stone or Metals.] It is not neceffary to lay them over with fize, but only to add a flight conch of colours before the defign is drawn on it: nor even is this done on, ftones, where you would have the ground appear, as in certain marbles and agates of extraodinary colours.

All the Colours ufed in Frefco.] Are good in oil, except white of lime and marble duft. Thofe chiefly ufed are white-lead, or cerufe, yellow and white maflicot, orpiment, vermillion, lacca, blue and green afhes, verdigrife, indigo, fmalt, black lead, ivory-black, lampblack, &c. As to oils, the beft of thofe are linfeed, walnuts, fpike, and turpentine. The drying oils are nut oil, boiled with litharge and fandarach, or otherwife with fpirit of wine, maftic and gum laca. In the preparation of oil-colours, care muft be taken that they be ground fine: that in putting them on a pallet, thofe which will not dry of themfelves be mixed with drying oil, or other ingredients of a drying quality: and that the fringed colours be mixed in as fmall quantities as poffible. As to the fituation of the colours, the pureft and ftrongeft muft be placed in the front of the piece, and the colouring varied according to the fubject, time and place. If the fubject be grave, melancholy or terrible, the general teint of the colouring muft incline to brown and black, or red and gloomy: but it muft be gay and pleafant in fubjects of joy and triumph.

Colour, in Dying, &c.] There are, in the art of

L 3

dying, five colours, called fimple, primary, or mother colours, from the mixture of which all other colours are formed : thefe are blue, yellow, brown, red and black. Of thefe colours, varioufly mixed and combined, they form the following colours, panfy, blue and fcar- let are formed : amaranth, violet, and panfy : from the fame mixture of blues, crimfon and red, are formed the columbine or dove colour, purple crimfon, amaranth, panfy, and crimfon violet. Here it is to be obferved that they give the name crimfon to all colours made with cochineal.

Of blue and red madder is died purple, pepper colour, tan colour, and dry rofe colour.

The fame blue with red half in grain, makes ama- ranth, tan colour, and dry rofe colour.

Blue and half red crimfon, compofe amaranth, tan colour, dry rofe, a brown panfy, and fun brown.

Blue and yellow, mixed together, compofe a yellow green, fpring green, grafs green, laurel green, brown green, dark green, as well as fea green, parrot green, cabbage green, &c. Thefe three laft colours are to be lefs boiled than the reft. It is to be noted, that as to green, there is no ingredient or drug in nature that will dye it : but the ftuffs are dyed twice, firft in blue, then in yellow.

Blue and brown.] Thefe two colours are never mixed alone, but with the addition of red, either of madder or cochineal, they form feveral colours.

Red and yellow.] All the fhades compofed of thefe two colours, as gold, yellow, aurora, marygold, orange, nacarat, granat-flower, flame colour, &c. are made with yellow and red of madder, fcarlet being lefs proper as well as too dear.

Red and brown.] Of thefe two colours are formed cinnamon colour, chefnut, mufk, bear's hair, and even purple, if the red be of madder.

Yellow and brown.] The colours formed fron thefe two, are all the fhades of feuillemort, and hair colours. But this may be taken notice of, that though it be faid that there are no colours or fhades made from fuch and such mixtures, it is not meant that none can be made, but that they are more easily formed from a mixture of other colours.

Dying in general.] The art of dying consists in giving a lasting colour to silks, cloths, and other substances, whereby the beauty is much improved, and value enhanced: and this art chiefly depends on three things, viz. 1. Disposing the surface of the stuffs to receive and retain the colours, which is performed by washing them in different lyes, digesting, beating them, &c. in which human urine putrified, a sharp salt of ashes, divers soaps, and galls of animals, are of principal use; by means whereof the viscous gluten of the silk-worms naturally adhering to their threads, is washed and cleansed from them, and thus they become fitted gradually to imbibe the colours. By these also the greasy foulness adhering to wool and flax is scoured off. 2. So to grind the colours, as that they may enter the body duly prepared, and preserve their brightness undiminished. 3. The third consists in having beautiful colours.

The Materials used in the Art of Dying.] Are iron and steel, or what is produced from them, in all true blacks, called Spanish blacks, though not in Flanders' blacks, viz. they use copperas, steel filings, and slippe; they also use pewter for bowe-dye scarlet, viz. they dissolve bars of pewter in aquafortis; litharge is also used by some, though acknowledged by few to add weight to dyed silk. Antimony is much used to the same purpose. Arsenick is used in crimson upon pretence of giving lustre, although those who pretend not to be wanting in giving lustre, to their silks, disown its use. Verdigrise is also used by linen dyers in their yellow and greenish colours; though, of itself, it strikes no deeper colour than that of a pale straw. Of mineral salts used in dying, the chief is alum; the true use whereof seems to be in regard to the fixation of colours. The next mineral salt is salt-petre, not used by antient dyers and but by few of the modern: nor is it yet used but to brighten colours, by back boiling of them, for which argol is more commonly ufed : lime is much ufed in working blue vats.

Of the animal family are ufed cochineal, urine of labouring men kept till it be ftale and ftinking, honey, yolks of eggs, and ox-gall ; the ufe of the urine is to fcour, and help the fermenting and heating of wool ; and is ufed alfo in blue vats inftead of lime : it difcharg-eth the yellow, and therefore is ufed to fpend well withall.

Dyers ufe two forts of water, viz. river and well water ; the laft, which is harfh, they ufe in reds and other colours wanting reftringency, and in dying mate-rials of the flacker contextures, as in callico, fuftian, and the feveral fpecies of cotton works ; but it is not good for blues, and makes yellows and greens look rufty.

River water is more fat and oily, and is therefore uf-ed in moft cafes, and muft be had in great quantities for wafhing and rinfing their cloths after dying. Water is called by dyers white liquor ; but a mixture of one part bran, and five of the river water boiled an hour and put into leaden cifterns to fettle, is what they call liquors abfolutely.

Gums have been ufed by dyers about filk, viz. gum arabic, tragacanth, maftic, dragon's blood. Thefe tend little to the tincture, any more than gum in writ-ing ink, which only gives it a confiftence : fo gum may give the filk a gloffinefs ; and laftly, to increafe the weight.

The three peculiar ingredients for black are coppe-ras, filings of fteel, and flippe ; the reftringent binding materials are alder-bark, pomegranate peels, walnut rinds and roots, oaken fapling bark, and faw-duft of the fame, crab tree bark, galls, and fumac.

The falts are alum, falt-petre, fal ammoniac, pot afhes, and ftone lime ; among which urine may be enu-merated as a liquid falt.

The liquors are well and river water, urine, aquavi-tæ, vinegar, lemon juice, aquafortis, honey, and maffes.

Ingredients of another clafs are bran, wheaten flour,

yolks of eggs, leaven, cummin feed, fenugreek feed, agaric and fenna.

The fmectics, or abfterfives, are fuller's earth, foap, linfeed oil, and ox-gall.

The metals and minerals are pewter, verdigrife, antimony, litharge, and arfenic.

The colourings are of three forts, viz. blue, yellow, and red; of which logwood, old fuftic, indigo and madder, are the chief.

General Obfervations upon Dying.] 1. All materials which of themfelves do give colour are either red, yellow, or blue; fo that out of them, and the primitive fundamental colour white, all that great variety which we fee in dyed ftuffs doth arife.

2. That few of the colouring materials, as cochineal, foot, wood, wax, woad, &c. are in their outward and firft appearance of the fame colour, which by the flighteft diftempers and folutions in the weakeft menftrua, they dye upon cloth, filk, &c.

3. That many of them will not yield their colours without much grinding, fteeping, boiling and fermenting, or corrofion by powerful menftrua, as red wood, weld, woad, arnotta, &c.

4. That many of them will of themfelves give no colouring at all, as copperas or galls, or with much difadvantage, unlefs the cloth or other ftuff to be dyed be as it were firft covered, or incruftated with fome other matter, though colourlefs aforehand, as madder, weld, brafil, with alum.

5. That fome of them, by the help of other colourlefs ingredients, do ftrike different colours from what they would of themfelves, as cochineal, brazil, &c.

6. That fome colours, as madder, indigo and woad, by reiterated tinctures, will at laft become black.

7. That although green be the moft frequent and moft common of natural colours, yet there is no fimple ingredient now ufed alone to dye green with upon any material, fap-green being the neareft, which is ufed by country people.

8. There is no black thing in ufe which dyes black,

though both the coal and foot of moſt things burnt or ſcorched be of that colour, and the blacker, by how much the matter before being burnt was whiter, as in ivory-black.

9. The tincture of ſome dying ſtuffs will fade even with lying, or with the air, or will ſtain with water only, but very much with urine, vinegar, &c.

10. Some of the dying materials are uſed to bind and ſtrengthen a colour ; ſome to brighten it ; ſome to give luſtre to the ſtuff ; ſome to diſcharge and take off the colour, either in whole or in part ; and ſome out of fraud, to make the material dyed, if coſtly, heavier.

11. That ſome dying ingredients, or drugs, by the coarſeneſs of their bodies, make the thread of the dyed ſtuff ſeem coarſer ; and ſome by ſhrinking them, ſmaller ; and ſome, by ſmoothing them, finer.

12. Many of the ſame colours are dyed upon ſeveral ſtuffs with ſeveral materials, as red-wood is uſed in cloth, not in ſilks ; arnotta in ſilks, not in cloth, and may be dyed at ſeveral prices.

13. That ſcouring and waſhing of ſtuffs to be dyed, is done with ſpecial materials, as ſometimes with ox-galls, ſometimes with fuller's-earth, and ſometimes ſoap ; this latter being, in ſome caſes, pernicious, where pot-aſhes will ſtain or alter the colour.

14. Where great quantities of ſtuffs are to be dyed together, or where they are to be done with any ſpeed, and where the pieces are very long, broad, thick, or otherwiſe, they are to be differently handled, both in reſpect to the veſſels and ingredients.

15. In ſome ſtuffs and colours the tingent liquor muſt be boiling, in other caſes blood warm, and in ſome it may be cold.

16. Some tingent liquors are fitted for uſe by long keeping, and in ſome the virtues wear away by the keeping.

17. Some colours or ſtuffs are beſt dyed by reiterated dippings in the ſame liquor, ſome by continuing longer, and others a leſſer time therein.

18. In ſome caſes, the matter of the veſſel wherein

the liquors are heated, and the tincture prepared, muft
be regarded, as the kettles muft be pewter for bow-dye.

19. There is little reckoning made how much liquor
is ufed in proportion to the dying drugs, it being rather adjufted to the bulk of the ftuffs, as the veffels are
to their breadth ; the quantity of dying drugs being
proportioned both to the colour, higher or lower, and
to the ftuffs : as likewife the falts are to the dying
drugs. Concerning the weight that colours give to
filk (in which it is moft taken notice of being fold by
weight, and a commodity of great price), it is obferved that one pound of raw filk lofeth four ounces by
wafhing out the gums, and the natural fordes. That
the fame fcoured filk may be raifed to above thirty ounces from the remaining twelve, if it be dyed black
with fome materials.

Of a thing very ufeful in dying, efpecially of black,
nothing increafes weight fo much as galls, by which
black filks are reftored to as much weight as they loft
by wafhing out their gum : nor is it counted extraordinary that blacks fhould gain about four or fix ounces
in the dying, upon each pound.

Next to galls, old fuftic increafes the weight $1\frac{1}{2}$ in
12 ; madder, about one ounce ; weld, half an ounce.
The blue vats in deep blues of the 5th ftall, give no
confiderable weight ; neither doth logwood, cochineal,
nor even copperas, where galls are not : flippe adds
much to the weight, and giveth a deeper black than
copperas itfelf, which is a good excufe for the dyers
that ufe it.

Dying of wool and woollen manufactures.] For black
in woollen manufactures, it is begun with a ftrong decoction of woad and indigo, that communicate a deep
blue ; after which the ftuffs being boiled with alum and
tartar, or pot-afh, are to be maddered with common
madder, then dyed black with Aleppo galls, copperas,
and fumac, and finifhed by back boiling in weld.
Wools for tapeftry are only to be woaded, and then put
in black. For fcarlet, wool and woollen manufactures
are dyed with kermes and cochineal, with which may

alfo be ufed agaric and arfenic. Crimfon fcarlet is dyed with cochineal, maftic, aquafortis, fal ammoniac, fublimate, and fpirit of wine. Violet fcarlet, purple, amaranth, and panfy fcarlets, are given with woad, cochineal, indigo, braziletto, brazil and orchal. Common reds are given with pure madder, without any other ingredient. Crimfon reds, carnations, flame and peach colours, are given, according to their feveral hues, with cochineal, maftic, without madder, or the like. Crimfon red is prepared with Roman alum with cochineal. Orange aurora, brick colour, and onion peel colour, are dyed with woad and madder, mixed according to their feveral fhades. For blues, the dark are dyed with a ftrong tincture of woad; the brighter with the fame liquor, as it weakens in working. Dark browns, minims, and tan colours, are given with woad weaker in decoction than for black, with alum and pot-afhes, after which they are maddered higher than black: for tan colours, a little cochineal is added. Pearl colours are given with gails and copperas; fome are begun with walnut tree roots, and finifhed with the former; though to make them more ufeful, they generally dip them in a weak tincture of cochineal. Greens are begun with woad, and finifhed with weld. Pale yellows, lemon colour, and fulphur colour, are given with weld alone. Olive colours of all degrees are firf put in green, and taken down with foot, more or lefs, according to the fhade that is required. Feulemort, hair colour, mufk, and cinnamon colour, are dyed with weld and madder. Nacarat, or bright orange, is given with weld and goats hair boiled with pot-afhes.

Dying of Silks.] This is begun by boiling them in foap, &c. then fcouring and wafhing them in water and fteeping them in cold alum water. For crimfon they are fcoured a fecond time before they are put into the cochineal vat. Red crimfon is given with pure co chineal, maftic, adding galls, turmeric, arfenic, and tartar, all mixed in a copper of fair water almoft boil ing: with thefe the filk is to be boiled an hour and a half, after which it is allowed to ftand in the liquor til next day. Violet crimſon is given with pure cochineal, arſenic, tartar and galls ; but the galls in leſs proportion than in the former : when taken out, it is waſhed and put in a vat of indigo. Cinnamon crimſon is begun like the violet, but finiſhed by back boiling, if too bright with copperas, and if dark, with a dip of indigo. Light blues are given in a back of indigo. Sky blues are begun with orchal, and finiſhed with indigo. For citron colours, the ſilk is firſt alumed, then welded with indigo. Pale yellows, after aluming, are dyed in weld alone. Pale and brown auroras, after aluming, are welded ſtrongly, then taken down with rocou and diſ-ſolved with pot-aſhes. Flame colour is begun with ro-cou, then alumed, and afterwards dipped in a vat or two of brazil. Carnation and roſe colours are firſt alum-ed, then dipt in brazil. Cinnamon colour, after alum-ing is dipt in brazil, and braziletto. Lead colour is given with fuſtic, or with weld, braziletto, galls and copperas. Black ſilks of the coarſer ſort, are begun by ſcouring them with ſoap, as for other colours ; af-ter which they are waſhed out, wrung, and boiled an hour in old galls, where they are ſuffered to ſtand a day or two : then they are waſhed again with fair water, wrung, and put into another vat of new galls ; after-wards waſhed again, and wrung, and finiſhed in a vat of black. Fine black ſilks are only put once into galls of the new and fine ſort, that has only boiled an hour : then the ſilks are waſhed, wrung out, and dipped thrice in black, and afterwards taken down by back boiling with ſoap.

The dying of thread.] This is begun by ſcouring it in a lye of good aſhes : afterwards it is wrung, rinſed out in river water, and wrung again. A bright blue is given with braziletto and indigo : bright green is firſt dyed blue, then back-boiled with braziletto and verdi-ter, and laſtly woaded. A dark green is given like the former, only darkening more before woading. Lemon and pale yellow is given with weld mixed with rocou. Orange Iſabella, with fuſtic, weld and rocou. Red, both bright and dark, with flame colour, &c. are given

M

with brazil, either alone, or with a mixture of rocou. Violet, dry rofe, and amaranth, are given with brazil, taken down with indigo. Feulemort and olive-colour are given with galls and copperas, taken down with weld, rocou, or fuftic. Black is given with galls and copperas, taken down and finifhed with braziletto wood.

A preparation for curing Wens, by which a perfon has acquired a confiderable fortune, and much reputation.] Take a quantity of fnow, that has been collected in the coldeft feafon, fufficient to produce a quart of water, when melted : add to this one ounce of Roman vitriol, and one drachm of camphire; thefe are to be put in the fnow water; after this is made warm over a moderate fire, let it ftand till fine ; and then add thereto four ounces of fpirit of wine, in which one drachm of the golden or July butter-flies have been infufed. Thefe infects are to be dried and powdered, before they are put into the fpirits of wine ; and care muft be taken to produce the right fort, as it appears that very much depends on them. They are to be had, in moft places where flowers abound, about Midfummer; and are then in their prime. With this liquid the wens are to be rubbed night and morning for a month fucceffively, and fuccefs will attend it, with very little pain or trouble to the patient. Snow, when ufed alone, is faid to have many valuable properties ; as may be feen at large in Bartholin's Treatife de nivis ufu medico. It has been obferved, in the cure of Wens, that if the patient anoint the part with oil of fweet almonds three or four days before ufing the above remedy, it will greatly forward the cure.

Method of colouring Brandy.] All brandies, when firft made, are as clear as water, and do grow higher coloured by long keeping ; however, they are artfully made of any colour feveral ways. To make a light ftraw colour, ufe turmeric or a little treacle : but the beft way is to give it a colour or tincture with a little burned fugar made to a confiftence ; or fyrup of elderberries may be ufed, which gives an admirable colour, and may be made deeper or lighter, according to the quantity you put in.

The way to make Sealing-wafers.] Take very fine flour, mix it with glair of eggs, ifinglafs, and, a little yeaft ; mingle the materials ; beat them well together, fpread the batter, being made thin with gum water, on even tin plates, and dry them in a ftove ; then cut them out for ufe. You may make them of what colours you pleafe, by tinging the pafte with brazil or vermillion for red ; indigo or verditer, &c. for blue.

Sympathetic powder.] The compofition of the famous fympathetic powder, ufed at Goffilaer by the miners in all their wounds, is this. Take of green vitriol, eight ounces ; of gum tragacanth, reduced to an impalpable powder, one ounce ; mix thefe together, and let a fmall quantity of the powder be fprinkled on the wound, and it immediately ftops bleeding. The vitriol is to be calcined to whitenefs in the fun, before it is mixed with the gum.

The virtues of a cruft of bread, eat in a morning fafting ; publifhed by an eminent phyfician.] In the above treatife, (which fells for 2s. 9d.) the author only afferts, that a great many obftinate diforders, are cured by this fimple remedy ; and gives many inftances of its great efficacy in the following cafes. viz. king's evil, cachexies, fcurvies, leprofies, rheumatic complaints, &c. The author orders about half an ounce of hard cruft, or fea bifcuit, to be eat every morning fafting, for five or fix weeks ; and nothing to be taken after it in lefs than three or four hours.

To purify butter, and make it of a moft fweet tafte.] Melt butter with a flow fire in a well glazed earthen veffel, which put to fair water, working them well together, and when it is cold take away the curds and the whey at the bottom. Do it again the fecond time, and if you pleafe, the third time in rofe-water, always working them very well together. The butter thus clarified will be as fweet in tafte, as the marrow of any beaft, and keep a long time, by reafon of the great impurity which is removed by this means, the drofs being near a quarter of the whole.

M 2

Conftruction of Almanacks.] The firft thing to be done, is to compute the fun's and moon's place for each day of the year, or it may be taken from fome ephæ-merides, and entered in the almanack; next, find the dominical letter; and, by means thereof, diftribute the calendar into weeks: then having computed the time of Eafter, by it fix the other immoveable feafts; adding the immoveable ones, with the names of the martyrs, the rifing and fetting of each luminary, the length of day and night, the afpects of the plane;s, the phafes of the moon, and the fun's entrance into the cardinal points of the ecliptic; that is, the two æquinoxes and folftices. And thefe are the principal contents of alma-nacks; befides which there are others of a political na-ture, and confequently different in different countries, as the birth-days and coronations of princes, tables of intereft, &c. As to the antiquity of almanacks, Du-cange informs us, that the Egyptian aftrologers, long before the Arabians, ufed the term almanack, and al-menachica defcriptio, for their monthly productions. Be that as it will, Regiomontanus is allowed to have been the firft who reduced almanacks to their prefent form. On the whole, there appears to be no myftery, or even difficulty, in almanack making, provided tables of the heavenly motions be not wanting

A neceffary POCKET ALMANACK, *by which the day of the month is known, at firft view, from the prefent time, to the year of our Lord* 1831.] Under the word years, find the year; above which is the dominical letter for that year———Then, againft the month, in the other table, find the fame letter, over which are placed the days of the month for every Sunday of that month.— Every blank fpace fhows the year following to be leap year———N. B. In every leap-year for January and Fe-bruary, ufe the letter above the blank fpace before for that year.

YEARS.								SUNDAYS.						
A	G	F	E	D	C	B		1	2	3	4	5	6	7
1758	59		60	61	62	63		8	9	10	11	12	13	14
	64	65	66	67		68		15	16	17	18	19	20	21
69	70	71		72	73	74		22	23	24	25	26	27	28
75		76	77	78	79			29	30	31				
80	81	82	83		84	85	Jan. Oct.	A	B	C	D	E	F	G
86	87		88	89	90	91	May.	B	C	D	E	F	G	A
	92	93	94	95		96	Aug.	C	D	E	F	G	A	B
97	98	99	1800	1	2	3	Fb.Mar Nov.	D	E	F	G	A	B	C
	4	5	6	7		8	June.	E	F	G	A	B	C	D
9	10	11		12	13	14	Sep.De	F	G	A	B	C	D	E
15		16	17	18	19		Ap.Jul.	G	A	B	C	D	E	F
20	21	22	23		24	25								
26	27		28	29	30	31								

To make an artificial Malaga wine.] Take a wine
veſſel well hooped with iron hoops, and one end open,
to which a cloſe cover muſt be fitted to put on and take
off at pleaſure, ſet it in a warm place, fill it full of fair
water, to every gallon of which put two pounds of
Malaga raiſins, firſt bruiſed in a ſtone mortar; and to
every twenty gallons of water a good handful of calx
vive: cover the veſſel cloſe, and keep it warm with
cloths: let it ſtand four or five days to work: then ſee
if the raiſins be riſen up, and beat them down, and co-

M 3

ver it again as before, beating them down every fourth or fifth day for three or four weeks: then put a tap in, four inches above the bottom, and see if it taftes like wine; if not, let it ftand a while longer; after which draw it off into another wine veffel, and to every twenty gallons put a pint or quart of the beft fpirit of wine (as you would have it in ftrength) two new laid eggs, and a quart or better of Alicant well beaten together. Let it ftand in a cellar as other wine till it is fine, and fit to be drunk.

To make an artificial claret.] Take water, fix gallons: choice cyder, two gallons: beft Malaga raifins bruifed, eight pounds: mix and let them ftand all in a warm place fourteen days, ftirring them well once every day. Then prefs out the raifins, and put the liquor into the veffel again, to which add juice of rafberries a quart: juice of black cherries a pint: juice of black berries a pint and a half: cover this liquor with bread, fpread thick with ftrong muftard; the muftard fide being downwards, and fo let it work by the fire three or four days; after which turn it up, let it ftand a week, and bottle it up, fo will it become a very brifk and pleafant drink, and far better and wholefomer than our common claret.

To make an artificial malmfy.] Take eight gallons of fpring water: honey two gallons: make them boil over a gentle fire for an hour: take it off, and when it is cold, put it into a runlet, hanging in the veffel a bag of fpices, and fet it in the cellar for half a year, at the end of which you may drink it.

To make rafberry wine.] Take Canary a gallon: rafberries two gallons: mix and digeft twenty-four hours: ftrain them out, and add raifins of the fun ftoned three pounds: digeft again four or five days, fometimes ftirring them together: then pour off the cleareft, and put it up into bottles, which put into a cold place: if it be not fweet enough you may dulcify it with fugar.

Another way to do the fame.] Take juice of rafberries, bottle it up clofe, and fet it in a cellar, and it will become clear, and keep all the year long, and be very fragrant; a few spoonfuls of this put into a pint of wine sweetened with sugar, will give it a full taste of the berry*: two or three ounces of the syrup of the juice will do the same.

To purify oil olive, that it may be eaten with pleasure.] Take fair water two quarts, oil olive a pint : mix and shake them well together for a quarter of an hour in a glass; then separate the water from the oil with a separating funnel. Do this four or five times or more, as you see occasion, till the oil becomes very pure; and the last time wash it with rose-water, then hang in the midst of the oil a coarse bag full of bruised nutmegs, cloves, and cinnamon, so will you give it an excellent taste.

To make sage, parsley, or pennyroyal butter.] When the butter is newly made, and well wrought from its water, milk, and wheyish part, mix therewith a little oil of sage or parsley, so much till the butter is strong enough in taste to your liking, and then temper them well together; this will excuse you from eating the plants therewith; and if you do this with the aforesaid clarified butter, it will be far better, and a most admirable rarity.

To purify and refine sugar.] In a strong lixivium of calx vive dissolve as much coarse sugar as it will bear, adding to every quart of liquor, two whites of eggs, beaten into glair, stir them well together, and make them boil a little, taking off the scum, as long as any will arise; then pass all through a great woollen cloth bag, then boil the liquor again so long till being dropt upon a cold plate, being cold, it is as hard as salt; this done, put it out into pots or moulds for that purpose, having a hole in the narrower end thereof, which must be stopped for one night, afterwards being opened, the molosses or treacle will drop forth; then cover the ends of the pots with potters' clay, and as that clay sinks down, by reason of the sinking of the sugar, fill them up with more clay, doing thus, till the sugar will sink no more. Lastly take it out, and being hard and dry, bind it up in papers.

To make a plant grow in two or three hours.] Take aſhes of moſs, which moiſten with the juice of an old dunghill (being preſſed out and ſtrained) then dry them a little, and moiſten them as before ; do this four or five times ; put this mixture, not being very dry nor very moiſt, into an earthen veſſel, and in it ſet ſeeds of lettuce, purſlane, or parſley, (for they will grow ſooner than other ſeeds) being firſt impregnated with the eſſence of a vegetable of its own ſpecies (ſome ſay the juice of the ſame plant, but eſpecially the ſpirit will do inſtead of the eſſence;) till they begin to ſprout forth ; which then put into the ſaid earth, with that end upwards which ſprings. Put the veſſel into a gentle heat, and when it begins to dry, moiſten it with the ſaid juice of dung : thus may you have a ſallad while ſupper is making ready.

To reduce a whole vegetable into a liquor which may be called the eſſence thereof.] Take the whole plant with flowers and roots, bruiſe them in a mortar, put all into a large glaſs veſſel, (but a wooden one is better) ſo that two of three parts may be empty ; cover it exceeding cloſe, and let it ſtand in putrefaction in a moderate heat for a year, and it will all be turned into a water.

To make the lively form and idea of any plant appear in a glaſs.] Take the former water, of vegetable, diſtil it in a good glaſs in aſhes, and there will come forth a water and oil, and in the upper part of the veſſel a volatile ſalt ; the oil ſeparate and keep by itſelf ; with the water diſſolve the volatile ſalt, and purify it by filtering and coagulating. This purified ſalt imbibe with the ſaid oil until it will imbibe no more ; digeſt them well together for a month in a veſſel hermetically ſealed ; ſo will you have a moſt ſubtle eſſence, which being held over a gentle heat, or the flame of a candle, by which means it may be made hot, you will ſee the fine ſubſtance (which is like impalpable aſhes or ſalt) ſend forth from the bottom of the glaſs, the manifeſt form and idea of the vegetable, vegetating and growing by little and little, and putting on ſo fully the form of ſtalks, leaves, and flowers, in ſuch perfect and natural wiſe, that ere would believe the fame to be real; when as in truth it is the fpiritual idea, arifing with the fpiritual effence of the plant; this, were it joined with its proper earth, would take to itfelf a more folid body. Now as foon as the veffel or glafs is removed from the fire, this idea or reprefentation vanifhes, becoming a chaos and confufed matter, returning to its fediment, from whence it arofe.

Another way to make the effence of a plant.] Put the herbs, flowers, feeds, fpices, &c. into rectified fpirit of wine: extract a very ftrong and deep tincture, upon which put ftrong oil of falt, and digeft in Balneo, till an oil fwim above, which feparate. Or elfe draw off the fpirit of wine in Balneo, and the oil or effence will remain at bottom: but before the fpirit of wine is abftracted, the oil or effence is blood red, and a true quinteffence.

Another way to make the true effence, or rather quinteffence.] Make the water, oil, and volatile falt, as before is taught; and from the faeces extract the fixed falt, which purify according to art; which falt refolve in a cellar upon a marble ftone to an oil, which is what we call per deliquium, filter it and evaporate, till the falt is white as fnow, with thefe falts imbibe as much of the oil as you can make it receive; then digeft till the oil will not feparate from the falt, but become a fixed powder, melting with an eafy heat.

To make the form of a firr tree appear in Colophonia.] Diftil turpentine in a retort gradatim: when all is diftilled off, keep the retort ftill in a reafonable heat, that what humidity is ftill remaining may be evaporated, and it become dry. Take it then off from the fire, and hold your hand to the bottom of the retort, and the turpentine which is dried, (called alfo colophonia or rofin) will crack afunder in feveral places, and in thofe cracks, or chaps, you fhall fee the perfect figure of firr trees, which will there continue many months.

To make hartfhorn feemingly grow in a glafs.] Take hartfhorn broken into fmall bits, and put them into a glafs retort to be diftilled, and you fhall fee the glafs

to be feemingly full of horns ; which will continue there
fo long, till the volatile falt be come over.

To make a durable and lafting oil.] 1. Take unflacked lime, bay falt, oil olive, of each a like quantity ; mix them well together, and diftil in fand : co-
hobate the oil upon the fame quantity of frefh lime and
falt; this do four times. 2. The oil by this means will
be clear, and impregnated with what falt was volatile
in the lime and falt. 3. If it be feven times diftilled,
it will be as pure, odoriferous, and fubtle, as many
diftilled oils of vegetables. 4. This oil whilft diftilling, has a moft fragrant fmell, and of a moft durable
quality, which durability comes from the faline im-
pregnation ; befides which, it is good againft any inveterate ache or pain in the limbs, or other parts. 5.
A lamp made with this oil, will burn fix or feven times
as long, as that which is made with other oil ; alfo it
burns very fweet. 6. You ought to be very cautious
in making of it, or elfe your glaffes will quickly break.
7. You muft take very ftrong lime, fuch as your dyers
ufe, and call Cauk.

To make a candle that fhall laft long.] Mix with your
tallow unflacked lime in powder ; or make your candles
of caftile-foap : fuch candles as thefe will be admirable
for lamp furnaces. Now it is the falt in the lime and
foap, that preferves the tallow from burning out fo faft,
as otherwife it would.

*To make the diftilled oil out of any herb, feed, flower,
or paper, in a moment, without a furnace.*] You muft
have a long pipe made of tin, or tobacco-pipe clay with
a hole in it as big as a fmall walnut, three or four inches
from one end of it, into which you muft put the matter, you would have the oil off ; fet it on fire with a
candle or a coal ; then put one end of the pipe into a
bafon of fair water, and blow at the other end, fo will
the fmoak come into the water, and the oil will fwim
upon it, which you may feparate with a funnel.

To reduce rofin into turpentine again.] Take oil of
turpentine and the colophonia, or rofin thereof, in powder ; mix thefe together, and digeft them, and you

shall have turpentine of the same consistency it was before; but of a more fiery and subtile nature: pills made thereof are more excellent for opening obstructions of the breast, lungs, kidnies, bowels, &c. than those that are made of raw turpentine.

To write or engrave upon an egg, pebble, flint, &c.] Write what you please with wax or grease upon an egg, pebble, flint, &c. then put it into the strongest spirit of vinegar, or oil of salt, letting it lie two or three days; and you shall see every place about the letters or writing, eaten or consumed away; but the place where the wax or grease was not at all touched.

To make a powder, which being wetted shall be kindled.] 1. Take a load-stone, powder it, and put it into a strong crucible; cover it all over with a powder made of calx vive and colophonia, of each a like quantity; put also some of this powder under it: when the crucible is full, cover it, and lute the closures with potters' earth, put it into a furnace, and there let it boil; after take it out, and put the matter into another crucible, and set it in a furnace also, this do till it becomes a very white and dry calx. 2. Take of this calx one part; sal nitre well purified four parts; and as much camphire, sulphur vive, oil of turpentine and tartar; grind what is to be ground to a subtile powder, and put all into a glass vessel, with as much well rectified spirit of wine, as will cover them two inches over. 3. Stop the vessel close up, and set it in horse-dung three months, so will all the matter become an uniform paste: evaporate all the humidity, until the whole mass becomes a very dry stone; which take out, powder it, and keep it very dry. 4. If you take a little of this powder, and spit upon it, or pour some water thereon, it will take fire presently, so that you may light a match, or any such thing by it.

To make a room seem to be on fire.] Take rectified spirit of wine, and dissolve camphire therein; evaporate this in a very close chamber, where no air can get in; and he that first enters the chamber with a lighted candle, will be amazed; for the chamber will seem to be full of fire, and very subtile, but of little continuance. This done in a clofe cupboard or prefs, will be much more perfpicuous and vifible.

To make the four elements appear in a glafs.] Take jet in fine powder an ounce and half: oleum tartari per deliquium (made without addition of any water) two ounces, coloured with a light green with verdigrife: add thereto fpirit of wine tinged with a light blue with indigo, two ounces: of the beft rectified fpirit of turpentine, tinged of a light red with madder, two ounces: mix all thefe in a glafs, and fhake them together, and you fhall fee the heavy black jet fall to the bottom, and reprefent the earth: next the oil of tartar made green falls, reprefenting the water: upon that fwims the blue fpirit of wine, reprefenting the air or fky; and uppermoft of all will fwim the fubtile red oil of turpentine, reprefenting the element of fire. It is ftrange to fee how after fhaking all thefe together, they will be diftinctly feparated one from another. If it be well done, (as it is eafy to do it) it is an admirable and glorious fight.

To reprefent the whole world in a glafs.] Take the fineft fal-nitre, what you pleafe; tin, half fo much; mix them well together, and calcine them hermetically: then put them into a retort, to which adjoin a glafs receiver, with leaves of gold put into the bottom thereof; lute them well together; put fire to the retort, until vapours arife that will cleave to the gold: augment the fire till no more fumes afcend; then take away the receiver; clofe it hermetically, and make a lamp fire under it: and you will fee reprefented in it, the fun, moon, ftars, fountains, trees, herbs, plants, flowers, fruits, and indeed, even all things, after a very wonderful manner.

To make regulus of antimony, for antimonial cups.] Take antimony in powder, nitre, of each a pound; crude tartar in fine powder, two pounds; mix, put them into a crucible, cover the crucible, and melt, fo will the regulus fall to the bottom, which pour into a brafs mortar fmeared with oil. Or thus: Take antimony powdered, two pounds; crude tartar in powder

four pounds; melt as before. This regulus you may
cast into cups, pictures, medals, or what figures you
pleafe : thefe infufed into two or three ounces of wine
in an earthen glazed veffel, or in a glafs, in a gentle
heat all night, gives you a liquor in the morning which
will vomit : dofe, from two drachms to two ounces and
a half ; you may fweeten it if you pleafe with a little
white fugar. Thefe cups or pictures will laft for ever,
and be as effectual after a thoufand times infufion as at
firft.

To make Barbers' wafh balls.] Take purified Venetian foap fix ounces, macaleb four ounces, ireos, amy-
lum, of each feven ounces, cloves two ounces, labdanum,
annifeeds of each one ounce, nutmegs, ma joram, Cy-
prefs powder, geranium mofchatum, camphire, of each
half an ounce, ftorax liquida half a drachm, mufk ten
grains, all being in fine powder, with a little fine fugar,
beat all in a mortar, and make them up into wafh balls.

To make common wafh-balls, the beft of that kind.]
Take Venice or Caftile-foap fliced very thin, four
pounds, fpirit of wine half a pint, beat all together ;
then add chemical oil of faffafrafs or lemons an ounce
or more ; and beat again very well : laftly, add white
ftarch made into a pafte with water, by boiling a fufficient
quantity to make all into an even and fmooth mafs,
which form into balls of four ounces a piece, with powder of white ftarch, dry them and keep them for ufe.

To make unguentum pomatum, or ointment of apples.]
Take hog's lard three pounds, fheep's fuet nine ounces,
bruifed cloves one drachm, aqua rofarum two ounces,
pomwaters pared and fliced one pound, boil all to the
confumption of the rofe-water ; then ftrain without
preffing, to every pound of which add oil of rhodium
and cinnamon, of each thirty drops.

To make a compound pomatum.] Take of the pomatum aforefaid (without the oils) four pounds, fpicknerk,
cloves, of each two ounces, cinnamon, ftorax, benjamin, of each one ounce, (the fpices and gums bruifed
and tied up in a thin rag) rofe-water, eight ounces ;
boil to the confumption of the rofe-water, then add

N

white wax eight ounces, which mix well by melting, ftrain it again being hot ; and when it is almoft cold mix therewith oil of mufk, then put it out, and keep it for ufe.

To cleanfe the Skin.] Wafh with warm water, and fweet fcented wafh bails very well ; then rub the fkin with a cloth, and wafh well with water in which wheat-bran has been boiled—Or thus, take fublimate one ounce, glair of fix eggs, boil them in a glafs veffel, till they grow thick, then prefs out the water, with which wafh the fkin.

To make the fkin foft and fmooth.] The fkin being very clean, as before directed, wafh it very well with a lixivium of falt of tartar, and after that anoint it with, pomatum ; or which is better, oil of fweet almonds, doing this every night going to bed.

A water to cleanfe the face from fcurf and morphew.] Take diftilled rain water fix ounces, juice of lemons twelve ounces, mix them, and wafh with it morning and evening, anointing after it at night going to bed with the oil or pomatum aforefaid.

An unguent which brings the fkin to an exquifite beauty.] Take of pomatum one ounce, falt of tartar one drachm, mufk twenty grains, mix them well, and (the face or fkin being very clean) anoint morning and evening.

To make the hair lank and flag that curls too much.] Anoint the hair thoroughly twice or thrice a week with oil of lilies, rofes, or marfh mallows, combing it after it very well.

To make the hair grow long and foft.] Diftil hog's greafe or oil of olive in an alembic ; with the oil that comes therefrom anoint the hair, and it will make it grow long and foft : ufe it for ufe.

To preferve the hair from fplitting at the ends.] Anoint the ends thereof with oil omphacine, or oil of myrtles ; they are eminent in this cafe to preferve the hair from fplitting, fo alfo an ointment made of honey, bee's-wax, and oil omphacine, or bear's greafe.

A fweet powder to lay among cloaths.] Take damafk-rofe leaves dried one pound, mufk half a drachm, violet leaves three ounces, mix them and put them in a bag

Another for the same, or to wear about one.] Take
rose leaves dried one pound, cloves in powder half an
ounce, spicknard two drachms, storax, cinnamon, of
each three drachms, musk half a drachm, mix them
and put them into bags for use.

An excellent perfuming powder for the hair.] Take
iris roots in fine powder one ounce and a half, benjamin, storax, cloves, musk, of each two drachms : being
all in fine powder, mix them for a perfume for hair-
powder. Take of this perfume one drachm, rice-flower
impalpable one pound, mix them for a powder for the
hair. Note, some use white starch, flower of French
beans and the like.

A perfume to smoak and burn.] Take labdanum two
ounces, storax one ounce, benjamin, cloves, mace, of
each half an ounce, musk, civet, of each ten grains, all
in fine powder, make it up into cakes with mucilage of
gum tragacanth in rose-water, which dry ; and keep
among your cloaths, which when occasion requires, you
may burn in a chafing-dish of coals.

To make red writing ink.] Take raspings of Brazil
one ounce, white lead, alum, of each two drachms,
grind and mingle them, infuse them in urine one pound,
with gum arabick two scruples, or a drachm at most.

Another way to make red ink.] Take wine vinegar
two pounds, raspings of Brazil two ounces, alum half
an ounce, infuse all ten days; then gently boil, to
which add gum arabick five drachms, dissolve the gum,
strain and keep it for use. *Note,* two drachms of the
gum in some cases may be enough.

☞ I forbear here to give a receipt for preparing a
most exquisite *Black Writing Ink,* having sold the property of it to WILLIAM SPOTSWOOD, Printer and Book-
seller, Philadelphia, who intends shortly to offer it to
the public ready prepared, at the same rate of the or-
dinary sort of black ink. It is free from the ill qualities
of the common black writing ink. I had it from a late
eminent and much celebrated chemist.

N 2

To make green ink to write with.] Make fine verdigrife into pafte with ftrong vinegar, an infufion of green galls, in which a little gum arabick hath been diffolved, let it dry, and when you would write with it, temper it with infufion of green galls aforefaid.

Another way to make green ink to write with.] Diffolve verdigrife in vinegar, then ftrain it, and grind it with a little honey and mucilage of gum tragacanth, upon a porphyry ftone.

To make blue ink to write with.] Grind indigo with honey mixed with glair of eggs or glue water, made of ifinglafs diffolved in water and ftrained.

To make red writing ink of vermillion.] Grind vermillion well upon a porphyry ftone, with common water; dry it and put it into a glafs veffel, to which put urine, fhake all together, let it fettle, then pour off the urine, and putting on more urine, repeat this work eight or ten times, fo will the vermillion be well cleanfed; to which put glair of eggs to fwim on it above a finger's breadth, ftir them together, and fettling abftract the glair; then put on more glair of eggs, repeating the fame work eight or ten times alfo, to take away the fcent of the urine: laftly, mix it with frefh glair, and keep it in a glafs veffel clofe ftopped for ufe. When you ufe it, mix it with water or vinegar.

To make printer's black.] This is made by grinding the beft lamp black with liquid varnifh, and boiling it a little, which you may make thick at pleafure. You muft make it moifter in winter, than in fummer; and note, that the thicker ink makes the fairer letter. If it be too thick, you muft put in more linfeed oil, or oil of walnuts, fo may you make it thicker or thinner at pleafure.

To make red printing ink.] Grind vermillion very well with the aforefaid liquid varnifh or linfeed oil.

To make green printing ink.] Grind Spanifh green with the faid varnifh or linfeed oil as aforefaid; and after the fame manner, may you make printer's blue, by grinding azure with the faid linfeed oil.

To make red foft wax.] Take white bee's-wax one

pound, turpentine three ounces, vermillion in powder well ground, oil olive, of each one ounce, melt the wax and turpentine; let it cool a little, then add the reft, beating them well together.

To do the fame otherwife.] This is done by taking away the vermillion, and adding inftead thereof red lead three ounces, to the former things.

To make green wax.] Take wax one pound, turpentine three ounces, verdigrife ground, oil olive, of each one ounce; complete the work as before directed.

To make black wax.] Take bee's-wax one pound, turpentine three ounces, black earth, oil olive, of each one ounce; mix and make wax as aforefaid.

To make wax perfumed.] This is done by mixing with the olive aforefaid, mufk, ambergrife, or any other eminent perfume, as oil of cinnamon, adeps rofarum, or the like, one drachm, more or lefs, according as you intend to have its fcent extended.

After the fame manner you may make foft wax of all colours, having what fcent you pleafe; by mixing the fcent intended, with the oil olive, and putting the colour in, in place of the vermillion.

To make hard fealing wax.] Take pure fine gumlack, melt it in an earthen veffel, and put into it a fufficient quantity of the colour you defign your wax to be of, ftir and mingle it well, then take it off the fire, and when it is a fit heat, you may make it up into rolls or fticks. To make red wax, you muft colour it with vermillion. Blue wax, with blue bice, fmalt, or ultramarine. Green wax with green bice, verdigrife, or fome other mixture of that colour. Black wax, with ivory or cherry ftone black. Purple wax, or of a dark red, with prepared caput mortuum, Indian lake, &c.

A ftrong glue for pipes and aqueducts.] Tobacco pipe clay, dried and reduced to powder, and mixed with good ftore of fhort flocks, and beat up with linfeed oil to a ftiff pafte, like kneaded dough, makes a ftrong and a lafting cement for pipes and aqueducts; and being made into pipes (though long a drying) is very ftaunch and lafting.

To make a very strong glue.] Soak the fineſt ichthyo-
colla (that is iſinglaſs) twenty-four hours in ſpirit of
wine, or common brandy ; then boil all very gently tó-
gether, continually ſtirring of it, that it burn not, ſo
long till it becomes one liquor or body (ſave ſome
ſtrings not very diſſolvable) which ſtrain whilſt hot,
through a coarſe linen cloth, into a veſſel where it may
be kept cloſe ſtopped ; a gentle heat will melt this glue
into a tranſparent liquor, with which you may glew
things ſo ſtrongly together, that they will rather break
in any other part, than in the place glued ; it much
exceeds the common glue.

To make artificial pearls.] Take ſublimate two ounces,
tin-glaſs one ounce, mix them, and ſublime them together, and you will have a ſublimate not inferior to
the beſt orient pearls in the world, of which, with
glair, you may form what you pleaſe.

END OF THE SECOND PART.

BEING THE

LABORATORY,

OR

HANDMAID to the ARTS.

CONTAINING

Such *Branches* of *Useful Knowledge,*

As nearly concerns all Kinds of People,

From the S QU I R E to the P E A S A N T :

AND WILL AFFORD BOTH

PROFIT and DELIGHT.

PART THE THIRD.

PHILADELPHIA:

PRINTED AND SOLD BY WILLIAM SPOTSWOOD,

AND H. AND P. RICE, MARKET-STREET.

1793.

THE
SCHOOL of ARTS.

Of the nature and compofition of GLASS:
and the art of counterfeiting Gems of
every kind.

PART the THIRD.

Of Glafs in general.

BY glafs, as here treated of, is to be underftood,
the artificial vitrifications of bodies, made to anfwer fome ufeful purpofe, either in domeftic neceffaries,
or other articles of commerce : and the obfervations
and directions given with regard to it, in this treatife,
are fuch only as refpect the improvement of the art of
preparing and compounding the kinds applicable to
thefe ends in the different manufactures of it. For
the more fpeculative and philofophic difquifitions on
its nature are avoided, where they lead to no principles
that are capable of being applied to practice. The me-
hods of modelling and forming it into all the variety
of veffels, and other figures, into which it is wrought
are likewife omitted : becaufe they are already, or may
be by other means, well known to thofe who have any
any concern with them as an employment ; or like all
other occupations of artifans, may be much more eafily
and better learned by fuch as are defirous to be initia-

ted into an operative knowledge of them, from an in
fpection of actual works, and trials to imitate what i
there to be feen done, than they can by the moft expli
cit verbal directions.

The manufactured glafs at prefent in ufe may be di
vided into three general kinds, white tranfparent glafs
coloured glafs, and common green or bottle glafs. O
the firft kind, there is a great variety of forts, accord
ing to the feveral purpofes intended to be ferved by it
either for making domeftic utenfils, or lights for inclo
fed places: and of the fecond, there is likewife a fti
greater multiplicity of fpecies, differing in their colou
or other properties, according to the occafions for whic
they are wanted: but of the laft, there is no diftin
guifhed difference of fort ; except what the accidenti
manner of preparation and management, practifed ac
cording to the fkill or art of particular directors
manufactories, may occafion.

In order, however, to fpeak more intelligibly of tl
nature of the manufactured glafs, to be here treated c
it is proper to give fome diftinct notion of vitrificatic
in general. But I fhall not endeavour to pufh the ma
ter to thofe almoft metaphyfical lengths to which B
eher, Stahl, and others, have endeavoured to carry i
even far beyond the conclufions which can be fupport
by inductions from fufficient experiments. Vitrificati
then (according to the more general and obvious n
tions of its nature) is a change which may be wrought
moft kinds of fixed bodies, or rather in all under for
circumftances, by the means of heat, applied in vario
degrees, according to the various nature of the bodie
from which change, they become fluid ; and contin
fo while kept in the fame, or any greater degree
heat ; and, when become cold, acquire tranfparenc
fragility, a great but not abfolute degree of inflexil
lity, a total want of malleability, and infolubility
water. All thefe qualities are infeparably attendant
perfect vitrification : though there may be many pret
rations of artificial glafs, even among thofe that are
common ufe, in which fome of them are wantir

But this is, nevertheless, only where the vitrification is immature; or where there is an admixture of other bodies with the vitrified matter: as in the case of the opake white glass; in which the matter giving the milky colour is in an unvitrified state, and consequently destroys the transparency; or, in the compositions where too great a proportion of salts is used, when the glass produced will be soluble in water, though perfect with respect to all the other qualities. In both these cases there is the presence of an heterogenous body, besides the proper glass; and therefore, if the whole mass be considered as if in a vitrific state, it must be deemed to be an imperfect one, though the composition, in the instance of the white glass, be adapted by this very circumstance to the œconimical purpose for which it is intended. The same principle will be verified on a due examination in all the other sorts of manufactured glass, as well as in accidental commixtures, where the appearances of the glass disagree with the system of qualities required, in the above given definition, to the perfect constitution of glass.

From the nature of vitrification, it therefore appears, that all fixed bodies are capable of being the materials of perfect glass under some circumstances. But as the means of vitrification are limited with regard to the manufactured glass, such bodies only are proper to become the ingredients of the perfect kinds of it, as are easily to be procured in due quantity, and admit of being vitrified by the heat of a furnace either alone, or by their commixture with others, which may promote this change in them: and in the case of the imperfect sorts, such as that above-mentioned, bodies that are not capable of being vitriated, by the means there employed, are also taken in as materials: where they are required to give the particular properties wanted in each peculiar sort. The principal substances, therefore, that are chosen for the composition of manufactured glass, are sand, flints, and other fossible bodies of a stony and earthy texture; metals and semi-metals of all kinds previously prepared by calcination, or other operations; arsenic and zaffer, which are prepared parts of a foffile ; and all falts of a fixed kind.

Among thefe fubftances there are fome which are ftrongly reluctant to the vitreous fufion, and could fcarcely alone be ever converted to glafs ; at leaft not by the heat of any furnaces ; and yet are fuch, as are moft capable of giving firmnefs and tenacity to that in which they are admitted ; as alfo of being more copi-oufly provided at a fmall expence. There are others, on the contrary, that vitrify in a much lefs heat than that commonly employed in the working of glafs ; and have likewife this attendant property along with their own pronenefs to vitreous fufion, that they accelerate and produce it in many of thofe that are otherwife more repugnant to it ; and caufe them, by their commixture, to vitrify in a greatly lefs degree of heat than they other-wife would. This property of promoting vitrification is called technically fluxing the bodies on which they fo act ; and on the proper application of this principle to practice lies the main ftrefs of fkill in the art of com-pounding glafs ; as the favings in the original coft of the ingredients, in time and in fewel, as well as the qualities of the glafs produced, depend chiefly on the thorough intelligence, in this view, of the nature of the bodies, proper to become ingredients of it. The next important relation, in which bodies ftand with refpect to the compofition of glafs, is the effect they may have on its colour by their admixture : in order to deftroy all kinds of which in fome cafes, and to produce them in others, ingredients are frequently added, that are not otherwife neceffary ; as being no way fubfervient to the general view. This conftitutes, therefore, the other great object of fkill in the art of making glafs for the knowing properly how to take away all colour from the tranfparent white glafs, and to impart any kind defired, to proper compofitions on other occafions is of the next great moment to the being able, by the moft cheap and eafy means, to procure a due vitrification

According to the above fpecified intentions, in which the feveral fubftances ferving for the materials of glafs are ufed, they may be properly diftinguifhed into three kinds, as making the body, flux, and colorific matter.

The fubftances which have been employed in forming the body of glafs are fand (by which is only to be underftood the white kinds) flints, talc, fpar, and feveral other ftony foffiles. All thefe vitrify of themfelves too flowly, to produce perfect glafs by the degree of heat that can be applied to them when in larger maffes: which makes them therefore require the addition of thofe other kinds, whofe fluxing power may remedy this defect in them: while they, on the other hand, being of low price, and to be procured in unlimited quantities, and giving that hardnefs, ftrength, and infolubility, which cannot be had in any glafs, formed of other fubftances without them, are yet effential and indifpenfibly neceffary ingredients in all kinds of manufactured glafs.

The fubftances which are ufed as fluxing ingredients in glafs, are red-lead, pearl-afhes, nitre, fea-falt, borax, arfenic, the fcoria of forges, commonly called clinkers, and wood-afhes, containing the calcined earth and lixiviate falts, as produced by incineration. The prefence of fome of thefe bodies is always equally neceffary with that of thofe which form the body, in all the compofitions of manufactured glafs. But the ufe of them, both with refpect to choice and proportion, is greatly varied in different works; even where the fame kind of glafs is intended to be produced: as the general nature of them has never been hitherto underftood by the directors of fuch works; and they have only implicitly followed the beft receipts they could procure, carefully keeping them fecret, when they happened either by communication or their accidental difcovery to be poffeffed of fuch improvements, as gave them any advantages over their fellow operators.

The fubftances which have been applied as colorific matter in manufactured glafs, are extremely numerous and various; as all the fpecies of metals and femi-metals, with many other mineral and foffile bodies, have been ufed for the producing fome colour or other; and make a large field of fpeculative and practical knowledge.

O

The art of ftaining glafs, with all the variety of colours
in the greateft degree of force and brightnefs, is not
however of fo much importance commercially confidered, as the knowing how to banifh and exclude, with
eafe and certainty, the colours which of themfelves arife
in moft of the compofitions for glafs intended to be perfectly tranfparent and colourlefs. For this laft purpofe,
nitre and magnefia are the principal fubftances employed,
in the manufactures of G. Britain ; and extremely
well anfwer the end : though not without enhancing
the expence of the glafs by the ufe of the firft ; and in
a fmall degree injuring its tranfparency by that of the
latter: as may be demonftrated by principles that are
unqueftionable in themfelves, though wholly unknown
to thofe who are practically concerned in thefe matters.

From thefe three kind of fubftances, duly combined
together by commixture and adequate heat, or in fome
cafes from the two firft only, all the forts of manufactured glafs at prefent in ufe are formed. The general
manner of doing which, is to reduce thofe kinds of bodies, that are in groffer maffes, to powder ; and then,
all the ingredients being thoroughly well mixed together by grinding, and put into proper pots, to place
them in a furnace where the heat is fufficient to bring
them to a due ftate of fufron; in which they are to be
continued till the vitrification be completed.

This proper degree of vitrification muft be diftinguifhed by the tranfparent and equal appearance of the
matter, when a fmall portion is taken out and fuffered
to cool : except in the cafe of thofe forts where the
glafs is not perfect, with regard to which, a judgment
muft be made from their having attained or wanting
that peculiar appearance, which the particular fort is
required to have. It may be proper to fubjoin, that in
all cafes, the vitrification is fooner and more eafily made
perfect in proportion as the ingredients are reduced
to the ftate of a finer powder, and more intimately
commixt.

Of the materials ferving for the body of glafs.] The
materials employed to give a body to glafs, are fand,

flints, talc, spar, and some other stony and terene fossiles.

Sand is, at present, almost the only kind of substance which is used in this intention in the British manufactures of glass; and with great reason, as it extremely well answers the purpose; and does not demand the previous preparation of calcination, that is necessary with respect to flints and other stones; and as it can be with certainty procured in any quantity demanded. The kind of sand most fit for making the white transparent kinds of glass, is that brought from Lynn in Norfolk, by the name of which place it is distinguished: and there is also another kind of this, but inferior, brought from Maidstone in Kent. It is white and shining; and examined by means of a microscope, appears to be small fragments of rock crystal; from which it does not seem, by any experiments, to differ in its qualities; and the glass formed of it may, therefore, properly be considered as made of crystal. The introduction of the use of it into the manufactures of glass in this country has almost wholly superseded that of flints: from which it no way differs in this application, but in the being somewhat slower in vitrifying; which makes it require in proportion a greater strength of flux and fire: but to compensate for this disadvantage, it is clearer in its own colour, and much freer from heterogeneous tinging bodies, which injure the colour of the glass; and frequently give embarrassment where flints are used. The sand requires no previous preparation for common and grosser purposes; especially where nitre is used; which burns out the sulphureous matter from any filth of the nature of animal and vegetable substances; and consequently calcines them to an earth no way injurious to the glass: but for nicer purposes, and where no nitre is used, it is proper to purify or cleanse the sand by washing: which may be thus done. Pour water upon it; and, having stirred them well about, incline the vessel immediately, in such manner, that the water may run off, and carry with it the filth that will float in it: by repeating which a few saving in the fluxing bodies which are to be added to them.

Flints are the next important article in the fubftances which are ufed for forming the body of glafs; and where indeed the only kind employed in larger works, where any better forts of glafs were manufactured, before the ufe of the white fand excluded them in all places where it is to be conveniently obtained. Since, for the reafons above given, it is a more eligible material, unlefs for experiments, or wheie very fmall quantities are required; in which cafe the calcined flints being more eafily reduced to an impalpable powder, may poffibly be more commodioufly employed than the fand. Flints yet, however, continue to be ufed wherever the proper fand cannot be procured at a reafonable charge, as the fole ingredient for forming the body of the better kind of glafs: fince they are, in moft places where they are naturally found, to be had in extreme great quantities; and the expence of calcining them does not enhance their whole coft to a degree beyond what the current price of glafs may bear. The goodnefs of flints with refpect to this ufe of them muft be diflinguifhed by their clear tranfparent black colour; and all fuch as are marbled with brown or yellowifh colour fhould be rejected, for fear of iron, which frequently lurks in them under that appearance, and is very injurious to the colour of glafs if it get admiffion into it. Such fhould, therefore be carefully picked out when found in parcelsof the clearer fort; but if the greater part of any parcel appear fo marked, it fhould not be ufed till trial be made in a fmall quantity, whether the difcolouring be owing to any fubftance detrimental to the colour of glafs or not. It is always neceffary, that flints fhould undergo a calcination before they be ufed in the compofi-tion of glafs: as well becaufe they are not otherwife tô

be reduced to a texture, which will admit of their being powdered, in order to their due commixture with
the other ingredients; as becaufe they are not fufceptible of vitrification till a proper change may be produced in them by calcination. This calcination muft be
performed by putting them into a furnace of a moderate heat, being firft dipped in water; and continuing
them there till they become entirely white, even to the
moft interior part: which will require a greater or lefs
time, according to their magnitude, and the degree of
heat of the furnace. When they are thus rendered
white, they muft be taken out of the fire; and inftantly immerfed in cold water; where they muft remain,
till they be again cold: and then they will be found, if
duly calcined, to be cracked and fhivered into flaky
pieces; and to become fo foftly brittle as to be eafily re-
ducible to powder. Some part will neverthelefs be always found infufficiently calcined; which may be diftinguifhed by their harder and more obdurate confiftence: and they muft be carefully feparated, in order
to be re-calcined; as they will otherwife greatly retard
and impede the powdering of the duly calcined parts.
Thofe which are properly calcined muft then be levigated, by means of mills or other implements, accordingly as the quantity or opportunity may make it expedient; and they will then be fit for ufing in the compofition for glafs.

Talc of various fpecies has been likewife ufed in the
fame intention as fand and flints: but feldom in large
works. It fometimes requires a calcination, in order
to its due preparation for entering into the compofition
of glafs: but neither fo great a heat, nor the quenching in cold water, are neceffary for bringing it to a
proper texture to bear powdering. Some forts of talc
are much more quickly vitrifiable than others; and,
fufing eafily with either falt of tartar or lead, may
therefore be ufed in default of flint, or fand fufficiently
white. But, with refpect to larger manufactures, the
ufe of flints is more eligible; as they are to be procured
in great quantities with more certainty; and will, in

general, require much lefs flux and fire to bring them to a due ftate of vitrification.

Several other, both earthy and ftony, foffiles have been likewife ufed for forming the body of glafs: and it has been obferved, that moft kinds of ftony fubftances, which will fcintillate or ftrike fire with fteel, are vitrifiable within the degree that fits them for this purpofe. But as they are neither ufed at prefent, nor promife to be any way advantageous in practice, as far as is hitherto known of them, I fhall omit enumerating them; as being foreign to the purpofe in hand : except with refpect to two kinds. The one of thefe is called *meilon* by the French ; and is found in great quantities, as an upper cruft in many freeftone quarries : and, as it may be ufed without any previous preparation, and is very quickly vitrifiable, may be ferviceable, on fome occafions, to thofe who may want to form glafs, or vitreous compofitions, where this may be procured with more eafe than any of the before-mentioned fubftances. The other is the white round femi-tranfparent river pebbles, which vitrify very foon ; and, if chofen colourlefs, make a very white glafs ; but they muft be calcined, as the flint, by putting them into the fire till they be red hot ; and then quench them in cold water, in order to bring them to a ftate fit to undergo powdering.

Kunckel confounds the calcined flints, and all other ftones ufed for making glafs, under the name of fand, in his receipts ; notwithftanding he admits of a great difference in their readinefs to be vitrified : as in the cafe of calcined flints, and the fofteft kind of natural fand ; where one hundred and forty pounds of falt are required to a hundred and fifty pounds of the calcined flints, and only one hundred and thirty pounds of falt to two hundred pounds of the fand.

Of the materials ufed as fluxes in the compofition of glafs.] The materials ufed for the fluxes in the compofition of manufactured glafs, are, lead, pearl-afhes, nitre, fea falt, borax, arfenic, fmith's clinkers, and wood-afhes,

Lead is the prefent moſt important flux in the Britiſh manufactures of what is called flint glaſs: but it muſt be brought, by previous calcination, to the ſtate of minium, or what is called red lead. This, uſed in a due proportion, makes a tougher and firmer glaſs than can be produced from ſalts alone : and is yet procured at a very ſmall expence. But all the glaſs formed of lead is tinged originally with yellow ; and therefore requires the addition of nitre to burn and deſtroy the ſulphur or phlogiſtic matter it contains, in order to bring it to a more colourleſs ſtate : which addition of nitre enhances again the coſt of glaſs ſo compoſed, that would otherwife be extremely low. There is another reafon, likewife, for the addition of nitre, or ſome other ſalt, to operate as a flux in the glaſs compounded with lead ; which is, that there may not be a neceſſity of uſing beyond a certain proportion of it. For, if glaſs have much lead in its compoſition, it will ſuffer a corro-ſion by the air ; which gives a greyiſh dulneſs to its ſurface, that is very injurious both to its beauty and utility. It is needleſs here, to teach the manner of cal-cining lead ; becaufe it is done in works appropriated to that purpofe ; and is ſold by the proprietors of theſe works, at a cheaper rate than any particular perfons could pretend to manufacture it for their private ufe. The perfection of red lead lies in its being thoroughly well calcined ; which is beſt diſtinguiſhed by its redneſs, inclining to crimſon, and in its being pure ; which may be adjudged of by the brightneſs of its colour. There is indeed no materials of a red colour cheap enough to adulterate it with, except powdered bricks, or ſome of the red okres ; and they would immediately ſhow themfelves, in the vitrification of the ſmalleſt quan-tity, by the ſtrong yellow tinge they would give the glaſs.

Pearl-aſhes is the next leading article among the fub-ſtances uſed as fluxes in glaſs : and they at prefent moſtly ſupply the place of the Levant-aſhes, the barillas of Spain, and many other kinds, which were formerly brought here, as well for making glass as soap. In the kinds of glass, where perfect transparency is wanted, as in looking-glass plates, and all kinds of window glass, salts are preferable as a flux to lead ; and, consequently, the pearl-ashes become the principal matter of the flux. For, as all the lixiviate or fixed alkaline salts of vegetables are the same for this purpose, when pure, and those called pearl-ashes are purer than any other which can be provided at a moderate expence, the use of them is more expedient than of any other. This kind of fixed alkaline salts, called pearl ashes, is prepared in Germany, Russia, and Poland, by melting the salts out of the ashes of burnt wood ; and, having reduced them again to dryness, evaporating away the moisture, and calcining them for a considerable time in a furnace moderately heated. But, as they cannot be prepared with advantage in this country, (tho' in America they unquestionably might, and indeed are of late) and are to be had at a reasonable price by those who may have occasion to use them in making glass. I shall wave entering more particularly here into the detail of the process, by which they may be best and most profitably produced ; as not properly falling within the intention of this work. The goodness of pearl-ashes must be distinguished by the equal and white appearance of them ; as it consists in their purity, and their having been calcined for a long space of time, of which the whiteness, and equal appearance, are marks ; unless in the case of some parcels that contain lumps of a bluish cast produced by the calcination ; which discolouring is not, however, any proof of their being bad : but any brownish cast in particular parts, or greyness in the whole, is a certain criterion of their not being good. This must, however, be confined to such as are perfectly dry ; which can only well be on the opening the casks they are brought over in : for, if the air have access to them, they soon deliquiate, and look brown or greyish, from a semi-transparency they acquire in that deliquiating state. There is one, and the most common adulteration, which is made in these salts, that is not easily

diftinguifhable by the appearance ; it is, the addition of
common or fea falt, to them ; which is fometimes copioufly made. This is not, however, very detrimental
in the application of them to the forming glafs. But
it is, nevertheless, a difadvantage confiderable enough
in large concerns, to buy one thing for another at fix
times its current price. As it is expedient, therefore,
to know how to diftinguifh this fraud, the following
method is propofed as eafy and certain.

Take a fmall quantity of the falt fufpected ; and,
after it has lain in the air fo as to be a little foftened
but not melted, put it in a fire fhovel and hold it over
the fire where the heat is pretty ftrong. If it contain
any common falt, a crackling, and, as it were flight
explofion will follow, as the falt grows hot : which decrepitation is a certain mark of common falt wherever
it is found.

The pearl-afhes require no preparation ; except where
extreme great tranfparency is required, as in the
cafe of looking glafs, and the beft window-glafs ; in
which cafes a purification is neceffary, in the manner
which will be fhown in fpeaking of thefe particular kinds.

Nitre in its refined ftate, in which it is commonly
called falt petre, has been formerly much ufed as a flux
in the finer kinds of glafs ; and is now likewife employed in moft compofitions of the fame nature. But
this is a noted one by thofe who are at all acquainted
with the principles of the art, fo much in the intention
of a flux, as in that of a colorific ingredient ; from its
power of rendering glafs colourlefs, by deftroying the
phlogifton in lead, or in any vegetable or animal matter, which may tinge the glafs ; as we fhall have occafion to obferve more particularly in its proper place. As
a flux, it is lefs powerful than fixed alkaline falts of vegetables : and being dearer by much, its ufe would,
therefore, be in proportion lefs expedient than that of
pearl-afhes, if it were to be employed in this view only.
The falt-petre that is ufed here, is brought from the
Eaft Indies, in the form of what is called crude nitre ;
and in commercial language rough-petre : in which ftate

obtained in cryſtals of a ſuch a ſize, th
them may be diſtinguiſhable, there is no
adulteration, but what would be very ap
heterogeneous matter can be made a p
ſuch cryſtals; and, therefore, if they
and colourleſs, the goodneſs cannot be

Sea-ſalt is alſo frequently uſed as a flux
glaſs of various kinds; and it has a ver
in promoting vitrification even in ſome ot
but, uſed in a large proportion, it does
ſtrong and tenacious a glaſs as lead, or
line ſalts of vegetables; and is therefore
aid of the others, when admitted as an
ſhould be brought to a dry ſtate by decr
is, keeping it in a moderate heat, till
ling, before it be put with the other i
the fuſing heat : otherwiſe, by the little
of its parts, it will drive ſome of the po
out of the pot. It muſt not, after ſuch
be again expoſed to the air; for, if it
gain its former quality of crackling in a

Borax is the moſt powerful flux of all
deed, of any known ſubſtance whatever
count of its great price, can only be ad
compoſition of glaſs deſigned for looking
other purpoſes, where a conſiderable val
the produce ; or where the quantity wan
It is brought from the Eaſt-Indies, u
of tincal; and the refinement of it in a
is hitherto known but to few perſons i
carefully keep it ſecret. The knowle
ever, is not important to the art of m
it is always procured for that purpoſe ir
and not uſed in very large quantitie
of it may be aſcertained by the largeneſs

the cryſtals: for when it is had in that ſtate, it may be always concluded good. The previous preparation of borax for the compoſition of glaſs, is to calcine it with a gentle heat, which converts it to a flaky feathery kind of ſubſtance like calcined alum: after which it ſhould be ground to powder, and is then fit to be commixt with other ingredients. This calcination of borax ſhould be with a gentle heat, and in a very large veſſel proportionably to the quantity; for it ſwells and riſes in inflated bladders, ſo as to occupy a very great ſpace.

Arſenic is alſo a powerful flux; but muſt not be added, neverthelefs, in too great quantity. For though when once vitrified perfectly, it greatly promotes the ſame change in other ſubſtances, yet, when added in a redundant proportion, it turns the glaſs milky or opake; and keeps it in that ſtate a confiderable time before it will duly aſſimilate; from whence the due vitrification is greatly retarded, ſo as to occafion an intolerable loſs of time and fewel. Though the glaſs in all ſuch cafes would become clear, if continued long enough in the fire, yet, on this principle of its ſlownefs in vitrifying when added to compoſitions of glaſs in a large proportion, it is uſed for giving an opake white colour to glaſs as we ſhall ſee below.

Wood aſhes, by which is to be underſtood, likewife, thofe of broom, furze, or any other burned vegetable, are uſed as a flux for the common bottle or green glaſs. The aſhes muſt be taken in their original ſtate, confiſting of the calcined earth of the vegetable, and their lixiviate or fixed alkaline ſalt; as their virtue lies in their original manner of commixture: for this very extraordinary circumſtance attends them, that though in their primitive ſtate they vitrify eaſily, and act as ſtrong flux to any of the vitrifiable earths or ſtones; yet, if the ſalts be ſeparated from the earth, by ſolution in water, the earth from that time becomes extremely repugnant to vitrification; and though the ſame ſalts which were taken away from it, or even a much larger quantity be again added to it, it refiſts their fluxing power, and diſplays a nature entirely different from that

which it appeared to have befo e its feparation from the
falts. There is no preparation necessary for thefe afhes,
in order to their entering into the compofition of glafs,
except the fifting them to free them from all the fragments of charcoal, or unburned parts of the vegetables
employed in their production : but they fhould be carefully kept from damp and moifture ; which would make
the falts deliquiate, and run off from the earth   The
goodnefs of thefe afhes mult be diftinguifhed by their
appearing free from impurities, and by their whitenefs ;
and their abounding in falt is, likewife, a proof of their
excellence ; which may be examined, by making a lixivium of any known fmall quantity, and judging of its
ftrength by its weight.

Of the materials ufed to make glafs colourlefs.] As the
fubftances ufed for producing the various colours in glafs,
will more properly come in queftion, when I treat particularly of that art, I will omit fpeaking of them here,
and only at prefent enquire into the nature of nitre and
magnefia, which are two ingredients ufed for rendering
the glafs colourlefs, that is intended to be fo : and
which, indeed, is the kind much the molt general y
ufeful, and what makes the only fubject of great manufactures.

The general nature of nitre, or falt-petre, has been
before obferved in fpeaking of it as a flux ; and it only
remains to explain that quality of it, by which it ope-
rates in deftroying the colour in thofe compofitions of
glafs, where it is ufed for that purpofe. This quality
is, the power of afcending and fupporting in a combuftible ftate all bodies, which contain phlogiftic and
fulphureous matter, if they be brought in contact with
it, in a certain degree of heat ; by which means fuch
fulphureous or phlogiftic matter is deftroyed. Or, in
other words, it has the fame combuftible power with
the air in making bodies burn till they be reduced to the
ftate of a calx. In this intention, therefore, falt petre
is made an ingredient in thofe compofitions for tranfparent colourlefs glafs, where lead is ufed as a flux : for
fuch glafs, having, otherwife, a ftrong tinge of yellow

from the phlogifton of the lead, requires, confequently, the deftruction of the phlogifton, at leaft to a certain degree, in order to its being freed from this tinge. This operation of the nitre on the lead, is moft obvioufly apparent, if a piece of falt-petre be thrown into melted glafs formed of lead.; for a detonation or explofive effect, immediately fhows itfelf: and continues till the acid contained in the falt-petre, be confumed.

The diftinct knowledge of this principle clearly points out in what compofitions of glafs, nitre is neceffary; and, in fome degree, what the proportions may be in which it fhould be added to each kind : as fuch proportion muft be regulated by the quantity of phlogifton to be deftroyed. For, as has been before obferved, confidered merely as a flux, if is dearer than the pearl afhes, without any advantage, but the being fomewhat more void of colour. This is obvious, as it is not only of double the price, but weaker in its action, unlefs where meeting with phlogiftic matter in any of the other ingredients, it be deprived, as was above intimated, of its acid fpirit ; and converted, as it then will be, to exactly the fame kind of fixed alkaline falt, with the pearl-afhes themfelves : but in the proportion of only one-third of its original weight. In glafs formed of lead, therefore, the ufe of nitre is abfolutely neceffary ; and, in glafs of falts only, where the colour is to be entirely deftroyed, and great tranfparency is wanted, as in the cafe of looking glafs, and feveral other kinds of plates, it is alfo requifite in a lefs proportion. For, tho' the appearance of any flight yellow tinge may be taken away by the ufe of the magnefia ; yet that (for the reafon we fhall fee below) is always attended with a proportionable lofs of the tranfparency.

Magnefia is the other fubftance employed for rendering glafs colourlefs. It is a foffile, that partakes of the nature of iron ores ; but does not contain any confiderable quantity of that metal, and fometimes only a very little. It is found in almoft every country amongft other iron ores : and frequently, alfo, above the beds of lead ore ; where, indeed, the beft feems to have

P

been always found ; probably from its being lefs replete
with iron, than fuch as is found in the beds of that
metal. The hills near Mendip, in Dorfetfhire, have
particularly afforded extremely good. It is not of any
peculiar fhape or figure, but fomewhat ftriated like antimony in its texture ; and of a brownifh black colour
like foot. The marks of its being good, is the deep-
nefs of the colour, and the being free from fpecks of a
metalline appearance, or a lighter caft : and that fhould
be particularly rejected, which has fpots of a reddifh
brown, or yellowifh colour, as being figns of the prefence of iron.

When fufed with glafs of any kind, it readily vitrifies, and tinges the glafs of a ftrong reddifh purple colour, but not clear and bright. In confequence of this
quality, it is ufed for deftroying any flight yellowifh or
greenifh tinge in glafs, that is required to be colourlefs,
on the following principle. The three primitive colours
of yellow, red, and blue, when mixed in due proportion, deftroy each other ; and produce the effect of
grey, in the cafe of opake bodies ; and of black, in
fuch as are tranfparent. Now the tinge of magnefia in
glafs being purple, which is a compound of blue and
red, and being added to the greenifh or yellowifh tinge
of the glafs, confequently deftroys the appearance of
it ; efpecially the greenifh, as the proportion of red in
it is greater than that of the blue : but a proportion of
black being produced, the glafs is obfcured in the fame
degree, though not fo as to be perceptable to the eye,
without comparing it with fome other more pellucid.
This is a reafon for ufing the magnefia fparingly, or
rather avoiding it entirely, in thofe compofitions of
glafs, where great tranfparency is demanded ; and for
forming them of fuch ingredients as are moft colourlefs,
or may be rendered fo by the ufe of nitre. Magnefia
requires to be well calcined in a hot furnace ; and then
to undergo a thorough levigation : for it ought to be
in the ftate of an impalpable powder, in order to its
perfect commixture with the other matter. It was
formerly practifed to quench the magnefia feveral times

in vinegar, after reiterated calcinations; with a view of freeing it from any iron that might be mixed with it: but this was needlefs; and is now entirely difufed. Its application to the colouring glafs, in which it is very efficacious for many purpofes, we fhall fpeak of in its proper place.

Of the inftruments and utenfils employed in the compo-fition and preparation of glafs.] The inftruments and utenfils employed in the compounding and preparing glafs are of two kinds: as they are fubfervient to two different purpofes: the levigation and commixture of the ingredient; and the fufion or vitrification of them.

The inftruments fubfervient to levigation, and the mixture of the ingredients, are horfe or hand-mills, mortars and peftles, and flat ftones and mullars.

The horfe, or hand-mills, may be fuch as are ufed for other purpofes: but the ftones fhould be of a very hard texture, in order that as little as poffible of the matter of them may be abraded and commixt with the glafs.

Where large mortars are ufed for fuch ingredients as are not employed in a fufficient quantity, to make it commodious to grind them in mills, they fhould be of caft iron, with peftles of the fame; and fhould be carefully kept from ruft. But for very nice purpofes where the quantity of the matter is fmall, mortars fhould be had of bottle or green glafs, or of flint or agate, as alfo a ftone and mullar of porphyry or agate, for levigating the calces of metals, or other ingredients ufed in colouring glafs.

Scarces or fieves of fine lawn fhould likewife be provided, for fifting fome of the levigated fubftances. They fhould be like thofe of the apothecaries and druggifts, with a cover fitted to the upper part; and a box to the under, for preventing that wafte of the matter which attends the fifting in the open air.

The utenfils employed in the fufing or vitrifying the matter of glafs are, furnaces, with the proper iron works; pots for containing the compofitions when put into the fire; with the iron inftruments for fhifting the matter from one to the other, in cafe of accident; and for taking out fmall portions, to judge of the progrefs of the vitrification, and the qualities of the glafs.

The ftructure of the furnaces for preparing and working glafs in large, is fo well and commonly known, that it is needlefs to enter into the detail of it here. Where fmaller quantities are prepared, as in the cafe of coloured glafs, or paftes in imitations of ftones, the common wind furnace, or the athanor of the chemifts may be ufed; or a furnace may be made for this particular purpofe, which may be conftructed in the following manner:

Mark out a circular area of one yard diameter; and let a cylindrical building be raifed upon it of good ftock bricks, and coal-afh mortar, of the height of twelve inches. This cylinder muft have an hollow area in the middle, of a round form, twelve inches in diameter; the reft of the fpace being filled with folid brick work. But an opening muft be left in the front at the bottom, which muft be fix inches broad and four high, for taking away the afhes; and it fhould likewife have an iron frame and door, like thofe commonly ufed for feeding the fire in furnaces, that it may be occafionally clofed, in order to check or extinguifh the fire. This cylindrical fabric being raifed to the height of twelve inches, a grate for bearing the fuel, compofed of a ftrong iron ring with bars let into it, muft be laid over the round hollow: and another cylinder, of the fame diameter and thicknefs of wall, muft be raifed in like manner to the height of eight inches above the bars. But this fhould be done with Windfor bricks, and the mortar formed of Windfor loom, where they can be obtained; and care fhould be taken, likewife, that the brick work may have good hold of the rim of the grate. At the height of about five inches above the bars, a frame and door fhould be fixed for feeding the fire. The door fhould be about five inches high, and eight long; and fhould have a ftrong latch going acrofs the whole breadth of it, by which it may be opened and fhut. When the cylindrical hollow over the bars is thus car-

ried eight inches high, a larger area muſt be taken of
twenty-four inches diameter ; and the brick work muſt
be carried up round it, in the ſame cylindrical manner
as at firſt, for ten inches more ; except, that four iron
doors and frames of the ſame form with thoſe for feeding the fire mult be fixed in the brick work. The di-
menſions of theſe doors ſhould be twelve inches high,
and eight in breadth ; and the loweſt part of them ſhould
be level with the flooring made by the brick work on
enlarging the area of the cavity of the furnace ; or, in
other words, where the brick-work of this wider cylinder begins. Theſe doors ſhould be placed at equal diſ-
tances from each other, and in ſuch manner, that the other
for feeding the fire may be exactly in the middle betwixt
the two neareſt to the front ; and the chimney betwixt
the others. A hole ſhould be likewiſe left for vent-
ing the ſmoke into the chimney, which may be fix inches
broad and three high : and after this the brick-work,
may be brought together, in the manner of an arch, till
the whole cavity be covered. For the whole of this upper
part, Windſor bricks and Windſor loom ſhould be uſed,
or, where they cannot be procured, ſuch other as are
moſt like them in their quality of bearing intenſe heat,
without either being calcined or vitrified. The manner of
uſing this furnace is too obvious to require explanation ;
it being enough apparent that the flooring in the enlarged cavity is intended for the pots, or crucibles containing the matter ; and the four doors for the more conveniently putting them in and taking them out. When,
however, they are to be placed in the furnace, it ſhould
not be on the parts before the doors ; for fear the ſtream
of cold air, on opening the doors occaſionally, may crack
them. But they ſhould be conveyed through one of
the doors to the oppoſite ſide, by means of an iron peel,
formed like thoſe of the bakers ; and put betwixt the
doors on that ſide ; by which means, they will not only
be much ſafer, but will be out of the way of impeding
the operator from ſeeing what paſſes in every part of the
furnace : and, by this means, likewiſe, room may be
found for many more pots and crucibles, than could be

introduced if the firft four ftood before the doors; and
blocked up the entrance againft any other. When this
furnace is wanted for calcinations, or other operations
that require lefs heat, the area of the cylinder fhould be
made lefs by bricks formed of Windfor loom and fand,
and adapted to the cylindrical figure of the cavity:
which bricks may be eafily put in, or taken out, by
means of the four doors in the upper part, and that in
the lower for feeding the fire. The dimenfions of this
furnace are calculated to anfwer the purpofe of thofe,
who may engage in thefe matters for profit; and may
be enlarged, if there be yet occafion: but for fuch as
meddle with them fpeculatively, and in the view of experiments only, they may be proportionably contracted;
as being much larger than needful.

The pots for containing the melted matter of the glafs
fhould be formed of the clay ufed for making tobacco-
pipes, or of the beft potter's clay that can be procured.
But as there are feldom any fuch clay found, as will
ftand the drying and burning well, without the admixture of fome earthy body, broken crucibles ground to
powder, or, in default of them, white fand, or calcined
flints duly levigated, may be added. Near London the
tobacco-pipe clay, or the Sturbridge clay, with a fourth
or fifth of ground crucibles or fand, are the beft materials that can be ufed: but care fhould be taken to free
the clay perfectly from ftones or gravel, and to incor-
porate the ground crucibles or fand well with the clay.
When the tobacco-pipe clay is ufed, it is previoufly
calcined, and then ground to powder; and afterwards
moiftened with water, then well beat in the manner of
mortar.

Small pots for making paftes or coloured glaffes, may
be formed on a wooden mould; and fhould be flowly
dried, and afterwards baked or burned, in a fire very
gradually increafed to a ftrong degree, and then fuffered
to extinguifh before the pots be taken out of the furnace.
This may be done commodioufly in a potter's kiln, along
with earthen or ftone ware. But the pots fhould be
placed in the hotteft part of the furnace. They other-

wife may be burned, where other conveniences are wanting, commodiously enough in the furnace above-mentioned; and if intended to be ufed in fuch furnace, the
largeft may be fix inches diameter, and ten or twelve
inches in height. However, they muft be formed a
little conical or narrower at the bottom than the top,
that they may be the more eafily drawn from the mould;
which need only to be a piece of wood turned into the
form and dimenfions of the cavity of the pot.

*Of the feveral kinds of white glafs ; and their compo-
fition in general.*] The feveral kind of white tranfparent glafs now ufed in moft parts of Europe are,
the flint-glafs (as it is here called) and the German
cryftal glafs, which are applied to the fame ufes and
purpofes ;—the glafs for plates for mirrors or looking-
glaffes ;—the glafs for windows and other lights ;—and
the glafs for phials, and fuch kind of fmall veffels.

Of each of thefe kinds there are feveral forts ; fome
only differing in the particular compofition and management of the directors of the works where they are manufactured, but alike in their price, and the ufes to
which they are applied ; and others, which are allow-
edly inferior forts, fold at cheaper rates, and employed
accordingly for coarfer purpofes.

The feveral kinds of glafs differ in the fubftances employed as fluxes in forming them, as well as in the
coarfenefs or finenefs of fuch as are ufed for their body.
The flint and cryftal, mirror, and beft window glafs, not
only require fuch purity in the fluxes, as may render it
practicable to free the glafs perfectly from all colour ;
but, for the fame reafon alfo, either the white Lynn-
fand, calcined flints, or white pebbles, fhould be ufed.
The others do not demand the fame nicety in the choice
of the materials ; tho' the fecond kind of window-glafs,
and the beft kind of phial, will not be fo clear as they
ought, if either too brown fand, or impure falts, be fuffered to enter into their compofition.

*Of the nature and compofition of flint glafs ; and the
German cryftal glafs.*] Flint glafs, is of the fame general kind with what is in other places called cryftal

glafs. It had this name from being originally made with calcined flints, before the ufe of the white fand was underftood ; and, though no flints are now ufed in its compofition, it retains ftill the name. This kind differs, however, from the German and other cryftal glafs, in being partly formed of lead ; whereas the fluxing bodies employed for the others, are only falts or arfenic ; and in having a white fand (which as is faid before, appears to be fragments of cryftal) for its body. Inftead of which, calcined flints, or the white river pebbles, or other fuch ftones, are ufed for the cryftal glafs in other places : there being no fand of this kind of equal goodnefs found out of England, as far as is hitherto known.

The compofition of flint glafs is, therefore principally the white fand and lead ; to which a due proportion of nitre is added, to burn away the phlogifton of the lead : which otherwife imparts a ftrong yellow tinge to the glafs ; and to this is added, for hiding the remainder of the colour, a fmall quantity of magnefia : as alfo in fome works a proportion of arfenic, to aid the fluxing ingredients. Flint glafs is not, however, a fimple glafs of lead : for where no other falts are added, yet the quantity of nitre ufed being confiderable, and fluxing a proportionable quantity of the fand, it muft be confidered as a compound glafs of falts and lead. But indeed it has been generally practifed, to add fome quantity of other falts to it ; and diminifh proportionably the quantity of lead otherwife neceffary. This quantity, though great in the glafs made fome time ago, feems to be much diminifhed in that manufactured lately ; at leaft in fome works : as appears from the fmall weight and tranfparency of what is now to be met with ; as well as from the veffels being blown much thinner, and of lefs fubftance, than the glafs in which leads abound could well bear to be. The admiffion of lead into glafs renders fuch glafs lefs hard and tranfparent, than that made of falts only. But there is in glafs of lead a power of reflecting the rays of light, of the fame nature with that of diamonds and topazes, that gives a luftre and brilliant appearance to veffels of a round figure, not found in the mere glafs of falts : where the too great tranfparency, and want of play, occafions a poornefs or deadnefs in the look, when feen by the other : and this likewife ex-tends itfelf in fome degree to the appearance of liquors contained in them. For polygonal veffels however, or thofe cut with flat fides, or fuch as are decorated with flowers, or other ornaments cut in them, or with gild-ing, the glafs of falts is preferable ; as may be obferved in the inftance of thofe brought from Germany. This muft not, neverthelefs, be extended to fuch pieces as are cut with a great number of angles for the parts of chan-deliers, or other purpofes where the play of the light is wanted : for in all fuch cafes, the glafs formed with lead again takes place of the other ; as producing a greatly ftronger and more beautiful effect, for the reafons before given.

It appears from what has been faid, that flint glafs may be, as in fact it is, formed of various compofitions, by altering the quantities of lead and nitre, and adding equivalent proportions of other falts or arfenic : in con-fequence of which, favings may be made in the expence, and a difference will arife in the hardnefs or foftnefs of the glafs. For the more the quantities of nitre or other falts are increafed, and that of the lead diminifhed, the more hard and firm the texture of the glafs will be ; and fo vice verfa. I will, therefore, give a recipe for the compofition of a glafs, according to each of the feveral manners, in which the proportion of the ingredients may be properly varied ; and diftinguifh, likewife, in each cafe, what the abfolute and comparative qualities of the glafs produced will be ; and with refpect to the comparative expence, the quantities of the feveral in-gredients being thus ftated, it will be very eafy for thofe who are acquainted with the market-price of them, to make a computation.

No. 1. *Compofition of the moft perfect kind of flint glafs.*] "Take of the white fand one hundred and twenty pounds, of red lead fifty pounds, of the beft pearl-afhes forty pounds, of nitre twenty pounds, and of magnefia five ounces."—If this compofition be fufed with a very ftrong fire, and time be given to it, a glafs will be produced, that will have the play of the beft flint glafs, and yet be hard and ftrong. It is not fo cheap as the compofitions below given, where arfenic or common falt is introduced, or where more of the pearl-afhes are ufed: in either of which cafes, favings may be made, by diminifhing proportionably the quantities of nitre. But the qualities of this glafs will be found to come nearer to the ftandard of perfection: which is to unite the luftre and hardnefs together in the greateft degree, they are compatible with each other.

If this compofition be, however, defired to flux with lefs heat and quicker, a powder or two of arfenic may be added: which will be found effectually to anfwer the purpofe.

No. 2. *Compofition of flint glafs, with a greater proportion of falts.*] " Take of fand one hundred and twenty pounds, of red lead thirty-fix pounds, of nitre twelve pounds, and of magnefia fix ounces."——This will require much the fame fire as the other: but will be harder in its texture; and have lefs of the refractive play of the light: it is, however, a very good compofition of glafs; and comes nearer to the kind now made: though I imagine the proportion of lead is ftill more diminifhed in fome I have feen than here. If it be defired, to be made more yielding to the fire, arfenic may be added as is directed for the preceding; or the quantity of fand may be leffened; but in that cafe the glafs will be fofter and weaker.

No. 3. *Cheaper compofition of flint glafs with arfenic.*] " Take of white fand one hundred and twenty pounds, of the beft pearl-afhes thirty-five pounds, of red lead forty pounds, of nitre thirteen pounds, of arfenic fix pounds, and of magnefia four ounces."—This glafs will require a confiderable time in the fire to become clear, and muft not, if it can be avoided, be ftrongly urged at firft: for the arfenic is apt to fublime away, if the heat be violent before the other ingredients run into fufion fo as to detain it. It is well, therefore, to mix a confiderable proportion of glafs, which has been wronght before, and is to be manufactured over again with this compofition when it is ufed ; which, running fooner than the new mixed ingredients, will take hold of the arfenic, and fix it. This compofition fhould, however, be afterwards fufed, with a confiderable heat ; and continued in that ftate till the milky appearance of the arfenic, which it will fometimes retain for a long time, be entirely gone. For notwithftanding this apparent reluctance to perfect vitrification, the arfenic never fails at length to become very tranfparent glafs ; and even to contribute greatly to render the other ingredients fo likewife. This glafs will not be fo hard as thofe of the above compofitions : but it will be very clear, and may be employed for the formation of large veffels, where a fufficient thicknefs can be allowed to give them ftrength.

No. 4. *Cheaper compofitions of glafs by means of common falt.*] " Take the proportions of the other ingredients given in the laft ; and, omitting the arfenic, add in its ftead fifteen pounds of common falt."—This will be more brittle than the laft ; and therefore cannot be recommended, unlefs for the fabrication of fuch kind of veffels, or other pieces, where the ftrength is of little moment.

No. 5. *Cheapeft compofition of flint glafs, by the addition of arfenic and common falt.*] " Take of the white fand one hundred and twenty pounds, of red lead thirty pounds, of the beft pearl-afhes twenty pounds, of nitre ten pounds, of common falt fifteen pounds, and of arfenic fix pounds."—This glafs will fufe with a moderate heat ; but requires time, like the laft, to take off the milky appearance of the arfenic ; it is yet fofter than the laft ; and may, therefore, be deemed the worft kind of flint glafs that can be made, preferving the appearance of good glafs to the eye ; which it will have equally with any other when properly managed.

No. 6. *Compofition of the beft German cryftal glafs.*] " Take of the calcined flints, or white fand, one hundred and twenty pounds, of the beſt pearl-aſhes ſeventy pounds, of ſalt petre ten pounds, of arſenic half a pound, and of magneſia five ounces."—If the pearl-aſhes be pure and good, this glaſs will equal the beſt of this kind that ever was made. Borax has been frequently uſed alſo in the compoſitions for this ſort of glaſs; but its great price, without any equivalent advantage, will deter from the employing it in large manufactures; as there is no ſort of tranſparent glaſs in common practice, that of which looking-glaſs plates is made excepted, can bear the expence of it

No. 7. *Cheaper compoſition of German cryſtal glaſs.*] "Take of calcined flints, or white ſand, one hundred and twenty pounds, of pearl aſhes forty-ſix pounds, of nitre ſeven pounds, of arſenic ſix pounds, and of magneſia five ounces."——This compoſition requires a long continuance of heat, on account of the arſenic, for the reaſon before given. It produces a glaſs equally, or more tranſparent and colourleſs than the preceding, but ſomewhat more brittle. The arſenic is, however, ſo diſagreeable an ingredient, from the deleterious qualities of the fumes, which will neceſſarily riſe copiouſly till the fuſion of the other ingredients check it, that, where the advantage is not more conſiderable than the ſaving ariſing from the difference of theſe two recipes, it is ſcarcely worth while to ſubmit to the inconveniencies of it.

Of the nature and compoſition of the glaſs proper for plates for mirrors or looking glaſſes.] The glaſs for forming the looking-glaſs plates in perfection, is the moſt nice and difficult kind to manage, of any whatever; there being no latitude, with reſpect to ſeveral of the qualities, as there is in the caſe of flint glaſs, without its goodneſs being really impaired. Theſe qualities are, to be entirely tranſparent and colourleſs; to have as little power of refracting the rays of light as poſſible; to be entirely free from bubbles, ſpecks and flaws, and to be fuſible with a moderate heat. Hardneſs of conſiſtence is of leſs conſequence in this kind of glaſs than in the flint; though it is an additional excellence; as far as it may be had along with the other qualities: since the plates may, in that cafe, be wrought thinner with the fame degree of ftrength, which is a confiderable advantage to mirrors made of them.

The white fand is the proper ingredient for forming the body of this kind of glafs, as well as of the flint: and the principal part of the flux fhould be the fixed alkaline falt of vegetables; which the pearl-afhes will beft furnifh, when duly purified. This falt muft, however, be aided by borax, or common falt; in order to facilitate the fufion, and prevent the glafs from ftiffening in that degree of heat, in which it is to be wrought into plates. Lead is by no means a proper ingredient in the compofition of this kind of glafs; on account of its augmenting the refracting power; and for the fame reafon arfenic, which has the like effect, though in a much lefs degree fhould be either omitted, or but fparingly ufed. The fand fhould be carefully cleanfed for this ufe, by the means before directed for that purpofe, and the borax fhould be firft calcined, and then rubbed to powder. The pearl-afhes muft likewife be purified for this ufe, which may be done in the following way:

Manner of purifying the pearl-afhes.] " Take any quantity of the beft pearl-afhes, and diffolve them in four times their weight of water boiling: which operation may be beft performed in a pot of caft iron. When they are diffolved, let the folution be put into a clean tub; and fuffered to remain there twenty-four hours or longer. Let the clear part of the fluid be then decanted off from the dregs or fediment, and put back into the iron pot; in which the water muft be evaporated away till the falts be left perfectly dry again. They fhould then, if not ufed immediately, be kept in ftone jars well fecured from moifture and air, till fuch time as they are wanted."—Great care fhould be always taken, in this treatment of the falts, to keep the iron pot thoroughly clean from ruft, which would give the yellow tinge to the glafs, not to be removed without greatly injuring it.

Q

No. 1. *Beſt compoſition of glaſs for looking-glaſs plates.*]
" Take of white ſand cleanſed ſixty pounds, of purified
pearl-aſhes twenty five pounds, of ſalt-petre fifteen
pounds, and of borax ſeven pounds."—This compoſition ſhould be continued long in the fire; which ſhould
be for ſome time ſtrong, and afterwards more moderate,
that the glaſs may be entirely free from bubbles before
it be worked. It will be entirely clear of all colour,
unleſs in caſe of ſome accident : but if any yellow tinge
ſhould, neverthelefs, unfortunately affect it, there is no
remedy, except by adding a ſmall proportion of magneſia, which ſhould be mixed with an equal quantity of
arſenic ; and after their being put into the glaſs, giving
it a conſiderable heat again, and then ſuffering it to free
itſelf from bubbles in a more moderate one, as before.
If the tinge be ſlight, an ounce of magneſia may be
firſt tried ; and if that prove inſufficient, the quantity
muſt be increaſed ; but the glaſs will always be obſcure,
in proportion to the quantity that is admitted ; though,
perhaps, not in a degree that may prevent it from paſſing
current with thoſe who do not examine with great
ſtrictneſs. This compoſition is not to be made without
expence, at the times when borax is dear ; but the great
price which looking glaſs plates, particularly ſuch as
are large, bear, will very well allow it : or even the adding a greater quantity of borax, when there is occaſion to have the glaſs run more eaſily, and roll in a leſs
degree of heat.

No. 2. *Cheaper compoſition for looking-glaſs plates.*]
" Take of the white ſand ſixty pounds, of pearl-aſhes
twenty pounds, of common ſalt ten pounds, of nitre
ſeven pounds, of arſenic two pounds, and of borax one
pound."——This glaſs will run with as little heat as
the former ; but it will be more brittle, and refract the
rays of light in a greater degree. It is, therefore, worſe
than the other in a greater degree, than is balanced by
the ſaving in an article, where the coſt of the materials
is not conſiderable in proportion to the return ; it being
the work and ſkill, and not the prime expence of the
ingredients, that make the high price of looking-glaſs

plates. It would be, confequently, unpardonable, while they continue to be fold at the prefent dear rates they bear in this country, to impair the quality of the glafs, for the fake of a trifling faving out of the original price of the materials.

Of the nature and compofition of window-glafs.] In order to have window-glafs in the utmoft perfection, the fame qualities and treatment are required, as for the looking-glafs plates; and the fame kind of glafs is, therefore, ufed for lights, where the expence can be allowed. But as that is only done in extraordinary cafes, inferior kinds of various rates of price are wanted for more common purpofes; where not only the coft of grinding may be faved, but even the glafs itfelf afforded cheaper, on account of its compofition. The belt of thefe kinds is called crown-glafs: the compofition for which may be as follows; the ingredients being previoufly prepared in the fame manner as for the looking-glafs.

No. 1. *Compofition of crown (or the beft window) glafs.*] "Take of white fand fixty pounds, of purified pearl afhes thirty pounds, of falt-petre fifteen pounds, of borax one pound, and of arfenic half a pound."— This will be very clear and colourlefs, if the ingredients be good: and will not be very dear. It will run with a moderate heat; but if it be defired to be yet more fufible and foft, half a pound or a pound more of arfenic may be added. If the glafs fhould prove yellow, the magnefia muft be ufed, as above directed for the looking-glafs.

No. 2. *Compofition for a cheaper kind of window glafs.*] "Take of white fand fixty pounds, of unpurified pearl afhes twenty-five pounds, of common falt ten pounds, of nitre five pounds, of arfenic two pounds, and of magnefia one ounce and a half."—This will be inferior to the above kind; but may be improved, where defired, by purifying the pearl-afhes. This operation will not only free them from the remaining part of the earth of the afhes they were extracted from: (which is

apt to give a fmall degree of opacity to the glafs, as it
will not vitrify in this ftate) but renders them alfo lefs
liable to impart a yellow tinge to the glafs; and, therefore, where the goodnefs of fuch afhes is known by
trial, an ounce of the magnefia, or perhaps more, may
be fpared.

No. 3. *Compofition of common or green window-glafs.*]
" 'Take of white fand fixty pounds, of unpurified pearl-
afhes thirty pounds, of common falt ten pounds, of arfenic two pounds, and of magnefia two ounces."——
This is a cheap compofition; and will not appear much
green, nor be very deficient in tranfparency.

No. 4. *Cheapeft compofition of common or green
window-glafs.*] " Take of the cheapeft kind of white
fand one hundred and twenty pounds, of unpurified
pearl-afhes thirty pounds, of wood-afhes well burned
and fifted fixty pounds, of common falt twenty pounds,
and of arfenic five pounds."—This compofition is very
cheap, and will produce a glafs with a greenifh caft;
but greatly fuperior to what I have frequently met with:
though nothing that will at all anfwer the end, can be
well prepared at lefs expence.

Of the nature and compofition of the glafs for phials.]
The glafs of which phials for the ufe of apothecaries,
ink-bottles, and many other fuch fmall veffels, are made,
is a kind betwixt the flint-glafs and the common bottle
or green glafs. A very good fort of which may be thus
prepared:

No. 1. *Compofition of the beft phial-glafs.*] " Take
of white fand one hundred and twenty pounds, of unpurified pearl-afhes fifty pounds, of common falt ten
pounds, of arfenic five pounds, and of magnefia five
ounces."——This will be a very good giafs for the purpofe; and will work with a moderate heat: but requires time to become clear, on account of the proportion of arfenic: when, however, it is once in good condition, it will become very near to the cryftal-glafs.

No. 2. *Cheapeft compofition of green or common phial-
glafs.*] " Take of the cheapeft kind of white fand
one hundred and twenty pounds, of wood-afhes well

burned and fifted eighteen pounds, of pearl-aſhes twenty
pounds, of common ſalt fifteen pounds, of arſenic one
pound."——This will be green, but tolerably tranſparent; and will work with a moderate fire, and vitrify
quickly with a ſtrong one.

*Of the commixture of the ingredients for the ſeveral
compoſitions of white tranſparent glaſs.*] The commixture of the ingredients for making glaſs muſt be performed by different methods, according to the nature
of the ingredients that enter into the different compoſitions.

When ſand, and fixed alkaline ſalts, whether in form
of pearl-aſhes, or of ſuch as are extracted from them,
or any other aſhes of vegetables, are uſed together, they
ought to be thoroughly mixed, by grinding them in a
place free from damp. When they are ſo mixed, they
ſhould be put into a proper calcining furnace, and there
continued in a moderate heat for five or ſix hours; being
in the mean time frequently turned over and ſtirred a-
bout, by means of a proper rake; and at the end of
that time taken out of the furnace, and either immediately uſed, or kept, where no moiſture can have acceſs
to them, till wanted. The matter in this ſtate is called
frit, and may be converted into glaſs without further
preparation, than being broken into groſs powder before
it be put into the pots; unleſs where other ingredients
are to be added to it: in which caſe the following methods may be purſued.

When nitre is to be added to the frit, it ſhould be
after the calcination: and if it be well powdered, it may
be mixed with the frit, without their being ground together.

If arſenic be alſo uſed, it ſhould, being previouſly
well levigated, be mixed with the nitre, at the time that
it is to be powdered; and they may be then added together to the frit. But if no nitre be uſed, it ſhould be
ground with ſome pounds of the frit; or rather with
ſome of the ſalts of which the frit is made; and then
put to it.

In the cafe of the flint-glafs, when large proportions
of lead and nitre are admitted into the compofition ; or
in other cafes of foft glafs, where very powerful fluxes
are ufed ; the calcining the frit is difpenfed with, and
the fand, alkaline falts, lead, nitre, and alfo arfenic, if
any be ufed, are thoroughly mixed together by grinding.
But if a calcined frit be ufed, the matter, after it has
undergone that operation, and been grofsly powdered,
muft be put into the pot with the other ingredients in
that ftate ; they being previoufly well commixt together
by grinding.

If borax be ufed with the frit alone, it fhould be
ground with a fmall part of it ; and then mixed with the
reft. But, if other ingredients are to be added, it may
be ground with them. It fhould, however, be always
firft calcined, that is, placed in a moderate heat, till the
ebullition it makes at firft be over, and it be left in a dry
ftate.

When common falt is ufed in the compofition of glafs
where the frit is prepared, it may be added to the alkaline falt and fand when they are to be ground together ; and calcined along with them, which will fpare
the trouble of the decrepitation, mentioned p. 146 to
be neceffary. The falt muft otherwife be put into a
proper veffel, and continued in a gentle heat till it ceafes
the crackling it will for fome time make : and, if it
be not ufed immediately, it muft be carefully kept from
all moifture, even that of the air. When no frit is previoufly made, fo as to afford an opportunity of calcining
the falt with it, being firft decrepitated, it may be mixed
with any of the other ingredients ; but muft not be fuffered to attract any moifture ; otherwife it will crackle
and decrepitate again in the pots, and wafte the matter,
by diffipating it with the numberlefs little explofions it
will make.

Magnefia, when admitted into the compofition of glafs
made of frit without any other addition, being well levigated preparatorily, fhould be intimately mixed by
grinding with fome pounds of the frit ; and then put
into the pots along with the reft. But where lead,

falt-petre, or other ingredients are to be added, it may
be mixed with them when they are ground; and then
put to the frit. If no frit be prepared, it may, neverthelefs, be mingled with any of the fluxing ingredients,
and fo commixt with the whole mafs.

*Of the manner of melting and fufing the feveral compo-
fitions, in order to their converfion into glafs : with the
means of judging when the vitrification is perfect.*] The
materials being all prepared and duly mixed, the matter
muft be put into the pots: and urged to fufion, by a
heat proportioned to the ftrength of the flux in the compofition : and this muft be continued till the whole mafs
become one uniform fluid ; and have acquired the qualities neceffary in that particular kind of glafs which is
intended to be produced. There is an attention to another object, however, required in the mean time ; which
is, the taking off the fcum and foulnefs that will arife
on the glafs in the action of the ingredients on each
other, and the coction of the matter. This is to be
done by means of proper ladles ; and fhould be effectually performed before the glafs be wrought : otherwife it will be fo fouled by this fubftance, as to be rendered of very little value. This matter is called fando-
ver: and is fold to the colourmen, who difpofe of it
to the potters ; and they ufe it in the compofitions of
their glazings.

The exact time for keeping the feveral compofitions
of glafs in fufion, in order to their perfect vitrification,
can by no means be fettled by rule. For there is fo
much variation in the difpofition of different parcels of
materials of the fame kind to vitrify ; and likewife fo
great an uncertainty, with refpect to the degrees of heat
maintainable even in the fame furnace, that it muft be
left to the judgment of the operator. But where the
power of the flux is weaker, as may be gathered from
the nature and proportions of the ingredients in the
compofition, or where the heat is lefs intenfe, a greater
time will neceffarily be required, than in the cafe of
ftronger fluxes, and brifker fires. No damage can,
however, accrue from allowing a longer fufion than may

be neceffary to give the glafs the appearance of being perfect, except the lofs of time and confumption of fuel: for with refpect to the white tranfparent glafs, it is always improved in its hardnefs and clearnefs, by a longer coction.

In order to examine, whether the glafs have attained to its due ftate of vitrification, an iron rod, of which the end fhould be bright, or at leaft entirely free from ruft, muft be dipped in the melted matter: and what adheres to it fhould be firft tried, with refpect to its ductility or readinefs to fuffer itfelf to be drawn out in long threads; and, if this quality be found in it to a fuffi-cient degree, being fuffered to cool, it fhould be care-fully infpected, to form a judgment of its colour and clearnefs. If it be tranfparent, colourlefs, and free from all fpecks and bubbles, it may be concluded per-fect, and fit to be wrought. But if it want thefe marks, more time muft be given, according to the de-gree of the defectivenefs; and, after a reafonable al-lowance of fuch time, it muft be examined again by the fame means: and, if not yet perfect, a further time muft be given, and then the fame trial made again. If, neverthelefs, after all reafonable allowance of time, and the application of a ftrong heat, which fhould be raifed as high as can be admitted conveniently, without detri-ment to the other operations that may be carrying on in the fame furnace, the glafs yet appear faulty, the means, below advifed, muft be called in aid; in order to remedy the defects, either in the materials themfelves, or the means of their compofition.

Of the means of promoting and accelerating the perfect vitrification of the ingredients, when the compofition proves defective in that point: with the means of removing any yellowifh or greenifh tinge that may arife.] If, after the treatment above advifed, fufficient time and heat having been given, according to the nature of the com-pofition, the glafs will not be brought to run into one equal fluid mafs, but appear yet turbid and milky, or to abound in bubbles after fome abatement of the fire, it muft be concluded, that the flux is too weak. An

tion of the whole of this additional quantity, must be regulated by the appearance of what may be wanted from the backwardnefs of the vitrification in the glafs. But it is better to try a fmaller quantity firft ; becaufe more may eafily be added, if found neceffary ; and an excefs, on the other hand, injures the qualities of the glafs ; and in the cafe of falts cannot be rectified, unlefs by a long continuance of the fufion. There is, moreover, this further reafon for trying only a fmaller quantity at firft ; that frequently much lefs will anfwer the end, than the appearance may feem to make neceffary.

It is the practice of fome, when the vitrification will not go forwards, to have recourfe to the following expedient. They take four, or perhaps fix ounces of arfenic, and mix with it an ounce of magnefia : and, wrapping them tightly in a piece of paper of feveral doubles, they faften the mafs to the end of their iron, and plunge it down to the bottom of the pot ; where, the fubftance of the paper being deftroyed, the matter is left. This will frequently fucceed ; and the glafs will grow clear firft, towards the bottom, and foon after quite to the top ; and gain the perfect ftate of vitrification. The magnefia, neverthelefs, however it may promote the fufing power of the arfenic, does not feem a very proper ingredient in all cafes. For where there is no yellow tinge in the glafs, it will neceffarily impart a purplifh caft ; which, though perhaps in too flight a degree to be eafily diftinguifhed on a common infpection, is neverthelefs an imperfection ; and would fhow itfelf if the glafs were to be compared with fuch as were abfolutely colourlefs. I fhould think it, therefore, better to join two or three ounces of calcined borax with the arfenic, which would anfwer the end without any kind of injury to the glafs, and would not greatly enhance the expence ; when it is premifed, how confiderable a return a pot of glafs makes when worked off.

When the glafs appears perfect in other refpects, but is found to have a green or yellow tinge, fuch tinge may frequently be diminifhed by the addition of one or two pounds of nitre; if none, or but a fmall proportion, have before been admitted into the compofition. The nitre, in this cafe, fhould be fluxed with fome frit, or with fome other glafs of the fame kind with that in the pot, before it be put to the other ingredients. This is requifite, in order that it may the readier mix with the matter; and not be partly blown out of the pot, by the ebullition it would make, in confequence of the water contained in its cryftals, or partly fwim on the furface; as would happen, if it were put in crude, without being preparatorily heated or mixed with any other body. But if this fail, or remedy only in part the fault, re-courfe muft be had to the magnefia; to which may be advantageoufly added two or three ounces of arfenic, and they may be conveyed into the pot by the means above directed; which prevents the powders from float-ing on the furface of the melted matter, where the ar-fenic would foon fublime away, and take no effect.

Of the compofition and treatment of the common bottle, or green glafs.] This kind, excepting the beauty of colour and tranfparency, is the moft perfect glafs at pre-fent manufactured; and, with refpect to its utility, is alfo equal in importance to any other. It is formed of fand of any kind, fluxed by the afhes of burned wood, or of any parts of vegetables. The afhes muft not have the falts extracted from them, but muft confift of them, and the calcined earth of the vegetable fubftances, whence they are produced. This earth, though when once feparated from the falts formed along with it in the incineration, it becomes abfolutely refractory to vi-trification; and refifts not only the fame falts which were taken from it, but even the ftrongeft fluxes; yet conjoined with thefe falts, in the manner in which it is originally produced in the incineration, it not only vi-trifies perfectly itfelf, but even acts as a flux on fand.

ents, fand and wood ashes : but where the scoria or clinkers of furnaces or forges can be obtained in suffic:ent quantity, they may be added with great advantage : as a much lefs proportion of wood-ashes will become neceffary, and the good qualities of the glafs be rather improved than impaired   The scoria to be obtained at large foundaries, are very proper for the purpofe : or thofe from any other fuch works, where large and ftrong fires are ufed.   The particular compofition of this glafs may be as follows; but the proportions here given fuppofe the fofteft fand : to procure which care fhould be taken, as a great faving is thence made in the quantity of wood-afhes neceffary.

Compofition of green or bottle-glafs.] " Take of wood-afhes two hundred pounds, and of fand one hundred pounds.   Mix them thoroughly well by grinding together."—This is the due proportion where the fand is good, and the wood-afhes are ufed without any other addition : but there are inftances of fand of fo kindly a nature for vitrification, that a greater proportion of it may be added.

Compofition of green-or bottle-glafs, with the addition of fcoria or clinkers.] " Take of wood-afhes one hundred and feventy pounds, of fand one hundred pounds, and of fcoria or clinkers fifty pounds.   Mix the whole well by grinding them together."—The clinkers fhould be well ground before they be ufed, if they admit of it.   But frequently they are too hard ; and in that cafe they fhould be broken into as fmall bits as can be done conveniently ; and mixed with the other matter without any grinding.   The harder they are, the lefs material will be the powdering them, as they will the fooner melt of themfelves in the furnace ; and, confequently, mix with the other ingredients.

The general manner of fufing, and converting this

compofition to glafs, is the fame as in the other kinds:
as are alfo the means of judging when the vitrification
is perfect; and the remedy of the defect when the firft
compofition will not produce it ; except with refpect to
colour, which is, in the cafe of this kind of glafs, entirely out of queftion. When clinkers are not to be
had in fufficient quantity, to allow of their being ufed
in the general compofition, it is well however to have
fome quantity, to employ occafionally, when the vitrification fails. For the adding fuch a proportion of them
as may appear neceffary, with an equal part of wood-
afhes, will anfwer the purpofe much better, than the
addition of more wood-afhes alone, where the flux is
found too weak ; as will happen fometimes from the
great variation in the different parcels, as well of the
afhes as fand.

*Of the general nature of coloured glafs : and of the
feveral compofitions proper for receiving the colours, in
order to the forming glafs, or paftes, in imitation of precious ftones ; with the qualities attendant on each.*] The
glafs, which is intentionally tinged with colours... may
be divided into three kinds: the white opake and femi-
tranfparent glafs : the tranfparent coloured glafs : and
the femi-tranfparent or opake coloured glafs.

The white opake glafs, as alfo fome tranfparent
kinds, are principally ufed for making fmall vafes, toys,
and fome forts of ufeful veffels, as cream-pots, &c. in
imitation of China-ware of any kind, of which we
fhall fpeak below. It is alfo frequently employed, as a
white enamel for grounds, by painters of enamel dial-
plates, fnuff-boxes, and other fuch pieces, as have not
occafion to pafs feveral times through the fire, in order
to their being finifhed.

The compofition of white opake and femi-tranfparent
glafs is very various ; as any kind of coloured glafs may
be made the body of fuch ; and the tinge may be given
by calcined tin or antimony; alfo by arfenic, calcined
hartfhorn or bones, and feveral other fubftances.

The tranfparent glafs, tinged with colours, is likewife of different kinds, as the body or ground may be

tranfparent colourlefs glafs, or any of the compofitions
above exhibited. But it is commonly diftinguifhed into
two forts only : the one called coloured glafs, and the
other paftes. The reafon of which diftinction lies in
this. The chief defign of all coloured tranfparent glafs
being the imitation of precious ftones, the qualities of
fuch glafs, when perfect, are to be very clear and tranfparent; to be free from all colour but the proper tinge ;
and to be very hard and tenacious in their texture. But
thefe qualities being not to be had, except in glafs that
is very difficult to be melted, and requires a long as well
as an intenfe heat, both to its own mature vitrification,
and that of the bodies added to give the colour to it ;
it became inconvenient to thofe who prepared thefe kind
of compofitions in fmall quantities, to maintain fuch
ftrong fires; and therefore fofter compofitions were
fought for, that would run with the heat of common
fmall furnaces ; and would likewife be brought to perfection in a much fhorter time. Thefe compofitions
were therefore called paftes, to diftinguifh them from
the harder glafs, which retained its proper appella-
tion.

The glafs moft proper for the imitation of precious
ftones, where the hardnefs, which is a moft valuable
quality in fuch as is intended for mock jewels, that are
expofed to much wear, is wanted, is a perfect glafs of
falts ; in which no more flux is admitted, than merely
what may be neceffary for the complete vitrification of
the glafs, and tinging fubftances ; but it fhould be abfolutely free from every kind of tinge, except that
which is intended to be given it.

The kind moft proper for forming paftes, is a mixed
glafs of lead and falts, which will run eafily ; and vitrify
in a fhort time the metalline or other bodies that are
employed for tinging it. But in order to make it yet
more fufible, without having fo large a proportion of
lead as may make the texture of the glafs too tender and
brittle, arfenic and borax may be admitted into the compofition. Befides the forming imitations of coloured

R

ftones, there is yet another purpofe to which this kind
of glafs is peculiarly adapted, which is the making
mock diamonds and topazes, that cannot be fo well
counterfeited by any other compofition ; as the lead,
according to what was before obferved, gives a very extraordinary refracting power to the glafs, of which it
is an ingredient. This fort might feem to belong to
the clafs of the white tranfparent kinds of glafs before
treated of : but as the application of that kind of compofition, which renders it properly a pafte according to
the above diftinction, is confined to the intentions of
imitating gems, it is more properly introduced amongft
the others, with which it has a common denomination.

The femi-tranfparent coloured glafs may have for its
body, either the compofitions of the harder kinds ; or
thofe of paftes : and it is principally applied to the imitation of the femi-tranfparent ftones, as lapis lazuli
chalcedony, jafper, agate, opal, or fuch others. The
manner of compofing them is much the fame, as that of
the tranfparent kinds ; except the adding fome opake
white body, which will endure the fufion of the glafs
without being vitrified, at leaft long enough to fuffer it
to be worked into the proper form. But the management of thofe of this kind, which are compounded of
a variety of colours, is much more difficult than that of
the tranfparent forts : which is moft probably the reafon
why they are fo little in ufe ; though fome of them have
a very beautiful effect for purpofes they might be equally
well applied to with the genuine ftones.

*Of the nature and preparation of the fubftances ufed
for tinging glafs.*] The fubftances employed for tinging
glafs, are, for the moft part, metallic and other foffibl
bodies ; or indeed all are fo, except tartar, which ha
been added to fome compofitions. The metals them
felves make the principal part ; and, properly treated
will produce all the colours, except a perfect blue. Bu
for cheapnefs and expedience, the femi-metals, an
preparations from other foffible bodies, are fometimes ad
mitted into the place of them ; particularly with re

fpect to yellow, where antimony fupplies the place of
filver:

The fubftances that have been ufed for producing any
opake whitenefs in glafs, are calcined tin, (commonly
called putty) calcined antimony, arfenic, calcined horns
or bones, and fometimes common falt. The fubftances
employed for red, are gold, iron, copper, magnefia
and antimony. The fubftances employed for blue,
are zaffer and copper. The fubftances that have
been employed for yellow, are filver, iron, antimony and magnefia, with tartar. The fubftances
employed for greens, are copper, Bohemian granate, and thofe which will produce yellow or blue.
The fubftances employed for purple, are all fuch as will
produce red and blue. The fubftances employed for
orange colour, are antimony, and all thofe which will
produce red and yellow. The fubftances employed for
black, are zaffer, magnefia, copper and iron, in various
combinations. The Bohemian granate requires no o-
ther preparation than to be well pulverized.

*Compofition of hard glafs and paftes, proper for re-
ceiving colours.*] Though almoft every kind of tranfparent colourlefs glafs will admit of being tinged ; yet
there are, as was obferved before, fome compofitions,
that are more peculiarly adapted to the purpofes for
which the coloured glafs is intended, either by their
hardnefs and tenacious texture ; or their being more
eafy to be wrought by thofe who manufacture them,
from their requiring lefs heat to fufe them, and fluxing
the colorific matter expeditiously. The clearnefs and
tranfparency of the glafs, and the being devoid of any,
colour but that intended to be given, are likewife neceffary in both the hard glafs and paftes which are to be
coloured : and therefore to have them in perfection, a
glafs of each kind fhould be purpofely prepared ; in
which more exact methods may be ufed for producing
thefe qualities, than are expediently compatible with the
difpatch and profit of groffer manufactures. The beft
compofitions for the hard glafs are as follows : but as
the extreme purity of the fixed alkaline falts is of very

beſt pearl-aſhes three pounds, and of ſalt-petre ſix ounces. Pound them together in a glaſs or marble mortar, till they are thoroughly well mixed ; and then put part of them into a large crucible, and ſet it in a furnace, where it may undergo a ſtrong heat. When the part of the matter, that was firſt put into the crucible, is heated red hot, throw in the reſt gradually : and if the crucible will not contain the whole, pour part of the melted matter out on a moiſtened ſtone, or marble ; and, having made room in the crucible, put in the reſt ; and let it continue there, likewiſe, till it be red hot. Pour it out then as the other ; and afterwards put the whole into an earthen, or very clean iron pot, with ten pints of water ; and heat it over the fire, till the ſalts be entirely melted. Let it then, being taken off the fire, ſtand till it be cold ; and afterwards filter it through paper, in a pewter cullender. When it is filtered, return the fluid again into the pot, and evaporate the ſalt to dryneſs, which will then be as white as ſnow ; the nitre having burnt all the phlogiſtic matter that remained in the pearl-aſhes after their former calcination.

No. 1. *Compoſition of the beſt and hardeſt glaſs for receiving colours.*] " Take of the beſt ſand, cleanſed by waſhing as directed in p. 147, twelve pounds, of pearl aſhes, or fixed alkaline ſalt purified with nitre as above, ſeven pounds, of ſalt-petre one pound, and of borax half a pound."—The ſand being firſt reduced to powder in a glaſs or flint mortar, the other ingredients ſhould be put to it, and the whole well mixed, by pounding them together.

No. 2. *Compoſition of the beſt glaſs for receiving colours ; but ſomewhat leſs hard than the above.*] " Take of white ſand cleanſed twelve pounds, of pearl-aſhes purified with ſalt-petre ſeven pounds, of nitre one pound, of borax half a pound, and of arſenic four ounces."—

Proceed as in the laſt ; but if the glaſs be deſired to
melt with yet leſs heat, a pound of borax may be uſed
inſtead of the half pound, and a pound of common ſalt
may be added ; but this laſt is apt to make the glaſs
more brittle ; which is an injury done to ſuch as is to
be cut into very ſmall pieces, and ground with ſo many
angles in the figure, as in the imitations of jewels.

No. 3. *Compoſition of ſoft glaſs or paſte, proper for
receiving colours.*] " Take of white ſand cleanſed ſix
pounds, of red-lead three pounds, of purified pearl-
aſhes two pounds, and of nitre one pound."—Proceed
in the mixture as with the foregoing.

No. 4. *Compoſition of glaſs, or paſte, much ſofter
than the above.*] " Take of white ſand cleanſed ſix
pounds, of red lead and purified pearl-aſhes, each three
pounds, of nitre one pound, of borax half a pound, and
of arſenic three ounces."—To be mixed as all the preceding. This is very ſoft, and will fuſe with a very
gentle heat, but requires ſome time to become clear,
on account of the arſenic. It may even be prepared
and tinged in a common fire without a furnace ; if the
pots containing it can be ſurrounded by burning coals,
without danger of their falling into it. The borax,
being a more expenſive ingredient than the others, may
be omitted, where a ſomewhat greater heat can be applied ; and the glaſs is not intended for very nice purpoſes. Or a pound of common ſalt may be ſubſtituted
in its place. But the glaſs will be more clear and perfect ; and free itſelf much ſooner from bubbles, where
the borax is uſed. This glaſs will be very ſoft, and
will not bear much wear, if employed for rings, buckles,
or ſuch imitations of ſtones, as are expoſed to much
rubbing. But for ear-rings, ornaments worn on the
breaſt, or ſuch others as are but ſeldom put on, it may
laſt a conſiderable time. In all theſe ſoft compoſitions,
care ſhould be taken, that part of the ſand be not left unvitrified in the bottom of the pot ; as will ſometimes
happen. For, in that caſe, the glaſs, abounding too
much with ſalts and lead, will not bear the air ; but
being corroded by it, will ſoon contract a miſtineſs, and

specks on the surface; which will entirely efface all the lustre of the paste. An unlucky instance of this particularly happened a few years ago, to the great loss, and almost ruin of many of the poorer lapidaries. For there being at that time a great demand for all kinds of ornaments decorated with false stones for the Spanish West-Indian trade, a person undertook to make them and furnish the lapidaries; who, glad of an opportunity of obtaining, on moderate terms, what they had found it difficult to procure before, (as the coloured glass had for the most part been imported from Venice) purchased as large quantities as they possibly could find money to pay for. But in a short time, both the unwrought paste, and that which they had been at the labour and expence of cutting, all turned foul, with a dull scum on the surface and little specks, which eat down into the substance; and took away the smoothness, as well as the lustre. It is proper, therefore, for those, who prepare such compositions, to be careful of adding more salts and lead than the proportions here given; and to watch that the sand, or other matter employed for the body of the composition, be really fluxed. And it is equally proper, that they who purchase such paste, should have some good ground of assurance of its being duly prepared; otherwise, they may throw away their money in the purchase, their time in cutting, and their credit in disposing, of such a faulty commodity. There is a very certain and good method of preventing the inconvenience arising from the separation of the salts in the preparation, as well of the hard kind of coloured glass, as the pastes; which is, by previously calcining the sand, and fixed alkaline salts, as in the manner of making the frit. This may be done, by putting the sand and salt, reduced to powder and mixed together, on a tile placed in a furnace of moderate heat; and turning over and stirring the matter with a tobacco-pipe, or small iron rod; for which purpose, the tile should be either placed near some proper opening into the furnace, or drawn to the door at due intervals. When the matter appears to coalesce strongly, and form a hard body on cooling, it may be taken out; and being kept entirely free from moifture, fhould be powdered. It fhould be then added to the other materials according to the proportion that would have been obferved, with regard to the ingredients of the frit, if they had been ufed without being combined previoufly, by means of this operation.

Compofitions of glafs, or pafte, of a red colour.

No. 1. *Compofition of a fine red glafs refembling the ruby.*] " Take of the hard glafs, No. 1. or No. 2. one pound, of the calx caffii, or gold prepared by precipitation, with tin 3 drachms. Powder the glafs ; and grind the calx of gold afterwards with it in a glafs, flint, or agate mortar ; and then fufe them together."——This may be made of a ftronger or more diluted colour, by varying the proportion of the gold : in adjufting which properly, regard fhould be had to the application of the glafs, when made. For where this glafs is fet in rings, bracelets, or other clofe work, where foils can be ufed, a great faving may be made, with regard to the colour of it, without much injury to the effect. But for ear-rings, or other purpofes, where the work is fet tranfparent, a full ftrong colour fhould be given : which may be effected by the proportions directed in this compofition.

No. 2. *Compofition of a pafte refembling the ruby.*] " Take of the pafte, No. 3. or No 4. one pound, of calx caffii, or precipitation of gold by tin, two drachms. Proceed in the mixture as with, the above."——This will be equally beautiful with the above ; and defective only in foftnefs. But as that greatly takes away the value for fome purpofes, fuch as is appropriated to them may be tinged in a cheaper manner by the following means.

No. 3. *Compofition of a cheaper pafte refembling the ruby.*] " Take of the compofition for pafte, No. 3. or No. 4. half a pound, of glafs of antimony half a pound, and of the precipitation of gold by tin one drachm and half. Proceed as with the others."—This will be confiderably cheaper ; and will have much the fame effect, except that it recedes more from the crimfon to the orange.

No. 4. *Compofition for hard glafs refembling the gar-nct.*] " Take of the compofitions for hard glafs, No. 1. or No. 2. two pounds, of glafs of antimony one pound, of magnefia, and of the precipitate of gold by tin, each one drachm "—This cempofition is very beautiful, but too expenfive, on account of the gold, for the imitation of garnets for common purpofes, on which account the following may be fubftituted.

No. 5. *Cheaper compofition of hard glafs refembling the garnet.*] " Take of the compofitions, No. 1. or No. 2. two pounds, of the glafs of antimony two pounds, and of magnefia, two drachms."——If the colour be found too dark and purple in either this and the preceding compofition, the proportion of magnefia muft be diminifhed.

No. 6. *Compofition of pafte of the colour of garnet.*] " Take of the compofitions for paftes, No. 1. or No. 2. and proceed as with the above."

No. 7. *Compofition of hard glafs refembling the vine-gar garnet.*] " Take of the compofitions No. 1. or No. 2. two pounds, of glafs of antimony one pound, of iron highly calcined half an ounce. Mix the iron with the uncoloured glafs, and fufe them together, till the mafs be perfectly tranfparent ; then add the glafs of antimony powdered, ftirring the mixture with the end of a tobacco-pipe ; and continue them in the heat, till the whole be perfectly incorporated."

No. 8. *Compofition of pafte refembling the vinegar garnet.*] " Take of the compofition for pafte, No. 3. or No. 4, and proceed as with the foregoing."—In this, as well as in all the fucceeding compofitions, it fhould be obferved, that fome allowance may be made in the proportion of the colorific, or tinging matter, for the greater variety of the paftes than the hard glafs, on the fcore of the lead which enters into the compo-fition. For, as the volume, in a pound weight of the pafte, is, confequently, lefs ; a lefs quantity of ting-ing matter is proportionably neceffary to give the fame force of colour to it.

Compositions of glafs and pafte, of a blue colour.

No. 1. *Compofition of hard glafs of a very full blue colour.*] "Take of the compofition for hard glafs, No. 1. or No. 2. ten pounds, of zaffer fix drachms, and of magnefia two drachms. Proceed as with the above."—If this glafs be of too deep a colour, the proportions of the zaffer and magnefia to the glafs may be diminifhed : and if it verge too much on the purple, to which caft it will incline, the magnefia fhould be omitted. If a very cool or pure blue be wanted, in-ftead of the magnefia, half an ounce of calcined copper may be ufed ; and the proportion of zaffer dimi-nifhed by one half.

No. 2. *Compofition of pafte of a full blue colour.*] "Take of the compofition for pafte, No. 1. or No. 2. ten pounds, and proceed as with the foregoing."

No. 3. *Compofition of hard glafs refembling the fapphire.*] "Take of the compofitions for hard glafs, No. 1. or No. 2. ten pounds, of zaffer three drachms and one fcruple, of the calx caffii, or precipitation of gold by tin, one drachm. Proceed as with the above."

No. 4. *Cheaper compofition of hard glafs refembling the fapphire.*] " As the foregoing ; only, inftead of the precipitate of gold, ufe two drachms and two fcruples of magnefia."——If this be well managed, the colour will be very good ; and the glafs, when fet and cut, will not be eafily diftinguifhable from the true fapphire : but the preceding will be a fine colour, as there is a foulnefs in the tinge of the magnefia, which will always diminifh, in fome degree, the effect of brighter colours, when mixed with them.

No. 5. *Compofition of pafte refembling the fapphire.*] "Take of the compofition for pafte, No. 3. or No. 4. and proceed as with the foregoing."—It is not worth while to beftow the expence of colouring paftes with the gold ; and it is, therefore, more expedient, in the cafe of fuch, to ufe the other method.

No. 6. *Compofition of hard glafs and paftes, refembling fapphires, by means of fmalt.*] "Take of the compofitions for hard glafs and paftes, any quantity ; and mix with them one-eighth of their weight of fmalt, the brighteft and moft inclining to purple, that can be procured."——If it be defired to give a more purple tinge, magnefia may be added in the proportion required.

No. 7. *Compofition of hard glafs re'embling the eagle marine (vulgarly called egg-marine.*] "Take of the compofition for hard glafs, No. 1. or No. 2. ten pounds, of copper highly calcined with fulphur three ounces, and of zaffer one fcruple. Proceed as with the foregoing."

No. 8. *Compofition of pafte refembling the eagle marine.*] "Take of the compofition for pafte, No. 1. or No. 2. ten pounds; and proceed as with the above."

Compofitions of hard glafs, and paftes, of a yellow colour.

No. 1. *Compofition of hard glafs of gold, or full yellow colour.*] "Take of the compofitions for hard glafs, No. 1. or No. 2. ten pounds, but omit the falt-petre; and for every pound add an ounce of calcined borax; or, if that do not render the glafs fufficiently fufible, two ounces, of red tartar, the deepeft coloured that can be procured, ten ounces; of magnefia two ounces; of charcoal of fallow, or any other foft kind, two drachms. Proceed as with the reft."——This colour may be prepared with filver: but as there is no advantage in that to counterbalance the expence, I wave giving the procefs.

No. 2. *Compofition of pafte of a gold or full yellow colour.*] "Take of the compofition for pafte, No. 3. or No. 4. prepared without the falt petre, ten pounds; of iron ftrongly calcined, one ounce and a half. Proceed as with the others."——The crude tartar and the charcoal muft not be ufed, where lead enters into the compofition of the glafs; and the nitre may be fpared; becaufe the yellow tinge given to the glafs by the lead, on account of which the nitre is ufed, is no detriment in this cafe; but only adds to the proper colour. This colour may alfo be prepared by crude antimony, as well as the calcined iron: but it is more difficult to be managed, and not fuperior in its effect.

No. 3. *Compofition of hard glafs refembling the topaz.*]
" Take of the compofition for hard glafs, No. 1. or
No. 2. ten pounds, and an equal quantity of the gold
coloured hard glafs. Powder, and fufe them together."—As there is a great variety in the colour of the
topaz, fome being a deeper yellow, and others flightly
tinged, the proportions of the yellow glafs to the white,
may be accordingly varied at pleafure: that here given
being for the deepeft.

No. 4. *Compofition of pafte refembling the topaz.*]
" This may be done in the fame manner as the preceding: but the falt-petre may be omitted in the original compofition of the glafs: and for the refemblance
of the very flightly coloured topazes, neither the gold
coloured pafte, nor any other tinging matter need be
added, that of the lead being fufficient, when not deftroyed by the nitre."

No. 5. *Compofition of hard glafs refembling the cryfolite.*] " Take of the compofition for hard glafs,
No. 1. or No. 2. ten pounds, of calcined iron fix
drachms. Proceed as with the above."

No. 6. *Compofition of pafte refembling the cryfolite.*]
" Take of the compofition for pafte, No. 3. or No. 4.
prepared without falt-petre, ten pounds, and of calcined iron five drachms. Proceed as with the reft."

Compofition of hard glafs, and pafte, of a green colour.
No. 1. *Compofition of hard glafs refembling the emerald.*] " Take of the compofition for hard glafs,
No. 1. or No. 2. nine pounds, of copper, precipitated
from aquafortis, three ounces, and of precipitated iron
two drachms."

No. 2. *Compofition of pafte refembling the emerald.*]
" Take of the compofition for pafte, No. 1. or No. 2.
and proceed as with the above: but if the falt-petre be
omitted in the preparation of the pafte, a lefs proportion of the iron will ferve."

Compofitions of glafs and paftes, of a purple colour.
No. 1. *Compofition of hard glafs, of a deep and very
bright purple colour.*] " Take of the compofition for
hard glafs, No. 1. or No. 2. ten pounds, of zaffer fix

drachms, of gold precipitated by tin one drachm. Proceed as with the rest."

No. 2. *Cheaper composition of hard glass of a deep purple colour.*] " Take of the compositions for hard glass, No. 1. or No. 2. ten pounds, of magnesia one ounce, and of zaffer half an ounce. Proceed as with the others."

No. 3. *Composition of paste of a deep purple colour.*] " Take of the compositions for pastes, No. 3. or No. 4. ten pounds; and treat them as the foregoing."

No. 4. *Composition of hard glass of the colour of the amethyst.*] " Take of the composition for hard glass, No. 1. or No. 2. ten pounds, of magnesia one ounce and a half; and of zaffer one drachm. Proceed as with the rest."

No. 5. *Composition of paste of the colour of the amethyst.*] " Take of the composition for paste, No. 1. or No. 2. ten pounds; and treat it as the preceding."

Of paste resembling the diamond.] " Take of the white sand six pounds, of red-lead four pounds, of pearl-ashes, purified as above directed, three pounds, of nitre two pounds, of arsenic five ounces, and of magnesia one scruple. Proceed as with the others: but continue the fusion for a considerable time, on account of the large proportion of arsenic."—If this composition be thoroughly vitrified, and kept free from bubbles, it will be very white, and have a very great lustre; but, if on examination it yet appear to incline to yellow, another scruple or more of the magnesia may be added. It may be rendered harder, by diminishing the proportion of lead, and increasing that of the salts; or fusing it with a very strong fire: but the diminution of the proportion of lead will make it have less of the lustre of the diamonds.

Composition of hard glass perfectly black.]—" Take of the composition for hard glass, No. 1. or No. 2. ten pounds, of zaffer one ounce, of magnesia, and of iron strongly calcined, each six drachms. Proceed as with the rest."

Composition of paste perfectly black.] " Take of the

eompofition for pafte, No. 1. or No. 2. prepared with
the falt petre, ten pounds, of zaffer one ounce, of magnefia fix drachms, and of iron highly calcined five
drachms. Proceed as with the others.''

Of the white opake, and femi-tranfparent glafs, and paftes.

No. 1. *Compofition of white opake glafs.*] " Take
of the compofition for hard glafs, No. 1. or No. 2. ten
pounds, of horn, ivory or bone, calcined perfectly
white, one pound. Proceed as with the others.''

No. 2. *Compofition of pafte of an opake whitenefs.*]
" Take of the compofition, No. 3. or No. 4. ten pounds,
and make the fame addition as to the above.''

No. 3. *Compofition of glafs of an opake whitenefs formed by arfenic.*] " Take of flint-glafs ten pounds, and
of very white arfenic one pound. Powder and mix
them thoroughly, by grinding them together ; and then
fufe them with a moderate heat, till they be well incorporated : but avoid liquifying them more, than to make
a perfect union.''—This glafs has been made at a confiderable work near London in great quantities ; and
has not only been manufactured into a variety of different
kinds of veffels, but, being very white and fufible with
a moderate heat, has been much ufed as a white ground
for enamel in dial-plates, fnuff-boxes, and other pieces,
which have not occafion to go feveral times into the fire
to be finifhed. It will not, however, bear repeated
burnings, nor a ftrong heat continued for any length
of time, when applied to this purpofe, without becoming tranfparent; to which likewife, the fmoke of a
coal fire will alfo greatly contribute : but it anfwers the
end very well in many cafes; though even in thofe,
enamel of the fame degree of whitenefs would be preferable ; as this is always brittle, and of lefs firm and
tenacious texture.

No. 4. *Compofition of hard glafs, or pafte, formed by
calk of tin or antimony.*] " Take of any of the compofitions for hard glafs or paftes, ten pounds, of calcined
tin, (commonly called putty) or of antimony, or tin
ealcined by means of nitre, one pound and a half. Mix
them well, by grinding them together ; and then fufe

S

them with a moderate heat."—The glafs of this kind, made with the compofition for paftes, differs in nothing from white enamel, but in the proportion of the calx of tin and antimony : and, if thofe calxes be prepared with nitre, (without which they cannot be made to produce a pure whitenefs in glafs) this compofition will be more expence and trouble than thofe above given, without any other advantage, than that it will bear the action of a much ftronger and longer continued fire, without lofing its opacity in any degree, than the others.

No. 5. *Compofition of femi-tranfparent white glafs and pafte, refembling the opal.*] " Take of any of the compofitions for hard glafs, or pafte, ten pounds, of horn, bone, or ivory, calcined to a perfect whitenefs, half a pound. Proceed as with the reft."—This white hard glafs is much the fame with the German glafs formerly brought here in porringers, cream-pots, vinegar-cruets, and other fuch pieces, of which we frequently meet with the remains.

Compofitions of fictitious or counterfeit lapis lazuli.] " Take of any of the above compofitions for hard glafs, or pafte, ten pounds, of calcined bones, horn or ivory, three quarters of a pound, of zaffer one ounce and a half, of magnefia half an ounce. Fufe the uncoloured compofition with the zaffer and magnefia, till a very deep tranfparent blue glafs be produced. The mafs being cold, powder it : and mix it with the calcined matter, by grinding them together. After which, fufe them with a moderate heat, till they appear to be thoroughly incorporated ; and then form the melted mafs into cakes, by pouring it on a clean bright plate of copper or iron."——If it be defired to have it veined with gold, it may be done, by mixing the gold powder with an equal weight of calcined borax, and tempering them with oil of fpike ; by which mixture, the cakes, being painted with fuch veins as are defired, they muft be put into a furnace of a moderate heat ; and the gold will be cemented to the glafs, as firmly as if the veins had been natural. If the counterfeit lapis lazuli be defired of a lighter hue, the quantity of zaffer and magnefia muft be diminifhed; or, if it be required to be more tranfparent, that of the calcined horn, bone, or ivory, fhould be leffened. Inftead of zaffer, where that cannot be obtained, a proper proportion of fmalt may be fubftituted. And in all cafes, indeed, it may be a more certain way, to form the zaffer and vitrifying ingredients into glafs alone, and then, having powdered them with the calcined bones or horns, infufe them a fecond time, and make them into cakes in the manner directed. For the fluxing power of the ingredients of the glafs is fo retarded by the calcined bone or horn, that it may, in fome cafes, fail to act fufficiently on the zaffer to vitrify it perfectly.

Compofition of hard glafs refembling the red cornelian.] "Take of the compofitions for hard glafs, No. 1. or No. 2. two pounds, of glafs of antimony one pound, of the calcined vitriol, called fcarlet oker, two ounces, and of magnefia one drachm. Fufe the glafs of antimony and magnefia with the other glafs firft together; and then powder them well, and mix them with the fcarlet oker, by grinding them together; and afterwards fufe the mixture with a gentle heat, till they be incorporated: but the heat muft not be continued longer than is abfolutely required to form them into a vitreous mafs."—If it be defired to have the compofition more tranfparent, a proportionable part of the red oker muft be omitted.

Compofition of pafte refembling the red cornelian.] "Take of the compofitions for paftes, No. 1. or No. 2. two pounds; and proceed as with the above."

Compofition of hard glafs refembling the white cornelian.] "Take of the compofitions for hard glafs, No. 1. or No. 2. two pounds, of yellow oker well wafhed, two drachms, and of calcined bones, each one ounce. Mix them well by grinding them together; and fufe them with a gentle heat, till the feveral ingredients be well incorporated in a vitreous mafs."

Compofition of pafte refembling the white cornelian.]

marine) ten pounds, of calcined bone, horn, or ivory, ·
half a pound. Powder and mix them well; and then
fufe them in a moderate heat, till they be thoroughly
incorporated."——If the colour be not fo deep as
may be defired, a fmall proportion of fmalt may be
added.

*Compofition of the brown Venetian glafs with gold
fpangles; commonly called the Philofopher's ftone.*] " Take
of the compofition for hard glafs, No. 2. and the compofition for pafte, No. 1. each five pounds, and of highly
calcined iron one ounce. Mix them well, and fufe them
till the iron be perfectly vitrified; and have tinged the
glafs of a deep tranfparent yellow brown colour. Powder this glafs; and add to it two pounds of glafs of
antimony, being powdered; and mix them well, by
grinding them together. Take part of this mixture,
and rub into it fourfcore or one hundred leaves of the
counterfeit leaf-gold, commonly called Dutch gold;
and, when the parts of the gold feem fufficiently divided, mix the powder containing it with the other
part of the glafs. Fufe the whole then with a moderate heat, till the powder run into a vitreous mafs fit to
be wrought into any of the figures, or veffels, into
which it is ufually formed: but avoid a perfect lique-
faction; becaufe that deftroys, in a fhort time, the
equal diffufion of the fpangles; and vitrifies, at leaft
part, the matter of which they are compofed; converting the whole to a kind of tranfparent olive-coloured
glafs."——This kind of glafs is ufed for a great variety
of toys and ornaments, and procured from the Veneti-
ans. A few years ago a very great demand arofe for
it to China, and raifed the price very high, till fuch
quantities had been brought from Venice, and fent
thither, as glutted the market. But there is no reafon
why it fhould not be equally well prepared here; and

at a small expence; as will be found, on a few trials, by those who will carefully execute what is here directed.

Of the fusion and vitrification of the several compositions of coloured glass; with the particular rules and cautions to be observed in the management of each kind.] The several compositions above-mentioned being prepared according to the directions respectively given; the matter should be put into proper pots, of which it should not fill above two-thirds; and then placed in the furnace, or in any other kind, where they may receive a sufficient heat, and be secured from any coals, soot, or any other filth, falling into them. In order to prevent which, it is expedient, with regard to the pots in which this kind of glass is prepared, to have covers over the tops of them, with a little return over the side. And it is also proper to have a hole in the side, a little below the return; through which an iron may be passed to take out a small quantity of the melted matter, for the judging of the progress of the vitrification. These pots, when put into the furnace above-mentioned, should be placed on the flooring or stage intended to support them in the part betwixt the doors, opposite to that through which they are passed into the furnace, according to the manner before directed; which should be done by means of a strong iron peel, like those used by the bakers. It is necessary to observe, likewise, that however well the pots may have been before baked, it is always proper, in the case of glass of greater value, where the clearness and beauty is of consequence, to give them another burning before they be used; and, at the same time, to incrust them over with any common colourless glass; which may be done in this manner: Having reduced the glass to powder, moisten all the inside of the pot with water; and, while it is yet moist, put in some of the powdered glass, and shake it about till the whole inner surface of the pot be covered by what will adhere to it, in consequence of the moisture. Throw out then the redundant part of the powdered glass; and, the pot being dry, set it in a furnace sufficiently

S 3

hot to vitrify the glaſs adhering to it ; and let it continue there ſome time : after which, care muſt be taken to let it cool gradually.

The pots, containing the compoſition, being thus placed in the furnace, a gentle heat, ſuch as will juſt keep the pots red hot, ſhould be given for the firſt hour or longer. There is, however, an exception to this, which is, where there is much arſenic in the compoſition, which requires that ſome degree of vitrification ſhould be brought on as quickly as poſſible, in order to fix it, and prevent its ſubliming away from the other ingredients ; which it will not ceaſe to do, ſo long as continued in the ſtate of a powder. But where a gentle heat is proper at firſt, after the expiration of an hour and a half, or two hours at furtheſt, the heat may be raiſed ſufficiently to produce a vitrification ; but not ſo as to render the melted matter very fluid at firſt ; which in this part of the proceſs would occaſion a ſeparation of the ingredients ; and greatly retard, if not intirely prevent, the perfect vitriſic incorporation of the whole.

The due degree or continuance of heat, for the perfecting theſe kinds of glaſs, cannot be ſettled by any ſtandard, as they are varied both by the nature of the compoſition, and the quantity of the matter. But in the caſe of pots which hold ten or eleven pounds, twenty or twenty-four hours may be allowed for hard glaſs, and fourteen or ſixteen for paſtes. And where much arſenic enters into the compoſition, though it is neceſſary to bring on a quicker vitrification, yet more time muſt ſometimes be given to the matter, than in other caſes, before all the cloudineſs be diſſipated.

In the fuſion of the tranſparent coloured glaſs, it is above all things neceſſary to avoid ſtirring the matter, or even ſhaking the pots ; as it would otherwiſe hazard the cauſing bubbles in the glaſs, to prevent which is the greateſt difficulty attending the preparation of counterfeit gems. But if the ingredients, by their action on each other, do yet, notwithſtanding all exterior concuſſion be avoided, produce bubbles, the glaſs muſt be continued in fuſion till they wholly vaniſh. And if, when bubbles do arife in the glafs, and time be given for it, there appear no tendency to their going away, the heat muft be gradually raifed to a greater pitch, that the glafs may be rendered more fluid, and that vicidity, which was the occafion of their detenfion, removed.

When a proper time has been given the glafs to attain to a perfect ftate of vitrification, it fhould be examined, by putting the fmall end of a tobacco-pipe to the furface of the glafs, thro' the hole in the fide of the pot ; which will bring away with it a little quantity of the glafs, from whence the qualities may be judged of. And if there appear any defects, that feem owing to the want of a due converfion of the ingredients to a vitrious ftate, more time and heat muft be given to it. But if no fuch defects are found, and the glafs appear perfect, the fire fhould be decreafed, and, by degrees, fuffered to go out ; and the pots continued in the furnace, till they become cold : after which, the pot fhould be torn off from the mafs of glafs contained in it. As, however, it is not always convenient to difcontinue the heat of the furnace, when one or more pots of the glafs may have attained to the due ftate of vitrification ; they may, on fuch occafions, be taken out. And if the glafs be not of great value, nor intended for very nice purpofes, it may be formed into cakes, by pouring it on a clean plate of iron or copper, or into rolls. Thefe cakes, or rolls, fhould be put into a moderate heat, before they grow cold ; and continued there for fome time, that they may gain a good temper, fo as to bear cutting or working in any way, according to the ufe they are intended for.

The tranfparent coloured glafs is in moft cafes improved, by continuing it in the heat, even for a confiderable time after the vitrification feems perfected ; as it is, by that means, rendered harder, and freer from fpecks and bubbles. But the femi-tranfparent kinds, and opake white, formed of arfenic, muft be taken juft at the point, when the ingredients are duly united ; for a more mature vitrification converts to tranfparent glafs

The far greater hardneſs of cryſtal than of any kind of glaſs, and the ſuperior luſtre of it to any but paſtes, which are deplorably ſoft, have rendered the art of imparting to it the colour of gems, an object of frequent and eager purſuit: as great advantages might probably have ariſen from it to the firſt inventors. There are two methods, by which it has been conceived there was a poſſibility of doing it : the one, by cementing ; that is, impregnating the cryſtals by means of heat, with the proper tinging particles, under the form of ſteam : the other, by bringing the cryſtal to a ſtate of fuſion, thro' the means of heat aided by a ſtrong flux ; and combining it in that ſtate with the proper colouring ſubſtances. Both of theſe have been pretended to be effected in a perfect manner : and very oſtentatious accounts of them have been given to the public : though it is much to be feared, that ſo far from having carried this art to any degree of perfection, there is not hitherto known one ſingle fact, or principle, that in the leaſt ſeems to lead to the attainment of it. As the world has been made to believe, however, as well more lately as formerly, by perſons of ſome authority, that both theſe methods have been practiſed with all the deſired ſucceſs. I will exhibit the particular manner in which each has been practiſed, by thoſe who have been believed to be moſt the maſters of theſe arts.

 " Take of very yellow orpiment, and white arſenic, each two ounces, and of antimony and ſal ammoniacum each one ounce ; and having reduced them to powder, mix them well together, and put them into a large crucible. Over this mixture, lay the pieces of rock cryſtal ; firſt ſuch as are of the leaſt ſize, then larger, and at the top the biggeſt ; taking care, that thoſe choſen for this purpoſe have no flaws nor foulneſs. This crucible

muft then be covered by a leffer turned upfide down
upon it, in the bottom of which, there fhould be previoufly made a little opening of the bignefs of a pea;
in order that this bottom, becoming now the top of the
veffel, formed by joining the two together, the fumes
of the matter contained may have vent through the
hole; and, confequently, being determined upwards,
may pafs through the cryftals, and act upon them. The
joints produced by inverting the leffer crucible into the
greater fhould be luted; and being dry, the veffel thus
formed muft be put in the midft of pieces of charcoal,
in fuch manner, that the undermoft crucible may be bu-
ried in them intirely; and the uppermoft half way.
The coals muft then be kindled, and the fire fuffered to
burn very gradually without blowing, unlefs it fhould
be neceffary to keep it from extinguifhing; to prevent
which from happening too foon, the pieces of charcoal
fhould be chofen large. As the fire rifes, the mixture
in the crucible will emit copious fumes: which being very
noxious, muft be carefully avoided: and to that end
this operation fhould be always performed under a chimney; the front of which fhould be brought fo low, that
all the fmoke may be determined up it; and not fpread
itfelf in the elaboratory, or other place. The fire muft
be kept up fo long as any of thefe fumes appear to rife;
and then permitted to go gradually out; and all accefs
of cold air muft be cautioufly prevented. When the
crucibles are grown intirely cold, but not before, the
uppermoft may be taken off; and the cryftal will be
found coloured, fome pieces like topazes, and fome like
rubies, and a variety of other ftones."

It has been faid, that the cryftals thus coloured have
been cut; and produced fine imitations of the true
ftones: but the truth of the matter is, (notwithftanding
all pretenfion to more) that they do appear, when taken
out of the crucible, to be well coloured and beautiful;
yet on further examination it is found, that the whole
effect is produced by a fallacious caufe. For the cryftals being cracked by the heat, it is almoft univerfally
the confequence of being expofed to this degree of heat,

the fumes having infinuated themfelves into thefe cracks, and there producing the fame effect as the paint ufed betwixt the two tables of doublets, the whole fubftance of the ftene has the appearance of being tinged. But on due infpection, neverthelefs, the cryftals are found to be neither fit to be cut, on account of the flaws, nor to have acquired any colour, but what would inftantly be deftroyed on the feparation of the feveral parts of the ftones, into which they are divided by the cracks : fo that this method, together with many others of the fame kind for giving colours to cryftals by cementation, will be found to elude the hopes of thofe, who try them with any confidence.

The other pretended method of colouring cryftals, by fufing them, and imparting the various tinges to them, while in a melted ftate, is thus performed :

" Take of rock cryftals any quantity ; and put them in a covered crucible in a ftrong fire ; where they muft be continued for fome time. Remove the crucible then out of the fire ; and immediately throw the cryftals into a veffel of clean cold water : from whence being again collected, they muft be re calcined ; and afterwards thrown into frefh water again in the fame manner : and this operation muft be repeated, till the cryftals be fo changed in their texture, by the flaws and cracks produced by the fudden change from heat to cold, that they may be eafily levigated. Powder the cryftals thus calcined ; and, to three pounds of them, add two pounds of purified pearl-afhes, or a pound and a quarter of red lead, together with any of the tinging fubftances above-mentioned, in the proportion directed for colouring glafs or paftes ; and fufe them in the fame manner alfo, as has been before advifed for other compofitions. If the matter be found too difficult to be brought to a vitreous ftate, by this proportion of pearl-afhes or lead, borax or arfenic may be added, as in other cafes, in order to form a more powerful flux."

The cryftal thus treated produces however nothing more than a glafs exactly of the fame kind with that formed of the Lynn fand ; which is in fact no other than a grofs powder of cryftal; and neither of them differ very effentially from fuch calcined flints, as are wholly free from colour. The fuppofition, therefore, that the cryftal can be fufed by this means, and being tinged while in that ftate, reduced afterwards to its original hardnefs, is wholly groundlefs. For it cannot be fufed by the heat of furnaces without the medium of fome fluxing body added to it; and then its texture and properties are fo changed, or rather the glafs produced by the compofition is fo different from the cryftal itfelf, that there does not appear to be the leaft advantage in employing rock-cryftal, in forming fuch a compofition, preferably to flints; even if they could be procured at the fame expence; and required no greater trouble or labour in their ufe.

Of doublets.] The impracticability of imparting tinges to the body of cryftals, while in their proper and natural ftate, and the foftnefs of glafs which renders ornaments made of it greatly inferior in wear to cryftal, gave inducements to the introduction of colouring the furface of cryftal, wrought into a proper form in fuch manner, that the furfaces of two pieces fo coloured being laid together, the effect might appear the fame, as if the whole fubftance of the cryftal had been tinged. The cryftals (and fometimes white tranfparent glafs) fo treated, were called doublets: and at one time prevailed greatly in ufe, on account of the advantages, with refpect to wear, fuch doublets had, when made of cryftal, over glafs, and the brightnefs of the colours, which could with certainty be given to counterfeit ftones this way, when coloured glafs could not be procured; or at leaft not without a much greater expence. Doublets have not indeed the property which the others have of bearing to be fet tranfparent; as is frequently required in drops of ear-rings and other ornaments. But when mounted in rings, or ufed in fuch manner, that the fides of the pieces, where the joint is made, cannot be infpected, they have, when formed of cryftal, the title to a preference to the coloured glafs: and the art of managing them is therefore in fome degree of the fame

importance with that of preparing glass for the counterfeiting gems; and is therefore properly an appendix
to it, as being intirely subservient to the same intention.
The manner of managing doublets is as follows: ' '

Let the cryſtal or glaſs be firſt cut by the lapidaries
in the manner of a brilliant: except that, in this caſe,
the figure muſt be compoſed from two ſeparate ſtones,
or parts of ſtones formed in the manner of the upper
and under parts of a brilliant, if it was divided in an
horizontal direction, a little lower than the middle.
After the two plates of the intended ſtone are thus cut,
and fitted ſo exactly, that no diviſion can appear when
they are laid together, the upper part muſt be poliſhed
ready for ſetting; and then the colour muſt be put betwixt the two plates by this method:

" Take of Venice or Cyprus turpentine two ſcruples;
and add to it one ſcruple of the grains of maſtic choſen
perfectly pure, and free from foulneſs, and previouſly
powdered. Melt them together in a ſmall ſilver or braſs
ſpoon ladle, or other veſſel, and put to them gradually
any of the coloured ſubſtances below mentioned, being
firſt well powdered; ſtirring them together as the colour
is put in, that they may be thoroughly commixt.
Warm then the doublets to the ſame degree of heat, as
the melted mixture; and paint the upper ſurface of the
lower part; and put the upper one inſtantly upon it;
preſſing them to each other; but taking care that they
may be conjoined in the moſt perfectly even manner.
When the cement or paint is quite cold, and ſet, the
redundant part of it, which has been preſſed out of the
joint of the two pieces, ſhould be gently ſcraped off the
ſide, till there be no appearance of any colour on the
outſide of the doublets: and they ſhould then be ſkilfully
ſet; obſerving to carry the mounting over the joint, that
the upper piece may be well ſecured from ſeparating
from the under one."

The colour of the ruby may be beſt imitated, by
mixing a fourth part of carmine with ſome of the fineſt
crimſon lake that can be procured: which may be beſt
made for this purpoſe of Brazil wood.

The fapphire may be counterfeited by very bright Pruffian blue, mixed with a little of the above-mentioned crimfon lake, to give it a caft of the purple. The Pruffian blue fhould not be very deep coloured, or but little of it fhould be ufed: for otherwife, it will give a black fhade that will be injurious to the luftre of the doublets.

The emerald may be well counterfeited by diftilled verdigrife, with a little powdered aloes. But the mixture fhould not be ftrongly heated, nor kept long over the fire after the verdigrife is added: for the colour is apt to be foon impaired by it.

The refemblance of the garnet may be made by dragon's blood: which, if it cannot be procured of fufficient brightnefs, may be helped by a very fmall quantity of carmine.

The vinegar garnet may be imitated with great fuccefs by the orange lake.

The amethyft may be counterfeited by the mixture of fome Pruffian blue, with the crimfon lake: but the proportions can only be regulated by difcretion; as different parcels of the lake and Pruffian blue vary extremely in the degree of ftrength of the colour.

The yellow topazes may be imitated, by mixing the powdered aloes with a little dragon's blood; or by good Spanifh anatto; but the colour muft be very fparingly ufed, or the tinge will be too ftrong for the appearance of that ftone.

The cryfolite, hyacinth, vinegar garnet, eagle marine, and other fuch weaker or more diluted colours, may be formed in the fame manner, by leffening the proportions of the colours, or by compounding them together correfpondently to the hue of the ftone to be imitated; to which end it is proper to have an original ftone, or an exact imitation of one at hand, when the mixture is made; in order to the more certain adapting the colours to the effect defired. When thefe precautions are taken, and the operation well conducted, it is practicable to bring the doublets to fo near a refemblance of the true ftone, that even the beft judges cannot

T

distinguish them, when well set, without a peculiar manner of inspection.

Where any kind of lake, or Prussian blue, is used for this purpose, it is best to grind or levigate it with spirit of turpentine instead of water: which will prevent its concreting again as it dries. The dragon's blood may be levigated with water: but the distilled verdigrise must be powdered dry. All the substances used as tinges for doublets or foils must, however, be powdered as finely as possible: the brightness of the counterfeit stones for which they are used, depending very greatly on that.

There is, however, an easy method of distinguishing doublets: which is only to hold them betwixt the eye and light, in such position, that the light may pass through the upper part, and corners of the stone; which will then show such parts to be white; and that there is no colour in the body of the stone.

Of the general nature and preparation of foils.] Foils are thin plates or leaves of metal, that are put under stones, or compositions in imitation of stones, when they are set.

The intention of foils is, either to increase the lustre or play of the stones, or more generally to improve the colour, by giving an additional force to the tinge, whether it be natural or artificial, by that of a ground of the same hue; which the foil is in this case made to be.

There are consequently two kinds of foils. The one is colourless; where the effect of giving lustre or play to the stone is produced by the polish of the surface, which makes it act as a mirror; and, by reflecting the light, prevent that deadness which attends the having a duller ground under the stone; and brings it, by the double refraction of the light that is caused, nearer to the effect of the diamond. The other is coloured with some pigment or stain of the same hue as the stone; or of some other, which is intended to modify and change the hue of the stone in some degree; as, where a yellow foil may be put under green, which is too much inclining to the blue; or under crimfon, where it is defired to have the appearance more orange or fcarlet.

Foils may be made of copper or tin : and filver has been fometimes ufed ; with which it has been advifed, for fome purpofes, to mix gold ; but the expence of either is needlefs, as copper may be made to anfwer the fame end.

Where coloured foils are wanted, copper may, therefore, be beft ufed ; and may be prepared for the purpofe by the following means :

" Take copper plates beaten to a proper thicknefs ; and pafs them betwixt a pair of fine fteel rollers very clofely fet; and draw them as thin as is poffible. to retain a proper tenacity. Polifh them with very fine whiting, or rotten ftone, till they fhine, and have as much brightnefs as can be given them ; and they will then be fit to receive the colour."

But where the yellow or rather orange colour of the ground would be injurious to the effect, as in the cafe of purples, or crimfon red, the foil fhould be whitened, which may be done by filvering it in the following manner :

" Take a fmall quantity of filver, and diffolve it in aquafortis ; and then put bits of copper into the folution, to precipitate the filver ; which being thus precipitated, the fluid muft be poured off : and frefh water added to it, to wafh away all the remainder of the firft fluid : after which, the filver muft be dried. An equal weight of cream of tartar, and common falt, muft then be ground with it, till the whole be reduced to a very fine powder : and with this mixture, the foils, being firft flightly moiftened, muft be rubbed by the finger, or a bit of linen rag, till they be of the degree of whitenefs defired : after which, if it appear to be wanted, the polifh muft be refrefhed."

Inftead of rolling, the more general practice is, to beat the copper plates, previoufly heated, betwixt two flat irons on an anvil, till they become of the thicknefs required ; and then give to them an even furface, by a planifhing hammer, before they are polifhed : but the ufe of the rollers is muchmore expeditious and effectual, where the quantity demanded can defray the expence of purchafing them, with the other neceffary work.

The tin foils are only ufed in the cafe of colourlefs ftones, where quickfilver is employed : and they may be drawn out by the fame rollers ; but need not be further polifhed ; as that effect is produced by other means in this cafe.

Of the colouring foils.] There have been two methods invented for the colouring foils : the one by tinging the furface of the copper of the colour required, by means of fmoke : the other by ftaining or painting it with fome pigment, or other colouring fubftance. The firft is limited only to colours where blue is prevalent, and, being troublefome and uncertain in the production, is not, on the whole, fo eligible, in any cafe, as the latter : and I fhall, therefore, omit giving any direc-tions for the practice of it ; as all colours defired may be given to the foils by the other method : that is, by laying a pigment or other colouring fubftance on the furface, by means of fome proper vehicle that may ferve for fpreading it, and fixing it to the copper as a cement.

The colours ufed for painting foils, may be tempered with either oil ; water rendered duly vifcid by gum Ara-bic, or fize, or varnifh : and as there is no preference of one method to the other, but in particular cafes, it is beft to perufe all of them, according to the occafions that may be beft ferved. Where deep colours are wanted, oil is moft proper ; becaufe fome pigments become wholly tranfparent in it ; as lake or Pruffian blue : but yellow and green may be better laid on in varnifh, as the yellow may be had in perfection from a tinge wholly diffolved in fpirit of wine, in the fame manner as in the cafe of laquers ; and the moft beautiful green is to be produced by diftilled verdigrife, which is apt to lofe its colour, and turn black with oil. In common cafes, however, any of the colours may be, with little trou-ble, laid on with ifinglafs fize, in the fame manner as the glazing colours ufed in miniature painting ; for which, ample directions will now be given. The beſt method of adapting foils to all the ſeveral purpoſes, is as follows:

For red, where the ruby is to be imitated, carmine, with a little lake uſed in iſinglaſs ſize, or ſhell-lac var-niſh, is to be employed, if the glaſs or paſte be of a full crimſon, verging towards the purple. But if the glaſs incline to the ſcarlet, or orange, very bright lake (that is not purple) may be uſed alone in oil.—For the garnet red, dragon's blood, diſſolved in ſeed-lac varniſh, may be uſed:——and for the vinegar garnet, the orange lake, tempered with ſhell-lac varniſh, will be found ex-cellent.

For the amethyſt, lake, with a little Pruſſian blue, uſed with oil, and very thinly ſpread on the foil, will completely anſwer the end.

For blue, where a deep colour, or the effect of the ſapphire is wanted, Pruſſian blue, that is not too deep, ſhould be uſed in oil: and it ſhould be ſpread more or leſs thinly on the foil, according to the lightneſs or deepneſs of which the colour is deſired to be.——For the eagle marine, common verdigriſe, with a little Pruſ-ſian blue, tempered in ſhell-lac varniſh, may be uſed.

For yellow, where a full colour is deſired, the foil may be coloured with yellow laquer, laid on as for other purpoſes: and for the ſlighter colour of topazes, the burniſh and foil itſelf will be ſufficiently ſtrong without any addition.

For green, where a deep hue is required, the cryſtals of verdigriſe, tempered in ſhell-lac varniſh, ſhould be uſed: but where the emerald is to be imitated, a little yellow laquer ſhould be added, to bring the colour to a truer green, and leſs verging to the blue.

The ſtones of more diluted colour, ſuch as the ame-thyſt, topaz, vinegar garnet, and eagle marine, may be very cheaply imitated by tranſparent white glaſs, or paſte, even without foils. This is to be done, by tem-pering the colours above enumerated with turpentine and maſtic, treated in the manner directed as before, for doublets; and painting the ſocket in which the coun-

T 3

terfeit ſtone is to be ſet with the mixture ; as well that
as the ſocket and ſtone itſelf being previouſly heated.
In this caſe, however, the ſtone ſhould be immediately
ſet, and the ſocket cloſed upon it, before the mixture
cool and grow hard.

The orange lake, abovementioned, was invented for
this purpoſe, in which it has a beautiful effect ; and
was uſed with great ſucceſs by a conſiderable manufac-
turer. The colour it produces is that of the vinegar
garnet ; which it affords with great brightneſs.

The colours, above directed to be uſed in oil, ſhould
be extremely well ground in oil of turpentine, and tempered with old nut or poppy oil ; or, if time can be
given for their drying, with ſtrong fat oil diluted with
ſpirit of turpentine, which will gain a fine poliſh of itſelf.

The colours uſed in varniſh ſhould be, likewiſe, thoroughly well ground and mixed : and, in caſe of the
dragon's blood, in the ſeed-lac varniſh and the laquer,
the foils ſhould be warmed before they are laid on.

All the mixtures ſhould be laid on the foils with a
broad ſoft bruſh ; which muſt be paſſed from one end
to the other ; and no part ſhould be croſſed, or twice
gone over ; or, at leaſt, not till the firſt coat be dry ;
when, if the colour do not lie ſtrong enough, a ſecond
coat, or even a third, may be given.

*Of foils for cryſtals, pebbles, or paſte, to give the luſtre
and play of diamonds.*] The manner of preparing foils,
ſo as to give colourleſs ſtones the greateſt degree of
play and luſtre, is, by raiſing ſo high a poliſh or ſmooth-
neſs on the ſurface, as to give them the effect of a mirror ; which can only be done in a perfect manner by
the uſe of quickſilver applied in the ſame general way,
as in the caſe of looking-glaſs. The method by which
it may be beſt performed, is as follows :

" Take leaves of tin, prepared in the ſame manner
as for ſilvering looking-glaſſes ; and cut them into ſmall
pieces of ſuch ſize as to cover the ſurface of the ſocket
of the ſtones that are to be ſet. Lay three of theſe
then one upon another ; and, having moiſtened the

infide of the focket with thin gum water, and fuffered
it to become again fo dry, that only a flight flickinefs
remains, put the three pieces of leaves, lying on each
other, into it, and adapt them to the furface, in as
even a manner as poffible. When this is done, heat
the focket, and fill it with warm quickfilver; which
muft be fuffered to continue in it three or four minutes,
and then gently poured out. The ftone muft then be
thruft into the focket, and clofed with it ; care having
been taken to give fuch room for it, that it may enter
without ftripping off the tin and quickfilver from any
part of the furface. The work fhould be well clofed
round the ftone, to prevent the tin and quickfilver,
contained in the focket, from being fhaken out by any
violence."

The luftre of ftones, fet in this manner, will continue longer, than when they are fet in the common
way ; as the cavity round them being filled in this
manner, there will be no paffage found for moifture ;
which is fo injurious to the wear of ftones treated in
any other way.

This kind of foil gives fome luftre to glafs, or other
tranfparent matter, which has little of itfelf : but to
ftones, or paftes, that have fome fhare of play, it gives
a moft beautiful brilliance. It has been but little practifed hitherto ; I fuppofe from an ignorance of the
manner of doing it : for, indeed, I never heard of
more than one perfon, and he is now fome time de-
ceafed, who performed it to perfection : and he gave
the ftones a furprifing luftre, that made them not diftinguifhable from diamonds even by day light. There
is, neverthelefs, at prefent, one difadvantage attending
this method, as it is now practifed : which is, that it
can be only performed in the cafe of ftones with a flat
bottom. In confequence of which, the rofe or table
diamonds, only, can be imitated by it. But though
the manner of doing it has not been hitherto difcovered,
yet it is certainly not impoffible to contrive fome way
of fetting ftones of the cut of brilliants in this manner :
in which cafe, if any of the cryftal fpecies, fuch as

thofe called Briftol ftones, Kerry ftones, &c. were to
be ufed, their far greater hardnefs, as well as much
higher luftre, when treated in this way, would render
them far fuperior to paftes.

Of Cements.

CEMENTS require to be of very various compofitions, and different with refpeƈt to the nature of the
ingredients, according to the different manner in which
they are to be applied ; and the fubftances they are to
conjoin. The kinds of cement ufed for common purpofes pafs under the denomination of glues, fizes, paftes,
and lutes : but fome, that are ufed for extraordinary occafions, retain only the general name of cements.

Preparation of infinglafs glue.] " Ifinglafs glue is
made by diffolving beaten ifinglafs in water by boiling ;
and, having ftrained it through a coarfe linen cloth,
evaporating it again to fuch a confiftence, that, being
cold, the glue will be perfeƈtly hard and dry."—A great
improvement is faid to be made in this glue by adding
fpirit of wine or brandy to it after it is ftrained, and
then renewing the evaporation till it gain the due confiftence. Some foak the ifinglafs in the fpirit of brandy
for fome time before it is diffolved, in order to make
the glue ; and add no water, but let the fpirit fupply
the place of it. But it is not clear, from trial, that
either of thefe praƈtices render the glue better. This
ifinglafs glue is far preferable to common glue for nicer
purpofes ; being much ftronger, and lefs liable to be
foftened either by heat or moifture.

Preparation of parchment glue.] " Take one pound
of parchment, and boil it, in fix quarts of water, till
the quantity be reduced to one quart : ftrain off the
fluid from the dregs ; and then boil it again, till it be
of the confiftence of glue."——The fame may be done
with glovers' cuttings of leather, which make a colourlefs glue, if not burned in the evaporation of the water.

Preparation of a very strong compound glue.] "Take
common glue in very small or thin bits, and isinglass
glue; and infuse them in as much spirit of wine as will
cover them, for at least twenty-four hours. Then melt
the whole together; and, while they are over the fire,
add as much powdered chalk as will render them an
opake white."—The infusion in the spirit of wine has
been directed in the recipes given for this glue; but the
remark on the use of it in the preceding article will
hold good also in this: and the mixture may be made
with water only.

*Preparation of a very strong glue that will resist mois-
ture.*] "Dissolve gum sanderac, and mastic, of each
two ounces, in a pint of spirit of wine; adding about
an ounce of clear turpentine. Then take equal parts
of isinglass, and parchment glue, made according to
the directions in the preceding article; and, having
beaten the isinglass into small bits, as for common uses,
and reduced the glue to the same state, pour the solution
of the gums upon them; and melt the whole in a vessel
well covered; avoiding so great a heat as that of boiling
water. When melted, strain the glue through a coarse
linen cloth; and then putting it again over the fire, add
about an ounce of powdered glass."—This preparation
may be best managed in balneo mariæ, which will prevent the matter burning to the vessel; or the spirit of
wine from taking fire: and indeed it is better to use the
same method for all the evaporations of nicer glues, and
sizes; but, in that case, less water than the proportion
directed, should be added to the materials. A very
strong glue, that will resist water, may be also made by
adding half a pound of common glue or isinglass glue
to two quarts of skimmed milk, and then evaporating
the mixture to the due consistence of the glue.

*Preparation of lip glue, for extemporaneously cement-
ing paper, silk, and thin leather, &c.*]—"Take of
isinglass glue, and parchment glue, each one ounce, of
sugar candy, and gum tragacanth, each two drachms,
Add to them an ounce of water, and boil the whole together, till the mixture appear, when cold, of the pro-

per confiſtence of glue. Then form it into ſmall rolls, or any other figure, that may be moſt convenient."— This glue being wet with the tongue, and rubbed on the edges of the paper, ſilk, &c. that are to be cemented, will, on their being laid together, and ſuffered to dry, unite them as firmly as any other part of the ſubſtance.

Of ſizes.] Common ſize is manufactured in the ſame manner, and generally by the ſame people, as glue. It is indeed glue left in a moiſture ſtate, by diſcoutinuing the evaporation before it is brought to a dry conſiſtence : and therefore further particulars reſpecting the manufacture of it are needleſs here.—Iſinglaſs ſize may alſo be prepared, in the manner above directed for the glue, by increaſing the proportion of the water for diſſolving it : and the ſame holds good of parchment ſize. A better ſort of the common ſize, which may be likewiſe made by treating cuttings of glovers' leather in the ſame manner.

Of paſtes.] Paſte for cementing is formed principally of wheaten flour boiled in water till it be of a glutinous or viſcid conſiſtence. It may be prepared of thoſe ingredients ſimply for common purpoſes : but when it is uſed by book-binders, or for paper hangings to rooms, it is uſual to mix a fourth, fifth or ſixth of the weight of the flower of powdered reſin ; and where it is wanted ſtill more tenacious, gum Arabic, or any kind of ſize, may be added. In order to prevent the paſte uſed for hanging rooms with paper, or where it is employed in any other way that may render it ſubject to ſuch accidents, from being gnawed by rats and mice, powdered glaſs is ſometimes mixed with it. But the moſt effectual and eaſy remedy is to diſſolve a little ſublimate, in the proportion of a drachm to a quart, in the water employed for making the paſte ; which will hinder, not only rats and mice, but any other kind of vermin and inſects, from preying on the paſte.

Of lutes.] Lutes are cements employed for making good the joints of glaſſes put together, or other ſuch purpoſes, in chemical operations. In a general view,

the preparation of them properly belongs to the art of
chemiftry only : but as they are neverthelefs fometimes
ufed in other arts, it may be expedient to fhow here the
manner of compounding them. In the making good
junctures, where the heat is not fufficient to burn paper
or vegetable fubftances, the following mixture, which
is eafily made, will effectually anfwer the purpofe. Take
a mixture of linfeed meal or wheaten flour and whiting,
in the proportion of one part of the firft to two of the
laft, tempered with a folution of gum Senegal or Arabic in water, and fpread upon the joint, a narrow piece
fmeared with the fame being put over it and preffed clofe.
A piece of bladder fmeared with gum water, or the
glair of eggs, and fitted to the glaffes over the joint,
will alfo anfwer the fame end. But in the rectification
of fpirit of wine, or other fuch volatile fubftances, where
the wafte made by the efcape of the vapour may be material, a ftronger lute formed of quicklime, tempered
to a proper confiftence with drying oil, fhould be ufed.
This mixture fhould be made at the time it is wanted,
as it very foon becomes dry and untractable : and great
care muft be taken, where it is employed, to manage
the heat in fuch manner, that the vapour may not rife
fo faft as to heat the veffels beyond the due point ; for
this lute renders the glaffes joined together by it as one
intire body ; and will refift the expanfive force of the
vapour to fo great a degree, that the glaffes will frequently burft before it will give way. Where lute is
to be ufed in places liable to be fo heated as to burn
vegetable or animal fubftances, it may be thus compounded. Take two parts of green vitriol calcined to
rednefs, one part of the fcoria or clinkers of a fmith's
forge well levigated, and an equal quantity of Windfor
loom or Sturbridge clay dried and powdered : temper
them to a proper confiftence with the blood of any
beaft ; fome fhort hair, of which the proportion may
be as a twentieth part to the whole, being beaten up
with them, and fpread them over the juncture. In
cafes of little importance, a compofition of fand, clay,
and dung of horfes tempered with water, may be ufed.

*Preparation of cement for joining broken glaſſes, china,
&c.*] The cement, which has been moſt approved for
uniting glaſs, china, or earthen ware, as alſo the parts
of metalline bodies (where foldering is not expedient)
is thus prepared.—" Take two ounces of good glue, and
ſteep it for a night in diſtilled vinegar: boil them together the next day ; and having beaten a clove of garlic with half an ounce of ox-gall into a foft pulp, ſtrain
the juice through a linen cloth, uſing preſſure, and add
it to the glue and vinegar. Take then of ſanderac
powdered, and turpentine, each one drachm, and of
ſarcocol, and maſtic, powdered, each half a drachm ;
and put them into a bottle with an ounce of highly
rectified ſpirit of wine   Stop the bottle ; and let the
mixture ſtand for three hours in a gentle heat; frequently ſhaking it.   Mix this tincture alfo with the
glue while hot ; and ſtir them well together with a ſtick
or tobacco-pipe, till part of the moiſture be evaporated :
and then take the compoſition from the fire ; and it will
be fit for uſe.   When this cement is to be applied, it
muſt be dipped in vinegar ; and then melted in a proper veſſel, with a gentle heat; and if ſtones are to be
cemented, it is proper to mix with it a little powdered
tripoli or chalk ; or, if glaſs is to be conjoined, powdered glaſs ſhould be ſubſtituted."——I ſee no reaſon
why common vinegar ſhould not be equally proper for
this purpoſe with the diſtilled ; nor indeed am I very
certain that vinegar improves at all the cementing property of the compoſition.   For the uniting the parts
of broken china or earthen ware veſſels, as alſo glaſs
where the rendering the joint viſible is not of conſequence, the following compoſition, which is much more
eaſily prepared, may be ſubſtituted for the foregoing :
" Take an ounce of cheeſe, devoid of fat : grate it as
ſmall as poſſible ; and put it, with an equal weight of
quicklime, into three ounces of ſkimmed milk.   Mix
them thoroughly together ; and uſe the compoſition immediately."—Where the broken veſſels are for ſervice
only, and the appearance is not to be regarded, the
joints may be made equally ſtrong with any other part

of the glafs, by putting a flip of thin paper, or linen, fmeared with this cement, over them,'after they are well joined together by it. This method will make a great faving in the cafe of glaffes employed for chemical, or other fimilar operations. A cement of the fame nature may be made by tempering quicklime with the curd of milk, till it be of a due confiftence for ufe. The curd, in this cafe, fhould be as free as poffible from the cream or oil of the milk. On this account it fhould be made of milk from which the cream has been well fkimmed off; or the kind of curd commonly fold in the markets, made of whey, and the milk from which butter has been extracted, commonly called butter-milk. This cement fhould be ufed in the fame manner as the preceding: and they may be applied to ftones, marble, &c. with equal advantage as the more compound one above given, and is much more eafily and cheaper prepared. Drying oil with white lead is alfo frequently ufed for cementing china, and earthen-ware : but where it is not neceffary the veffels fhould endure heat or moifture, ifinglafs glue with a little tripoli or chalk is better.

Preparation of common cement for joining alabafter, marble, porphyry or other ftones.] " Take of bee's wax two pounds, and of refin one pound. Melt them; and add one pound and a half of the fame kind of matter powdered, as the body to be cemented is compofed of; ftrewing it into the melted mixture, and ftirring them well together; and afterwards kneading the mafs in water, that the powder may be thoroughly incorporated with the wax and refin. The proportion of the powdered matter may be varied, where required, in order to bring the cement nearer to the colour of the body on which it is employed."—This cement muft be heated when applied; as muft alfo the parts of the fubject to be cemented together; and care muft be taken, likewife, that they be thoroughly dry. It appears to me, that the proportion of the bees wax is greater than it ought to be : but I received this recipe from too good an authority to prefume to alter it. When this compofition is properly managed, it forms an extremely good ce-

ment, which will even fuſpend a projecting body of
conſiderable weight, after it is thoroughly dry and ſet :
and is therefore of great uſe to all carvers in ſtone, or
others who may have occaſion to join together the parts
of bodies of this nature.

*Of cements for rock-work, reſervoirs, and other ſuch
purpoſes.*] A variety of compoſitions are uſed as cements for purpoſes of this kind : in the application of
which, regard ſhould be had to the ſituation where they
are employed with reſpect to moiſture and dryneſs; as
well as to the magnitude of the bodies to be conjoined
together, or the vacuities or fiſſures that are to be made
good. Where a great quantity of cement is wanted
for coarſer uſes, the coal-aſh mortar (or Welſh tarras
as it is called) is the cheapeſt and beſt ; and will hold
extremely well, not only where it is conſtantly kept wet
or dry ; but even where it is ſometimes dry and at others
wet. But where it is liable to be expoſed to wet and
froſt, this cement ſhould, at its being laid on, be ſuffered to dry thoroughly before any moiſture have acceſs
to it ; and, in that caſe, it will likewiſe be a great improvement to temper it with the blood of any beaſt.
This mortar or Welſh tarras muſt be formed of one part
lime and two parts of well-ſifted coal aſhes ; and they
muſt be thoroughly mixed by being beaten together :
for, on the perfect commixture of the ingredients, the
goodneſs of the compoſition depends. Where the cement is to remain continually under water, the true tarras is commonly uſed ; and will very well anſwer the
purpoſe. It may be formed of two parts of lime, and
one part of plaiſter of Paris : which ſhould be thoroughly well beaten together ; and then uſed immediately. For the fixing ſhells, and other ſuch nice purpoſes, putty is moſt generally uſed. It may be formed
for this purpoſe of quicklime, and drying oil, mixed
with an equal quantity of linſeed oil; or, where the
drying quicker is not neceſſary, it may be made with
lime and crude linſeed oil, without the drying oil. The
ſtone cement, prepared as above of the bees wax and

refin, is alfo an extremely good compofition for this purpofe. But refin, pitch, and brick-duft, in equal parts, melted together and ufed hot, are much the cheapeft cement for fhell-work ; and will perform that office very well, provided the bodies they are to conjoin be perfectly dry when they are ufed.

Enᴅ *of the* T H I R D   P A R T.

BOOKS. *printed and fold by* H. & P. R I C E, No. 50, *Market-ftreet*, Pʜɪʟᴀᴅᴇʟᴘʜɪᴀ.

The Poetical Works of Peter Pindar, Efq. a diftant Relation to the Poet of Thebes. To which are p·e-fixed Memoirs and Anecdotes of the Author, 2 vols.
Knoxe's Moral and Literary Effays, 2 vols.
Buchan's Domeftic Medicine, A new Edition with many Additions.
Goldfmith's Hiftory of the Earth and Animated Na-ture, 8 vols. with beautiful plates. `
Goldfmith's Hiftory of England, 4 vols.
———————Abridged for the Ufe of Schools.
———————Hiftory of Rome, 2 vols.
———————————Abridged for the Ufe of Schools.
Entick's Pocket Dictionary.
Fables of Æfop, and other Allegorical Writers. Tranf-lated into Englifh : with proper Applications and a fuitable Defign to each Fable. By Samuel Croxall, D. D.

www.ingramcontent.com/pod-product-compliance
Lightning Source LLC
Chambersburg PA
CBHW030733280326
41926CB00086B/1330

9 783337 258030